AUSTRALIAN
CONFEDERATES

TERRY SMYTH

AUSTRALIAN CONFEDERATES

HOW 42 AUSTRALIANS JOINED
THE REBEL CAUSE AND FIRED THE
LAST SHOT IN THE AMERICAN CIVIL WAR

EBURY
PRESS

An Ebury Press book
Published by Random House Australia Pty Ltd
Level 3, 100 Pacific Highway, North Sydney NSW 2060
www.randomhouse.com.au

First published by Ebury Press in 2015

Random House Books is part of the Penguin Random House group of companies whose addresses can be found at global.penguinrandomhouse.com.

National Library of Australia
Cataloguing-in-Publication entry

Smyth, Terry, author.
Australian confederates/Terry Smyth.

ISBN 978 0 85798 655 9 (paperback)

Shenandoah (Cruiser)
Confederate States of America. Navy.
Australians – Confederate States of America.
United States – History – Civil War, 1861-1865 – Participation, Australian.
United States – History – Civil War, 1861-1865 – Naval operations.
Confederate States of America – History.

973.757

Cover illustration © Chicago History Museum, ICHi-62492, 'Confederate States Cruiser *Shenandoah* in the Harbor of Melbourne, Australia, 1865', by Christian Poulsen
Cover design by Luke Causby, Blue Cork Design
Internal design by Midland Typesetters, Australia
Typeset in 11/17pt Sabon by Midland Typesetters, Australia
Printed in Australia by Griffin Press, an accredited ISO AS/NZS 14001:2004 Environmental Management System printer

Random House Australia uses papers that are natural, renewable and recyclable products and made from wood grown in sustainable forests. The logging and manufacturing processes are expected to conform to the environmental regulations of the country of origin.

For Kate, Ben, Sophie and Acky
And for my mother

Contents

We call a ship 'she' and other tongues call a ship 'it'.
'She' implies that the ship carries us and is in some manner alive,
as a sailor in his heart privately believes.
– Captain James Iredell Waddell

Introduction

This is a tale of two lands: one, not yet a nation; the other, never to be a nation. The destinies of colonial Australia and the Confederate States of America crossed in the watershed year of 1865 – a year of cultural shifts and scientific advances that would change the world. It was also the last year of the American Civil War, and the year Australians became actively involved in that war, when the Confederate raider *Shenandoah* visited these shores.

In the Australia of the 18th and 19th centuries, while Europe remained the white man's Dreaming, American virtues – and vices – were greatly influential on the young societies of colonial Australia. The newcomers desperate to tame the southern continent looked to the New World for inspiration. And whenever Australian history was being made, there often seemed to be an American involved somehow.

On Australia's Cape York Peninsula, on 29 June 1770, where the explorer Captain James Cook was forced to beach his ship, the *Endeavour*, for repairs in a river mouth after she struck a reef,

Midshipman James Matra was out shooting when he spotted what he thought was a wolf. Matra, who was probably the first white person to see a dingo on the east coast of the continent, and who shot at it but missed, was an American.

Matra might have been the first American to leave his mark (or almost) on Australia, but he was certainly not the last. There were Americans among the convicts of the First Fleet that founded Sydney in 1788. Americans were among the earliest sealers and whalers working off the Australian coast. Americans flocked to Australia during the gold rushes of the 1850s and 1860s – mostly to Victoria – and American diggers of the California Revolver Brigade were among the rebels at the Eureka Stockade.

By the 1860s, there were more than 3,000 Americans living in Victoria alone. When the rush was over, the numbers of American immigrants declined, but their legacy lived on through their progeny, their prejudices and their politics.

When Australia became a nation in 1901, lessons learnt from America's political upheavals were enshrined in the new Constitution. The Preamble to the Australian Constitution states: 'Whereas the people of New South Wales, Victoria, South Australia, Queensland and Tasmania, humbly relying on the blessing of Almighty God, have agreed to unite in one indissoluble Federal Commonwealth under the Crown of the United Kingdom of Great Britain and Ireland, and under the Constitution hereby established.' The word 'indissoluble' was added to the final draft of the Constitution at the federation convention of 1898, specifically to avoid a calamitous secession such as that which led to the American Civil War.

Throughout the 19th century, Western Australia made a habit of threatening to secede, and Queensland made the threat at least once. In April 1885, on the eve of an official inquiry into blackbirding, Queensland plantation owners and their support- ers, fearful the inquiry could lead to restriction on 'Kanaka' slave labour, threatened to split from Queensland and form a new, sep- arate state in the north, with Townsville as its capital. These were no idle threats.

For the drafters of the Constitution, the American war was within living memory. They had based Australia's Constitution on the American model, but were mindful that although the United States Constitution of 1787 protected states' rights while creating a national government, it had not prevented the Civil War. The Southern states considered the Constitution to be no more than a contract that could be broken, and claimed the sov- ereign right to secede.

Debate raged over the best way to prevent an Australian civil war, and in the end the delegates came up with a one-word solution – 'indissoluble'.

Footprints still appear when the dead man marches. No matter how deep we bury those betrayed by birth and circumstance to be on the losing side of war – the side history and sensibility has pro- claimed the wrong side – and no matter how desperately we might try to wipe their very existence from memory, from history, they refuse to be forgotten, evident in the many Confederate memorials and historical societies in the American South today, and in the continuing worldwide interest in that period of American history.

Now, as then, the conflict that tore America apart in the years 1861 to 1865 excites debate and inflames passions. Even its name remains contentious. Depending on whom you ask, it was the American Civil War, the War Between the States, the War of Northern Aggression, the War of the Rebellion; the War of Southern Independence, the War of Secession, the Freedom War, the Lost Cause.

Regardless of how you name it, the world has had a century and a half of hindsight to satisfy itself why and how the Confederate cause was lost. We can confidently assure ourselves that the American slave states which proclaimed a sovereign nation in 1861 were at best misguided romantics or, at worst, merchants of evil. But back then there were no ready assurances. History makes sense when you're reading it, but not when you're living it.

This story is about 42 Australians who willingly, and well aware they were breaking the law, secretly enlisted in the Confederate States Navy when the notorious rebel raider *Shenandoah* visited Melbourne in 1865.

It's fair to ask what on earth possessed them. If it was adventure that motivated them – well, that's something we can understand. A thirst for adventure has driven countless reckless Australian youths to fight other men's wars. But if it was heartfelt sympathy for the Confederate cause which inspired them, that's quite another matter. That's something contemporary Australians might find difficult to accept. Upholding slavery doesn't sit comfortably with our image of ourselves.

The trouble is, the Confederate cause was not all black and white. And yes, the pun is intended. The effects of the American Civil War on Australia – and there were many, as we'll discover – must be considered in the context of the institution of slavery. To do otherwise would be to dilute and diminish the evidence of history.

Since history and hindsight are not always the best of

bedfellows, there's cause for caution here. Looking back on that war with 21st-century eyes, and, for Australians, from the perspective of an outsider looking in, it's a reasonable assumption that the Confederacy – in seceding from the Union and defending, by force of arms, its right to perpetuate the obscenity of human bondage – was perversely out of touch with tolerant attitudes prevalent not only in the Northern states but in the enlightened wider world. In 1865, when the tide of war was turning against the Confederacy, it's tempting to see the Civil War in terms of good versus evil; of a backward American South at odds with a forward-thinking Britain – and by default its empire – where slavery had been officially abolished almost 60 years earlier. However, in one far corner of the Empire – colonial Queensland – slavery under another name would continue.

Like other parts of the British empire, in 1865, when the *Shenandoah* sailed into Port Phillip Bay and controversy, Australian colonies were obliged to follow the policy of the British Government, which had remained strictly neutral throughout the war. The British people largely backed the North, as did the majority of people in New South Wales and South Australia. In Victoria and Queensland, arguably, opinion was polarised.

The Northern cause inspired renewed calls for democratic reform in Britain, with faint echoes in Australia. Industrialisation and social change in Britain had seen a shift in wealth and political clout from the landed gentry to the urban middle class. The working class, too, was demanding a bigger say in the running of the country.

Curiously, though, support for the anti-slavery North did not foster concern for the plight of the slave – quite the opposite, in fact. Earlier in the 19th century, prejudice against people of colour had been rare in Britain, and popular sympathy for abolitionists and missionaries was widespread. By the 1860s, however, racial discrimination was common.

The reason for the change in attitude in Britain was not the same as in America and Australia, where so-called scientific race theory was cynically used to excuse the exploitation and subjugation of 'inferior' peoples. In mid-Victorian Britain, black residents and visitors were rare, and the public's only sources of information on the nature of black people were soldiers, sailors, explorers and adventurers pushing the boundaries of empire. As white people of the middling sort clawed their way up the social ladder, aping the manners and arrogance of the aristocracy, they viewed black people as another species of humanity but one they could look down upon; one rung below the great unwashed. In lock-step, the great unwashed did likewise, and with relish. At last, someone to feel superior towards! In other words, for the British in 1865, racism was rife but snobbery ruled.

In Germany that same year, an Augustinian monk named Gregor Mendel was conducting experiments with plants that would earn him the title of the founder of the science of genetics. Not in his lifetime, however. Mendel's laws of heredity would be ignored until the 20th century.

Meanwhile, Charles Darwin's *The Origin of Species*, published in 1859, continued to foment controversy. For those who took literally the Bible's version of creation, Darwin's theory of evolution was blasphemy. Opponents popularised the claim that Darwin insisted man was descended from apes. Darwin, even though he made no such claim, was met with ridicule and derision. Darwin's work, like Mendel's, would one day be generally accepted as the basis for understanding that all humans are the same species, but in the 1860s it was widely believed that differently coloured humans were different species.

Throughout the Caucasian-dominated western world, many people accepted as scientific fact the view of Swiss zoologist Carl Vogt and other 'polygenist evolutionists' that blacks were related to apes but whites were not. In the American South, polygenism was used by prominent scientists such as Samuel Cartwright to justify slavery. Cartwright, a Louisiana doctor and plantation owner, diagnosed runaway slaves as suffering from 'drapetomania', a psychiatric disorder that could be cured by whippings and cutting off toes.

The Great Emancipator himself, Abraham Lincoln, often declared that while he believed the United States must put an end to slavery – and that all men were created equal, with equal rights to life, liberty and the pursuit of happiness – he did not believe white and black could co-exist in harmony. 'God made us separate,' he said. 'We can leave one another alone and do much good thereby.'[1]

Lincoln, like most white Americans, North and South, and indeed like most white people everywhere, was convinced that blacks were naturally inferior to whites, and that the two 'races' could never be on equal social or political terms. In other words, blacks had a perfect right to enjoy the fruits of freedom, but not on the same street, train or public place as whites enjoying the fruits of freedom.

Before the Emancipation Proclamation – arguably more a war measure than a humanitarian initiative – Lincoln made no attempt to free slaves, and favoured the deportation of freed slaves to Africa.

Lincoln's views on slavery were not so different from those of Confederate General Robert E. Lee. Both were emancipationists

but not abolitionists. Both believed that to abolish slavery overnight would mean social and economic disaster.

Lee expounded his views on slavery in a letter to his wife,
Mary:

> In this enlightened age, there are few I believe, but what
> will acknowledge that slavery, as an institution, is a moral
> and political evil in any country. It is useless to expatiate
> on its disadvantages. I think it however a greater evil to the
> white man than to the black race, and while my feelings are
> strongly enlisted in behalf of the latter, my sympathies are
> more strong for the former.
>
> The blacks are immeasurably better off here than in
> Africa, morally, socially and physically. The painful
> discipline they are undergoing is necessary for their
> instruction as a race, and I hope will prepare and lead
> them to better things. How long their subjugation may
> be necessary is known and ordered by a wise Merciful
> Providence.
>
> While we see the course of the final abolition of human
> slavery is onward, and we give it the aid of our prayers
> and all justifiable means in our power, we must leave the
> progress as well as the result in His hands who sees the end;
> who chooses to work by slow influences; and with whom
> two thousand years are but as a single day. Although
> the Abolitionist must know this, and must see that he has
> neither the right or power of operating except by moral
> means and suasion, and if he means well to the slave, he
> must not create angry feelings in the master; that although
> he may not approve the mode which it pleases Providence

to accomplish its purposes, the result will nevertheless be the same; that the reasons he gives for interference in what he has no concern, holds good for every kind of interference with our neighbours when we disapprove their conduct. Still I fear he will persevere in his evil course.[2]

Such attitudes were generally shared by Australians in 1865, no less so than in colonial Victoria, a rich yet raw society where political disputes with the mother colony of New South Wales, and antipathy towards advocates of federation, echoed those between the antebellum American North and South.

In Victoria, the gold rush and the Eureka rebellion had forged an anti-establishment spirit that found sympathy with the Confederate cause. It was a cause that in the view of some Australians was not about slavery but about sovereignty, and thus a romantic cause; a cause with which they could identify – for the moment, at least.

The men who sailed away on the *Shenandoah* in the summer of 1865 were men of their times. We will never know their thoughts on slavery or sovereignty or secession, but we do know they braved the worst Neptune could throw at them; that they fired the last shot of the American Civil War; that they destroyed 32 Yankee merchant ships worth an estimated AU$1.5 million, ransomed six and captured more than a thousand prisoners; that one of their number would be the last man to die in the service of the Confederacy. And, that while hunted as pirates, they would sail their ship 60,000 miles around the world to make history as the last rebels to surrender.

This is a tale of the sea, of war, of vainglory.

Chapter 1

Lands of cotton

You might say it was all because of Caty's cat – the unwitting provider of the Eureka moment that led to the explosion in the cotton industry. That was really what started off the whole sad, terrible business.

That's why the Mason-Dixon line – once merely ink on a map, marking borders between states – became a colossal cultural divide, alienating Americans humming 'Yankee Doodle' from Americans whistling 'Dixie'.

That's why, in 1861, the drums of war drowned out the voices of concord, and that's why now, in January of 1865, the tally in blood for a nation divided has posted numbers to make the head spin. Of more than three million men who have fought in the American Civil War so far, some 620,000 have lost their lives. Total casualties on both sides are reckoned at 1.5 million, including soldiers and sailors killed or wounded in battle, those missing in action and those who died of disease. There has been no accounting for the civilian toll a later age will coldly call collateral damage. And it isn't over yet.

That's why North and South, once unfamiliar names, have been etched forever into memory. Places such as Manassas, Shiloh, Fredericksburg, Gettysburg, Cold Harbour. Men such as Robert E. Lee, William T. Sherman, Stonewall Jackson, Ulysses S. Grant.

That's why, as the United States Congress debates the Thirteenth Amendment – to abolish slavery – the Confederate raider CSS *Shenandoah* is sailing into Australian waters, bound for the port of Melbourne.

And that's why the *Shenandoah*'s master, Lieutenant Commander James Iredell Waddell, striding the quarterdeck of his rakish black warship as it slices its way into this notionally neutral port – with the Roaring Forties behind him and an Antipodean summer haze on the shore ahead – has no way of knowing if he will be welcomed as a warrior in a desperate cause or hanged as a pirate.

Had destiny taken a different turn, this 41-year-old native of Orange County, North Carolina, would likely still be Second Lieutenant on USS *Saginaw*, serving in the peacetime navy he had joined as a boy but is now his sworn enemy. So here he is, captain of the scourge of the Yankee merchant fleet, seeking safe harbour in a strange land; a raw and remote place that is not so much a country as a curiosity.

A lifetime earlier and half a world away, in 1792, a 27-year-old farmer's son from Westborough, Massachusetts, took ship for South Carolina. Eli Whitney had always known that a life on the land was not for him. As a youth, during the Revolutionary War, he had turned a modest profit manufacturing nails on his father's farm, and dreamt of earning fame and fortune as an inventor and engineer. However, after graduating from Yale with a law degree but little enthusiasm to practise the profession, and short of money and opportunity, Eli set his dreams aside and took a job as a children's tutor on a plantation in South Carolina.

But Eli Whitney never made it to South Carolina. Fate stepped in in the form of Catherine Littlefield Greene, a passenger on the same ship. Like Whitney, Catherine Greene was blessed with an inventive mind, and during the voyage the pair became fast friends. She invited him to abandon his plan to become a tutor in South Carolina and tutor her children instead, at her plantation in Georgia. As an incentive, she offered to provide him with a workshop where he could tinker with his inventions. Whitney accepted with gratitude.

'Caty' Greene, as she was widely and fondly known, was the widow of General Nathanael Greene, a hero of the Revolutionary War. Like her late husband, Caty was a Northerner, from Rhode Island. As arguably the most capable general after George Washington, Nathanael Greene emerged from the war covered in glory, but his campaigns against the British had left him financially ruined. To provide rations for his troops, he had guaranteed large sums of money to merchants through a middle-man who turned out to be a fraudster. When, at the end of the war, the merchants demanded their money, Nathanael had no choice but to sell the family's northern estate to pay his debts and, with Caty and their five children, move south to a Georgia plantation granted to him in gratitude for his war service.

Mulberry Grove plantation, on the Savannah River, had been a successful rice plantation, and Nathanael hoped to restore the family's fortunes cultivating that crop. But the plantation had been deserted for 10 years. Its former owner, British loyalist John

Graham, the Lieutenant Governor of Georgia, fled in fear for his life after Britain lost the war. Although the mansion house and outbuildings were in fair order, the rice fields were choked with weeds and marsh grass, and all the slaves had run away.

Still, Nathanael and Caty were determined to make the plantation a going concern once more. The task proved arduous and, for Caty, became doubly so when, in 1786, Nathanael died suddenly of sunstroke.

To pay his respects, President Washington visited the plantation, noting in his diary that he 'called upon Mrs Green, the widow of the deceased General Green, (at a place called Mulberry Grove) and asked her how she did.'[1]

And it seems that within three years of her husband's death she was doing well. The plantation was thriving, its success credited to Caty's courage and determination, although in truth its prosperity – like that of all plantations throughout the South – was built on slavery.

While, in Georgia, slaves toiled in the rice fields and at the crop-cleaning machines in the cause of Caty's wealth and comfort, in England, the renowned abolitionist William Wilberforce rose in Parliament to condemn the slave trade as irredeemably wicked. Presenting his Abolition Bill to the House for the first time, he warned, 'You may choose to look the other way but you can never again say you did not know.'[2] Year after year, Wilberforce reintroduced the Bill until it was finally passed – albeit by a slim majority – in 1807, making the slave trade illegal on British ships. In Britain's former American colonies, however, lawmakers continued to either look the other way or to look the institution squarely in the eye and, as God-fearing Christians, heartily approve of it, citing the Bible for justification.

Both the Old and New Testaments have references to slavery as an acceptable practice. According to the Scriptures, some people were born to be chattel and others to be masters. It was simply nature's way; part of God's great plan: 'Slaves, obey your earthly masters with fear and trembling, with a sincere heart, as you would Christ.'[3] The fact that Jesus himself spoke not a word against slavery was cited as proof that he approved of it, while Biblical passages opposing slavery – and there are several – were conveniently ignored.

That's not to say American voices were not raised in opposition to human bondage. After the Revolutionary War, abolitionist sentiment slowly gained traction in the North. In the South, too, church leaders loudly echoed Methodist founder John Wesley's denunciation of slavery as 'the sum of all villainies'.[4]

But for every voice supporting Wesley's view, there were many more favouring that of another founder of Methodism, Englishman George Whitfield. A famed preacher and evangelist on both sides of the Atlantic, Whitfield successfully campaigned in 1751 for the relegalisation of slavery in Georgia, where it had been banned since 1735. Although Whitfield preached the usual claptrap about slavery being God's will, the main thrust of his argument was that it was an economic necessity – for the South in general and for himself in particular. He intended to buy a plantation in Georgia and become a slave-owner.

In his opinion, 'hot countries cannot be cultivated without negroes. What a flourishing country might Georgia have been, had the use of them been permitted years ago? How many white people have been destroyed for want of them, and how many thousands of pounds spent to no purpose at all?'[5]

An apologist for the brutal trade, he apparently believed that as a paternalistic master, he would be doing his kidnapped, captive workers a favour. 'And though it is true that they are brought in a wrong way from their own country, and it is a trade not to be approved of, yet as it will be carried on whether we will it or not, I should think myself highly favoured if I could purchase a good number of them, in order to make their lives comfortable, and lay a foundation for breeding up their posterity in the nurture and admonition of the Lord.'[6]

The re-introduction of slavery in Georgia, largely due to the influence of George Whitfield, caused the enslaved population to grow from less than 500 in 1750 to 15,000 within five years, as more and more slaves were brought from Africa to boost the production of Georgia's staple crops: rice, tobacco and indigo.

At Mulberry Grove, for example, during the years slavery was outlawed in Georgia, the plantation's workforce was a small number of white indentured labourers. In 1792, when Eli Whitney arrived at Mulberry Grove, there were a dozen or so slaves toiling in Caty's fields. They numbered among some 30,000 throughout Georgia – more than a third of that state's total population, yet this was a fraction of what was to come. By 1860, on the eve of the Civil War, the slave population of Georgia – the state with the largest number of slaves – would swell to more than 462,000. Nationally, of a total population of just over 31 million, almost four million would be in bondage.[7]

In 1792, the 2,000-acre Mulberry Grove estate grew corn and orchard fruits, but rice was still the prime cash crop, and the plantation's slaves had dug by hand a massive system of irrigation and drainage canals for the rice fields. But the South's rice economy was about to be upset by an upstart.

As promised, Eli Whitney was given a workshop in an upper room of the mansion in which to turn his ideas into practicalities.

And one of his ideas was to find some way to improve the production of what was then a very minor crop. Cotton.

Potentially, cotton was extremely valuable. The cotton mills of northern England, centred on the 'Cottonopolis' of Manchester, had an insatiable appetite for the fibre, and Britain's main source of the crop, India, was struggling to meet demand. The trouble was that even in areas ideally suited to its cultivation – such as the American South, with its long, hot summers, moderate rainfall and rich soils – removing the seeds by hand from the fibres in the fluffy seed pods, called 'bolls', was a slow and laborious process. Producing a single bale of cotton needed more that 600 hours of labour, and, even with slave labour, large-scale production in the United States was unviable.

So the story goes, one day at Mulberry Grove plantation, in 1793, Eli Whitney, in an idle moment, stood staring at a brood of fluffy chicks in a slat chicken coop, perhaps struck by their similarity to fluffy cotton bolls.

Just then, according to a presumably embroidered tale told and retold: 'Along came Tabby the house cat. Tabby reached in to claw a chick out of the coop, but as she did so the old mother hen pecked at her. That caused the cat to make a sweeping swipe at one of the chicks, with her claws exposed.

'She did not get the chick, but she withdrew her paw with a bunch of fluff clinging to her claws.'

This was Whitney's Eureka moment. 'He cried, "At last I have a plan for separating cotton from the seed! What we need is a machine that will act like a cat's paw. The cat struck at the chicken and removed its feathers. I want a machine that will strike at the cotton and remove it from the thing to which it is fastened."

'So he invented a machine which had a multiple of fine teeth revolving rapidly in a cylinder, and when the cotton was fed through it the teeth tore all the cotton from the seed in much the same way as the cat's claws stripped the fluff from the baby chick.'[8]

Whitney's prototype cotton gin ('gin' being short for engine) was a failure. Its 'teeth' were made of wood and broke off. Caty Greene suggested he try again using metal wire teeth, and it worked like a charm. Where previously it had taken hundreds of hours, now it took only 10 to 12 hours to produce a bale of cotton.

It was a revolution. By the 1820s, cotton had become the United States' biggest agricultural export and, in the South, the main source of wealth. By the 1840s, India could no longer compete on price or quality with American cotton. By 1860, Southern plantations supplied more than 75 per cent of the world's cotton, shipping directly to England – the global hub of the industry – from Savannah, Charleston, Mobile, New Orleans and other Southern ports.

But there was a catch: more cotton under cultivation required more slaves to pick the crop. As the Southern economy became dependant on cotton, its very survival depended on the institution of slavery. The once minor crop had become the basis of an economy, a society, and the justification for an abomination.

At the same time, a longstanding dispute over the role of the federal government was gaining heat. On one side were those who believed the powers of the national government should have pre-eminence over the powers of the states. On the opposing side were those who held the view that states should retain their sovereign rights within the federation.

Whereas, in Australia, a similar dispute between rival colonies would eventually be resolved – albeit grudgingly and imperfectly – by compromise in a federal constitution, the American debate over states' rights was hamstrung by the issue of slavery. There might well have been wriggle room on taxation and tariffs, but on the matter of slavery the South was immovable.

Northern states had been gradually abolishing slavery since the Revolutionary War, and by 1840 almost all slaves north of the Ohio River and the Mason-Dixon line – the border between Maryland and Pennsylvania, and, generally, free and slave states – had been freed. Unlike the industrial North, however, the agricultural South would not, could not, consider dispensing with the unpaid labour force that was the engine of its economy. In Dixie, a popular term for the South, 'abolition' was a dirty word. It was just plain unthinkable.

The dispute grew hotter still when new states were added to the Union. On the question of whether these former territories would be free states or slave states, tempers flared and sabres were rattled.

Could it lead to war between the states? Not likely, scoffed Senator James Henry Hammond of South Carolina, in 1858. 'Without firing a gun, without drawing a sword, should they make war on us, we could bring the whole world to our feet.

'What would happen if no cotton was furnished for three years? England would topple headlong and carry the whole civilised world with her save the South. No, you dare not make war on cotton. No power on the earth dares to make war upon it. Cotton is King.'[9]

Hammond, who owned several plantations and more than 300 slaves, was an influential pro-slavery advocate before the war. He firmly believed slavery was 'commanded by God through Moses, and approved by Christ through his apostles'.[10] But his faith in King Cotton was misplaced.

When the presidential election of 1860 put the anti-slavery Republican Abraham Lincoln in the White House, the enmity between Northern and Southern interests reached breaking point. Of the 15 slave states – the United States of America was comprised of 33 states at that time – South Carolina was first to secede from the Union. Ten more followed – Mississippi, Florida, Alabama, Georgia, Louisiana, Texas, Virginia, Arkansas, Tennessee and North Carolina – and on 9 February 1861, the rebel states proclaimed a new nation: the Confederate States of America.

Two months later, when the first shots of the Civil War were fired in the Confederate attack on Fort Sumter, in Charleston Harbor, it was blindingly obvious that King Cotton could not prevent a war. And, as it would soon become depressingly clear, neither could King Cotton help to win a war.

The Confederates hoped to gain the support of Britain and France, which were heavily dependant on Southern cotton, by restricting exports, creating economic crises in those markets. 'Cotton diplomacy', it was called, and it backfired spectacularly. Britain and Europe, with warehouses bulging with surplus cotton, enjoyed hefty profits as the price of cotton shot up, and saw no sense in picking a fight with the United States. And with the US Navy imposing a blockade on Confederate ports, the South could not ship its cotton regardless. The result was an economic crisis, not in Britain and Europe, as expected, but in the Confederacy. For a one-note economy, this spelt disaster not only in the treasury but on the battlefield.

Bad news for the Confederacy meant good news for other lands of cotton, and India, Egypt and Argentina massively increased production. Not so for the mill towns of Northern England, however. In Lancashire towns such as Oldham, the drying up of the supply of affordable American cotton led to what came to be known as the 'cotton famine'. Thousands of workers, laid off by the town's mills, were forced to rely on soup kitchens and charitable handouts for survival. Nevertheless, at a public meeting in Oldham, sacked workers declared they would rather starve than support slavery – a commendable but curious claim, given that the town had thrived on spinning and weaving slave-grown cotton since the turn of the 19th century.

In an aspiring land of cotton – Australia – the fledgling colony of Queensland sought to capitalise not only on the woes of the American South but on England's cotton famine. To attract investment by British mill owners and manufacturers, the colonial government guaranteed the price of raw cotton, which had soared since supplies from the South were cut off. And to attract unemployed English mill workers, Queensland offered free passage and grants of land to grow cotton. Some 1,000 families took up the offer, but they were urban factory workers, not farmers, and for many the task of carving out cotton fields from the rugged bush of south-eastern Queensland proved too much. The scheme was a failure.

Undaunted, Australia looked elsewhere for labour. In 1863, shipping magnate and entrepreneur Robert Towns established a cotton plantation on the Logan River, in Queensland. Convinced the venture would never turn a profit if he paid white man's wages, he sent a schooner to the South Pacific to recruit islanders. The ship returned with 67 Melanesian men who were put to work picking Towns' cotton. 'Kanakas', they were called – originally Hawaiian for 'free man' but used by whites as a derogatory term akin to 'nigger'. Although Towns' islander labourers were offered wages, food and housing and a promise they could return home if they wished, the practice of so-called indentured labour, as it spread throughout eastern Australia, soon degenerated into a form of slavery called 'blackbirding'.

For more than 40 years, blackbirding ships would carry human cargoes from Vanuatu, Tonga, the Loyalty Islands, Samoa, Kiribati, Tuvalu, Papua New Guinea and the Solomon Islands to toil on the cotton plantations and later in the sugar-cane fields of Queensland and Fiji. Regulations required that only willing recruits could be taken aboard the traders' ships, but in reality officialdom turned a blind eye to a corrupt and brutal practice of kidnapping. Often, islanders would be tricked into coming aboard with promises of trade, then forced below as the ship set sail or rounded up at gunpoint in their villages, in the manner of African slave raids. On Queensland plantations, living and working in appalling conditions, islanders often died young: worked to death in the fields; struck down by disease; destroyed by despair; or murdered by Australians who claimed the islanders were taking white men's jobs.

The Queensland planters modelled their estates on those of the American South, with grand houses surrounded by cotton fields where – so white society was led to believe – docile darkies sang happily at their work, content to toil from dawn till dusk under the paternal eye of their beloved masters.

As in the American South, Australian planters branded their field hands. But unlike in America, where branding was mostly used as a punishment for recaptured runaway slaves, Australian planters branded people as they did cattle. Wielding the branding iron was simply a means of identifying property, a practice that had an important bearing on an 1868 court case in Rockhampton,

Queensland, in which a certain John Tancred was charged with stealing an islander boy named Towhey, the property of Arthur Gossett. The complainant swore he could prove his ownership of the boy because he had branded him not once but twice – on the leg and on the side – which he demonstrated to the court. The judge fined Tancred £10 for theft, and Gossett walked away with his young slave in tow. The press report of the case heartily approved of the outcome, helpfully suggesting: 'perhaps it may not yet be too late for the Assembly to insert a "branding" clause in the Polynesian Labourers Bill'.[11]

Blackbirding meant handsome profits to ship owners, ship's masters and planters, and untold misery to the islanders. Despite often spirited opposition from missionaries, humanitarian groups, the British Government and elements of the Australian press, the trade would not be outlawed until 1903, by which time some 60,000 islanders had been taken to Australia – victims of greed, exploitation and violence, even wholesale murder.

While the most notorious of the blackbirders was the American pirate William 'Bully' Hayes – of whom much has been written and too often romanticised – the worst atrocity of the blackbirding era was carried out by a Melbourne doctor, James Patrick Murray. As master of the brig *Carl*, Murray's favourite trick was to send his crew ashore disguised as missionaries. When the islanders assembled for a religious service, the raiders would draw weapons and force them aboard ship. On one occasion, in 1871, when his captives attempted to escape from the ship's hold, Murray ordered them all shot. For several hours, the doctor and his men fired indiscriminately through the hatch. All the while, Murray, revolver in one hand and mug of coffee in the other, was lustily singing 'Marching Through Georgia' – a song about the Union Army's 1864 march to the sea to capture Savannah, Georgia. In an obscene irony, a verse of the song begins, 'How the darkies shouted when they heard the joyful sound.'

The *Carl* massacre claimed 70 lives – 35 killed by gunfire, and 35 wounded who were thrown overboard with their hands tied. Murray escaped prosecution. Guaranteed immunity for testifying against members of his crew – two of whom were hanged – and still registered to practise medicine, he abandoned his family and fled the country.

'Dr Murray was last seen in Sydney on the 20th of January last and now cannot be found,' the press reported. 'It is generally believed that he has gone to England. He has a wife and two children in Victoria, having been married there to a lady who formerly resided at St Kilda. So ends the colonial history of a man whose name will go down to posterity as one of the most vile offenders that ever disgraced the annals of any country.'[12]

Murray did indeed go to England. He practised medicine in Manchester until struck off the register, then hung out a shingle as a dentist until struck off. Rumour had it that he turned up next in Africa, and history loses sight of him after his name appears on the passenger list of a ship bound for Boston. Murray never paid for his crimes but it's likely the taint of the *Carl* massacre followed him to the grave, wherever that may be.

On the morning of 25 January 1865, as the *Shenandoah* sails through the heads of Port Phillip Bay, Captain James Waddell, easing his ship towards an anchorage at Sandridge – now Port Melbourne – is as yet unaware that the city a few miles distant harbours pro-Confederacy sentiments or that the institution of slavery, on the verge of collapse in the American South, has been reborn in Australia's north. He is about to find kindred spirits in Melbourne, but a whole lot of trouble, too.

As to why destiny, those many years earlier, had set in motion the events leading to the *Shenandoah*'s voyage to the bottom of the world, Captain Waddell would no doubt be surprised to learn it began when a man with time on his hands and invention on his mind stood staring at a chicken coop. Of course, Eli Whitney and Caty Greene were long dead and gone when King Cotton went to hell in a hand-basket and Union soldiers marching through Georgia burnt to the ground Mulberry Grove plantation. Whitney's cotton gin had not made him rich, as he had hoped. While his invention changed the world in its way, its very simplicity, along with the primitive patent laws of those days, made it easy to copy.

He did win fame, however. In his lifetime, Eli Whitney was feted as an engineering mastermind, which surely brought him some satisfaction. And although he gave no credit to Caty for her invaluable collaboration, he did at least give an honourable mention to the cat.

Chapter 2

Daughter of the stars

It is the afternoon of Wednesday 25 January 1865. On Hobson's Bay, in a light wind and clear weather, it's just another busy day at Melbourne's main port. Sailing out through Port Phillip Heads, the schooner *Lady Robilliard* has departed for Belfast, the barque *Theordore Dill* for Batavia, the *Wasp* for Western Port, the *Natal* for Newcastle and the *Derwent* for Hobart Town.

Arriving earlier today, to anchor in the bay, the brig *Eliza Goddard* sailed in from Java, the *Orwell* from London and the *Sir Isaac Newton* from South Australia. Also in port is the warship *Victoria*, pride of the Victorian colonial navy.

At two o'clock, at the Melbourne port station, news comes in by telegraph from the Cape Otway lighthouse that a large screw steamer, flying no colours but thought to be the *Royal Standard*, 52 days out from Liverpool, is inward bound. That message is soon corrected. The incoming vessel is not the *Royal Standard* but the *Shenandoah*, a Confederate warship known to have captured and destroyed at least 11 Yankee merchant ships.

By the time the *Shenandoah* has entered the west channel, the city is already abuzz with the news. The ship's assistant surgeon, Fred McNulty, will later recall, 'Never was conquering flag at peak hailed with half such honours as we were given upon that bright tropical morning. Steamer, tugboat, yacht – all Melbourne, in fact, with its 180,000 souls, seemed to have outdone itself in welcome to the Confederates. Flags dipped, cannon boomed, and men in long thousands cheered us as we moved slowly up the channel and dropped anchor. The telegraph had told of our coming from down the coast, where we had been sighted with Confederate flag flying . . . Evidently the heart of colonial Britain was in our cause.'[1]

The 'conquering flag' is the naval ensign of the Confederacy. Known as 'The Stainless Banner', it features a white field with the Confederate battle flag as a saltire: a diagonal cross in the top left-hand corner, known as the 'Stars and Bars'. So called because of the white field, the Stainless Banner is also known as 'Jackson's flag' because the first of its kind was used to enfold the body of General 'Stonewall' Jackson. It is popular with those in the South who believe it symbolises white supremacy. More practically minded Southerners are concerned that it could too easily be mistaken for a flag of truce.

On spying the Confederate vessel's flag fluttering in the breeze, most Yankee ships in the bay haul down 'Old Glory', presumably to avoid making themselves a target, and one ship raises instead the flag of the Ionian Islands – a blue flag bearing a winged lion with a Union Jack in the corner. A couple of American ships run up the 'Stars and Stripes' in a show of defiance, but their symbolic protest is a sideshow of the *Shenandoah*'s travelling Confederate circus.

Like McNulty, Master's Mate Cornelius Hunt is impressed by the reception. His memoir records, 'As soon as it became generally known in Melbourne that a Confederate cruiser had arrived in the offing, a scene of excitement was inaugurated which baffles all adequate description. Crowds of people were rushing hither and thither, seeking authentic information concerning the stranger, and ere we had been an hour at anchor, a perfect fleet of boats was pulling towards us from every direction.'[2]

Lieutenant Frank Chew recalls: 'Among our fair visitors there were many very pretty girls. It is useless to say that we vied with each other in showing them attention, and I might venture to add that some of our officers might have left their hearts in the "Golden Empire".

'Upon every steamer's approaching the ship we would look out for pretty faces and if found we stood near the gangway so as to take them in charge. If they were particularly agreeable we took them after to the cabin and requested the pleasure of a glass of wine with them.'[3]

Not all Victorians are enthused. One goldfields newspaper, the splendidly named *Creswick & Clunes Advertiser and County of Talbot Agricultural Journal*, huffs: 'We fail to see that more glory attaches to this band of marauders than to the pirates of Morocco.'[4]

Immediately upon arrival, Captain Waddell despatches one of his officers, Lieutenant John Grimball, with a letter for Victoria's Governor, Sir Charles Darling. It reads: 'I have the honour to announce to your Excellency the arrival of the Confederate States Steamer *Shenandoah*, under my command, in Port Phillip, this afternoon, and I have also to communicate that the steamer's machinery requires repairs, and that I am in want of coals. I desire your Excellency to grant permission for me to make the necessary repairs, to take in a [load] of coals, to enable me to get to sea as quickly as possible. I desire also your Excellency's permission to land my prisoners. I shall observe the neutrality.'[5]

What Waddell doesn't tell the Governor, of course, is that the need for repairs is a convenient excuse. While it's true that damage to the propeller shaft was discovered during the voyage south, the real reason for coming to Melbourne is to secretly recruit men to join his short-handed crew.

Later that afternoon, in Victoria's Parliament, during yet another tedious and interminable debate on import tariffs, Minister for Justice Archibald Michie is handed a telegram informing him of the arrival of the *Shenandoah*. Michie, who is also Melbourne correspondent for *The Times*, rushes off to report the incident to his London editors. *The Times* will not publish Michie's report until 13 March, followed four days later by a pompous editorial cautioning the colonials to judiciously observe the neutrality laws when dealing with their uninvited guests. It's a waste of ink and bombast. By then, the Confederate cruiser is long gone from Melbourne, steaming from the bottom of the world to the top, with the ultimate aim of destroying the Yankee whaling fleet.

At anchor, newspapers are pitched aboard the *Shenandoah* as, Captain Waddell will later write, 'cheer after cheer greeted us from the generous, brave-hearted Englishmen and Australians, who believed in the justice of our cause. We were prepared for the reception. The pilot [who came aboard when the ship entered the Heads of Port Phillip Bay] has said, "You have a great many friends in Melbourne."'[6]

Waddell is soon to find he has enemies, too, in Melbourne. Powerful enemies. And the newspapers pitched aboard give him little cheer. Having been at sea since the previous October, he was unaware of the re-election of Abraham Lincoln; of Sherman's march to the sea, leaving a path of destruction for 300 miles from Atlanta to Savannah; of the Confederates' crushing defeat at Nashville.

To old salts in port, there's something familiar about the warship, and a close look at her stern reveals the faded lettering of her former name: the *Sea King*, a British merchant ship that had visited Australia about a year earlier. Refitted as an eight-gun man-of-war, the auxiliary screw vessel – capable of both sail and steam power – has been renamed the *Shenandoah*, after the river and valley of that name in western Virginia, part of the Union. It is an ironic choice, though probably not deliberately so. The word is believed to mean 'Daughter of the Stars' in a Native American language; in 1865 the stars are no longer favouring the South.

Control of the valley, running north to south between the Blue Ridge and Allegheny mountains, is strategically vital to both sides. For the North, the Shenandoah had been the 'Valley of Humiliation' early in the war, while the triumphant rebels called it the 'Breadbasket of the Confederacy'.[7] Mainly thanks to Stonewall Jackson, who in 1862 fought off three Union armies there, the valley remained the back door for Confederacy forays until late in 1864, when Union forces under General 'Little Phil' Sheridan defeated Jubal Early's Confederates at the battle of Cedar Creek, and closed the back door; currently, the breadbasket is no more.

William Conway Whittle, the ship's executive officer, writes, 'I do not know why the name *Shenandoah* was chosen, unless because of the constantly recurring conflicts, retreats and advances through the Shenandoah Valley in Virginia, where the brave Stonewall Jackson always so discomforted the enemy, causing, it is said, one of the distinguished Federal generals to say of that valley that it must be made such a waste that a crow to fly over it would have to rake its rations.

'The burning there of homes of defenceless women and children made the selection of the name not inappropriate for a cruiser which was to lead a torch-light procession around the world and into every ocean.'[8]

Perhaps now, for Captain Waddell and his crew, the name is symbolic of a forlorn hope; a talisman to bring back glory days, and take revenge for the destruction visited on the Shenandoah Valley by Federal forces.

And on the journey to the far side of the world, the crew of this Daughter of the Stars wished upon a bright light moving slowly across the night sky. Discovered on January 17 by a Tasmanian ex-convict, watchmaker and amateur astronomer Francis Abbott, the Great Southern Comet of 1865 was so bright it would be visible to the naked eye until the end of February.

There is no guiding star, nor hope nor glory for a troop of the 5th Colored Cavalry driving a herd of cattle to Louisville, Kentucky. On a narrow road outside Simpsonville, the black Union soldiers are ambushed by Confederate guerrillas.

The 5th Colored Cavalry, under the command of General James Sank Brisbin, a prominent abolitionist, consists mainly of former slaves. Kentucky, although a slave state, has stayed in the Union. Since Abraham Lincoln's Emancipation Proclamation freed only slaves in the rebel states, many black men in Kentucky have gained a measure of freedom by joining the regiment.

Attacked from behind, 35 black soldiers are gunned down after their white officers run away. The wounded are shot dead by the rebel irregulars, whose habit it is to execute any wounded or captured black soldiers.

The press will report that one of the white officers hid under a store until the attack was over then rode off for Louisville without looking back, and that other officers were found 'loafing in the tavern'. The report, based on eye-witness accounts, continues:

> The ground was stained with blood and the dead bodies of negro soldiers were stretched out along the road. It was evident that the guerrillas had dashed upon the party guarding the rear of the cattle and taken them completely by surprise. They could not have offered any serious resistance, as none of the outlaws were even wounded. It is presumed that the negroes surrendered and were shot down in cold blood, as but two of the entire number escaped – one of them by secreting himself behind a wagon, the other by running, as he was met several miles from the scene of tragedy, wounded and nearly exhausted. Thirty-five dead bodies were counted lying in the road and vicinity. It was a horrible butchery, yet the scoundrels engaged in the bloody work shot down their victims with feelings of delight.
>
> After the wholesale murder, they took good care to secure the arms and ammunition of the slain. The officers in command of the negro troops should be held responsible for the slaughter, for it is certain that if they had been with their men, and enforced a proper discipline, the outlaws would have been whipped with ease.[9]

None of the white officers would be disciplined for deserting their men.

That same day, in a Confederate prisoner-of-war camp in Florence, South Carolina, one of the captured Union soldiers dies of pneumonia. Given that more than 2,000 of the 16,000 Union prisoners in the Florence Stockade have died of disease or starvation during the past four months, the death of one more Yankee bluecoat might pass without remark, but for the fact that this soldier was a woman disguised as a man.

Florena Budwin, of Philadelphia, dressed as a man and enlisted in the Union army to be with her husband, Captain John Budwin. After John was killed in battle, Florena – the male alias she used is not known – was captured and imprisoned, firstly in the notorious Andersonville prison camp in Georgia – where almost 13,000 of the 45,000 Union prisoners would die during the war – then in the Florence Stockade in South Carolina. There, she tended to sick prisoners until falling ill herself. It was only then that a doctor discovered her sex, and by that stage she was beyond help.

Private Florena Budwin died on 25 January 1865, just a few weeks before all the sick prisoners at the camp were released. She was 20 years old.

And Florena wasn't the only woman to take up arms out of love, loyalty or patriotic fervour. While there are no exact figures because presumably not all were discovered, it's estimated that on both sides at least 600 women disguised as men fought in the American Civil War, and that more than 60 were killed or wounded.[10]

In Australia, oceans away from all this carnage, confusion and despair, smaller life-and-death dramas are being acted out. In what is still a frontier society, the public is fascinated by the exploits of bushrangers, vacillating between hero-worship and outrage. The

1860s were the halcyon days of the Australian bushranger. It's as though the bush and the byways are alive with outlaws, all bound and determined to blast their way into folklore.

The murderous and deranged 'Mad Dan' Morgan is terrorising southern New South Wales and northern Victoria, robbing coaches and pastoral stations, shooting and killing anyone who gets in his way. From the Hunter Valley north to Queensland and west as far as Bourke, Captain Thunderbolt is carrying out daring robberies of mail coaches, travellers, inns, stores and stations, yet has never shot or killed anyone. In the western and southern districts of New South Wales, Ben Hall and his gang are kings of the road, bailing up travellers and gold escorts, and raiding towns and homesteads. Like Thunderbolt, Ben Hall has never killed anyone, but tomorrow, January 26, one of his gang will gun down a policeman in the New South Wales village of Collector, tarnishing Hall's Robin Hood image.

And at Avenel, a tiny settlement 80 miles (130km) north of Melbourne, a seven-year-old boy, son of the local publican, sets off for school as usual. But for reasons unknown, he diverts from the usual path. Instead of crossing the creek by the bridge near his father's hotel, he follows a track leading to a large tree that has fallen across the creek, close to the schoolhouse.

Like other local children, Dick Shelton has probably crossed on the log many times before. On this day, however, the creek below it is rushing and roiling after heavy rain. Dick has hardly taken a step when his hat blows off. Instinctively, he reaches for it and in doing so loses his balance and falls into the water. Dick cannot swim.

Swept away and failing fast, Dick seems fated to drown when another boy, walking along the opposite bank, spots him, dives in and swims to him. With difficulty, the boy manages to drag Dick onto the bank, where both sit awhile, heaving with exhaustion and relief before making their way, wet and bedraggled, to the Royal Mail Hotel.

Dick's 10-year-old saviour is an instant local hero, and Dick's grateful parents, Esau and Elizabeth Shelton, present him with a trophy and a green silk sash. The boy treasures the sash, and will be wearing it years later when his own fate takes a dire turn.

The boy's name is Ned Kelly.

Chapter 3

Welcome strangers

In Sydney, it's Anniversary Day, a celebration of the arrival 77 years ago of the First Fleet at Sydney Cove on 26 January 1788. Events marking the occasion include a regatta on the harbour, a cricket match, a variety of excursions and amusements for the public, and a chance to gawk at the inmates of the Hyde Park Asylum, all regaled in festive frippery whether they like it or not.

The Sydney Morning Herald, never missing a chance to take a backhanded swipe at the rival colony south of the border, opines, 'In celebrating this Anniversary we have the satisfaction to know that transportation [of convicts to Australia] – a great source of discord between England and the colonies – is virtually abolished, and all the miseries which have resulted from it are thus in a fair way of abatement. The elementary character of the colonies is probably far less diverse than their history would imply. We suspect, for example, that in Victoria a greater number are to be found who were formerly in bonds than are gathered in any other section of Australia.'[1]

In Melbourne, where the anniversary later to be renamed Australia Day is studiously ignored, John Egan, publican of The Wild Duck, has offered a £10 reward leading to the conviction of the rogue who stole his 'slightly flea-bitten' thoroughbred grey mare.[2] The publican's chances of gaining public attention to his plight today are slight indeed. Today, all the talk in town is of the Confederate warship that arrived yesterday afternoon.

Throughout the day, the ship is besieged by Melburnians coming alongside in steamers, yachts and rowboats, begging to be allowed aboard. All are refused except for a few set to leave port that day, including two officers of the Royal Navy.

Annie Baxter Dawbin, the wife of a British Army officer posted to Melbourne, writes in her diary, 'I went out to Mrs Armytage's soon after breakfast and sat there for some time, but came back for lunch, as I had to go to Sandridge to see the Confederate man-of-war *Shenandoah* – the late famous *Sea King*. I remained some time there, but the weather proved too stormy, and Captain Waddell sent a message on shore to say it would be unsafe to go.'[3]

Escaping the crowds, the *Shenandoah* officers go ashore, where they find fate has brought them to a place much like, yet at the same time alien to their homeland. This is a British colony named after an invisible monarch: a queen and empress who, since the death four years earlier of her beloved husband, Prince Albert, has shut herself away in Balmoral Castle, wallowing in what her private secretary Charles Grey has described as 'constant and ever increasing grief'.[4] Those close to the Queen fear she is not so much mad with grief as just plain mad. Parliamentarians have called for her to abdicate, and the people say she is dead to them.

Following the Australian convention of naming towns and geographical features after mediocre British politicians, the colony's capital city is named for William Lamb, Lord Melbourne. Melbourne was Queen Victoria's first prime minister, and the young Queen had quite a crush on him, hanging off his every word and, in her private time, drawing portraits of him in her sketch book. Victoria was much influenced by Melbourne, although it's not known whether or not she shared his view that the poor were not worth bothering with and were best left alone or that Lord Shaftesbury's efforts to ban child labour were a waste of time. He also distrusted newfangled contraptions of any kind, disliked railways and hated the Irish.[5]

For all that, his lordship is best remembered as the cuckolded husband of Lady Caroline Lamb, the mistress of Lord Byron, and for whipping orphan girls taken into his household, supposedly as an act of charity.[6]

The rebels have booked into Scott's Hotel, laid aside their swords, and are walking the streets of the capital, suitably impressed by its wide streets, grand houses, fine carriages and handsome public buildings.

Much is comfortably familiar. They see women in the high-brimmed 'spoon' bonnets fashionable in the South. It being high summer, many wear bonnets made of straw and woven horsehair, elaborately trimmed with laces and wide ribbons. Others wear their hair in gathered nets. The belles of Melbourne promenade in bell-shaped dresses with tiny waists. Underneath are crinolines – whalebone or steel cages that create the bell shape of the petticoats and dress. Beneath all that is a whalebone and fabric corset hooked or buttoned tightly at the front to make the waist look smaller. The women here, like those of the South, are veritable ironclads.

The Confederates note that many men here wear trousers in the American style, sporting a narrow waistband with a strap and buckle at the back, some with braces, some without. Despite the summer heat, gentlemen of quality strut about in frock coat and waistcoat with pocket watch, silk cravat or bow tie, top hat and walking cane.

This being a town the gold rush built, miners are a common sight. They go about in shirts and neckerchiefs, high boots and wide-brimmed hats, wearing trousers held up with a belt, braces or rope. Of the diggers on the streets, some – clearly down on their luck – are in threadbare clothes. Others, more fortunate, are almost as fashionably clad as city toffs, gold being the great leveller of class – at least until the money runs out.

Most women wear their hair curled and waved by mechanical contraptions worn overnight. Men mostly wear their hair long, with big moustaches, sideburns or beards. A few, presumably Yankees or Yankee sympathisers, sport a beard but no moustache, like Abraham Lincoln.

The Southerners see no black faces on the streets of Melbourne. They know there are no slaves here – not this far south, anyway – but where are the natives they have heard so much about? Where are the Aborigines?

Had they asked why, they would have recognised clear parallels between the treatment of, and attitudes towards the native peoples of Australia and those of North America. White colonisers on both continents share a belief that Anglo-Saxons are innately superior to indigenous races, and are thus ordained by divine providence to spread throughout the land, displacing or erasing native populations. White Americans call it 'Manifest Destiny'. White Australians, echoing the ideals of Victorian

England, call it 'Progress' – with a capital P – and are equally as convinced that in the path of Christian civilisation the fate of so-called inferior races is subjugation or extermination. Resistance is futile.

It is generally supposed that indigenous peoples are doomed to extinction. It's accepted as scientific fact – simply survival of the fittest – and thus it is the duty of the white race to ensure these lesser mortals pass into the fossil record as painlessly as possible and with a minimum of fuss.

In Australia, the notion of what the poet Rudyard Kipling would later call the 'white man's burden' underlines official policies of Protection – again with a capital P. Discrimination disguised as paternal concern, it is used to justify the forced relocation of peoples to isolated reserves where they are denied basic freedoms and their culture is ruthlessly suppressed, supposedly for their own good.

Typical of the hypocrisy of the age is an opinion piece, in a Melbourne newspaper, on the 1865 report of the Board for the Protection of Aborigines. The board has total control over the lives of Victoria's Aborigines, including the power to forcibly remove children from their families to be taught the white man's ways.

It begins: 'The condition of the aboriginal inhabitants of this continent is a subject full of interest to their white successors,' and goes on to commend 'the humanity and good feeling of the colonists in their treatment of the small remnant which still exists of these once numerous races of Victorian natives.

'On the whole, the report does not speak of any marked improvement in the condition of the blacks. As a general rule they are comfortable and healthy, but in their moral state they show they are but slightly reclaimed from savagery.'

The article concludes that 'the large majority' of Aborigines – the 'majority' presumably being those who had survived half a century of decimation through disease, dislocation and murder – are 'beyond the power of improvement'.

'It seems, indeed, that the race only shows a tendency to improvement in those branches of it which are nearest extinction.'[7]

Melbourne, founded in 1835, has grown rapidly since the discovery of gold in Victoria in 1851. Now, in 1865, its population has overtaken that of Sydney, and, thanks to the flow of gold, the city boasts streets studded with grand civic buildings, and inner suburbs linked by boulevards and gardens. To its proud inhabitants it is Eldorado Down Under.

In 1865, Victoria has been an independent colony for only 14 years. Previously, it was part of New South Wales, which originally covered two-thirds of the continent. The colonies differ in origin, wealth and stages of development; jealousies are rife and rivalry is intense.

In 1851, when Victoria separated from New South Wales, the border between the adjoining colonies was determined to be the top of the south bank of the Murray River. This meant that none of the river was in Victoria, yet the Murray is wont to change its course now and then, as rivers tend to do, and has been the cause of sometimes bitter disputes ever since, even threats of war.

Victoria and New South Wales cannot even agree on the gauge of railway tracks. People travelling between the colonies have to change trains at the border because Victorian tracks are wider than New South Wales tracks. Travellers also have to undergo customs and baggage checks at the border, with each side enforcing differing rules on what you can and can't bring in. Merchants are frustrated by the different tariffs and customs duties imposed, making trade between the colonies slow and often uneconomical.

Despite all those difficulties, talk of federation falls on deaf ears. No colony is willing to surrender its legislative rights. While there are no guns aimed across the Murray River, the defence of states' rights is as fierce as in America, and the Confederates would find the arguments eerily familiar. New South Wales, calling for tariffs on manufactured goods to be scrapped, supports free trade. Victoria, believing the colony should be self-sufficient, champions protectionism.

The dispute reminds the Confederates that back home, before the war, when the North pressed for tariffs as protection against foreign imports, the South reacted angrily, asking why the South should pay more for goods to the advantage of the North. The labels adopted by the opposing political camps in Australia – Free Trader and Protectionist – are familiar to American ears, having been coined by Southern slaveholders.

Particularly familiar is an ongoing dispute over the tax on tea. The import duty on tea charged by Victoria is sixpence a pound, whereas New South Wales and South Australia charge only half that amount. There have been no protests in the style of the Boston Tea Party, however. Duty-dodging Victorian traders send tea from Melbourne to Adelaide, then ship it down the Murray River to Melbourne. In other words, Victorians are smuggling Victorian tea into Victoria.

In their light grey uniforms, with gold braid, gilt buttons, and blue silk shoulder strap with a single star, the rebels turn heads as they stroll down Collins Street, with its imposing architecture, past the Town Hall; along Little Collins Street, where wigged and gowned lawyers flit between bars and chambers; up lively Bourke Street, with music halls such as the Alhambra Dance Hall and the Haymarket Theatre one of several theatres. In the foyer of the Haymarket, in the days to come, the Confederates will often gather to meet local ladies and discover that flattery will get them everywhere.

At the nearby Theatre Royal, tonight is 'positively the last night' of the 'burlesque extravaganza' *King Turko the Terrible*, followed by the musical farce *A Loan of a Lover*, and concluding the evening's entertainment with the 'very laughable farce', *A Ghost in Spite of Himself*.

When it comes to light-hearted diversions, distractions from the serious business of waging war, and dalliances of a romantic nature, the welcome strangers are spoilt for choice.

Back at Scott's Hotel, the drink flows freely and it's not too long before most of the rebel officers are three sheets to the wind. Surgeon Lining, for one, already feeling no pain, accepts an invitation to a party, staggers back to Scott's at around 11pm and falls into bed.

During one drinking session at Scott's, an American merchant – a Northerner whose girth is exceeded only by his self-regard – is overheard by the Confederates calling them 'a damned set of piratical scoundrels'. One of the rebels calmly gets up from his seat, grabs the merchant by the nose, leads him to the door and kicks him in the arse, sending him tumbling down the stairs. Reporting the incident with obvious glee, the *Creswick & Clunes Advertiser* comments, 'It may be presumed that the Northerner retired, like the generals of his country, solely for strategic reasons, for it is reported that he did not offer any resistance against his forcible expulsion. And yet it is singular that a citizen of the mighty Union, about – as he was wont to say – to annex Canada and Ireland, should allow himself to be so used by a "damned pirate".'[8]

While the ship's officers are being duchessed by Melbourne's quality folk, and throwing fat Yankees downstairs, her sailors and marines are sampling the city's flesh-pots. There are prostitutes on almost every corner, catering for all tastes, and brothels on most city streets, ranging from the upscale – such as Mother Fraser's opulent bordello on Stephens Street – to humble parlours in dank laneways.

On Bourke Street – with its all-night bars, dance halls with wall-to-wall girls, and hotels renting rooms by the hour – pimps, touts and spruikers compete for the patronage of thirsty and sex-starved sailors. The Southerners have seen nothing like this since New Orleans' French Quarter, and, readily led into temptation, they make the most of it.

Chapter 4

Other men's battles

William Kenyon is casting a weather eye down the columns of classified ads in Friday's paper when, between an ad for quarrymen and stonebreakers, and one placed by a young man seeking 'a situation, early hours preferred', he spies an intriguing notice.

It reads, 'Wanted, two or three respectable young men to be generally useful to travel up new country, apply personally to Mr Powell, No 125 Flinders Lane east, between 9 and 10 or 12 and 1 today.'[1]

Kenyon, born in the seaside village of Rye, south of Melbourne, but now living in the city, is 21 years old, at a loose end and craving adventure. A volunteer member of the Victorian Naval Brigade – a reservist unit supplementing the colony's permanent navy – he has been trained in artillery and infantry drill, ashore and afloat, but has never ventured further than Port Phillip Heads. He decides to go and see what Mr Powell has to offer.

Across Hobson's Bay, in Williamstown, Samuel Crook makes the same decision. Crook, better known as 'Little Sam', is a local waterfront character; an archetypal seadog. He has modest lodg-ings in Waterman's Row, but when home from the sea can usually be found propping up the bar at the Pier Hotel or down on the steamboat jetty, spinning rollicking seafaring yarns to anyone who'll listen.

Kenyon and Crook have no way of knowing, of course, that the door to a run-down boarding house at 125 Flinders Lane opens into peril and infamy or that not merely 'two or three respectable young men' but many more men of various ages and repute share their curiosity.

Melbourne sailor Thomas Strong is one. Sandridge stevedore John Collins is another. Also from Sandridge come waterman James McLaren, bootmaker William Green and fireman Thomas McLean. They are joined, from Williamstown, by shipwright John Kilgower and carpenter John James; from suburban Melbourne by seamen James McLaren and John Spring; by David Alexander; by many more from parts unknown; and by one mysterious charac-ter who will be the last man to die in the service of the Confederacy.

Of some 120 Australians known to have fought in the American Civil War, the vast majority joined US infantry regiments or the US Navy. Of those, most are listed as having been born in Sydney, with less than a dozen from Victoria, Tasmania, South Australia and Western Australia. The exact birthplace of many veterans is unknown, recorded only as Australia. About 20 New Zealanders also fought in the war, all on the Union side.[2]

A roll call of Australian Confederates is problematic, but that's hardly surprising. The lists do not take into account overseas-born Australian residents who took up arms for the South, nor can they include those men who secretly and illegally joined the crew of the *Shenandoah*, some of them using aliases, and whose fates are shrouded in mystery.

It's uncertain how many were native-born and how many were overseas-born Australians. This is not unusual. Australia, at that time, was the name of a continent but not of a nation. There was no such thing as an Australian passport, nor a colonial passport, nor even a British passport. Britain had abolished passports for travel within the Empire back in 1826.

Australian colonials, old and new, tended to identify with their ethnic origins first, their colony second, and the continent hardly at all. Thus, they would commonly refer to themselves as say, English, Irish, Scottish or German, even if they had been born in Australia. For example, William Kenyon, of Irish heritage but born in Victoria, is listed on the *Shenandoah*'s crew register as Irish, presumably because he identified himself as such.

(To add further confusion, many among the crew of the *Shenandoah* will later hope to avoid the noose for piracy by pretending to be Dixie born and bred.)

And it's no surprise that so many men find Mr Powell's vague temptation irresistible. The 1851 Victorian gold rush brought a flood of adventurous and desperate men from other Australian colonies and from overseas. Now, 14 years on, the easily won alluvial gold is running out and the roaring days are fading fast. Yet many of the adventurers and desperados are still here, as are the thousands of Melburnians who fled to the goldfields in the 1850s – leaving the city almost a ghost town – and have now returned with empty pockets and bleak prospects.

The smoke of the Eureka Stockade Rebellion has long since cleared but the wounds are still raw. In 1854, on the Ballarat goldfields, under a flag of the Southern Cross, diggers outraged by the imposition of miner's licences and government abuses took up arms against the colonial authorities. The diggers had sworn by the Southern Cross 'to stand truly by each other, and fight to defend our rights and liberties'.[3]

On Sunday 3 December, a force of redcoats and police troopers laid siege to the stockade. The battle was bitter and bloody, and cost the lives of 22 diggers and six soldiers and police. But while the rebellion was mercilessly put down and its wounded leader, Peter Lalor, and 12 other survivors charged with treason, the spirit of Eureka prevailed. It was surely present at the treason trials of Lalor and the others, when, after only 25 to 40 minutes' deliberation, and despite all evidence to the contrary, the juries found all 13 men not guilty.

The American writer Mark Twain, after visiting the Ballarat goldfields, would call the rebellion 'the finest thing in Australian history . . . It was a revolution small in size but great politically; it was a strike for liberty, a struggle for a principle, a stand against injustice and oppression.' Comparing the Eureka Rebellion to the standoff between the barons and King John that led to Magna Carta, and the battles of Lexington and Concord that marked the outbreak of the American War of Independence, Twain said, 'It was another instance of a victory won by a lost battle. It adds an honourable page to history; the people know it and are proud of it. They keep green the memory of the men who fell at Eureka Stockade, and Peter Lalor and his monument.'[4]

That memory is very green indeed in 1865. It may be that hard times and the spirit of Eureka have kindled in some an emotional attachment to the Confederate cause and empathy with the underdog, but for how many we can only guess. What we do know for sure is that idle hands and broken hearts make ideal fodder for foreign wars, and, for Australians, it wouldn't be the first time.

Colonial Australia, despite being an outpost of the powerful British Empire, is dogged by insecurity. Britannia rules the waves, but the Mother Country is so very far away. Napoleon has gone but France is still seen as a threat, as is America.

Lingering suspicion of American intentions harks back to the morning of 30 November 1839, when Sydney woke in fright to find a squadron of American warships anchored in the harbour – having slipped in uninvited and unnoticed during the night. The arrival of the American ships, which were not hostile but on a voyage of exploration, set off frantic moves to strengthen coastal defences. In Sydney Harbour, Pinchgut Island, which had been used to isolate troublesome convicts, was fortified in 1841 and renamed Fort Denison.

And then there were the Russians. Many in the young colonies were convinced that the Czar of all the Russias was plotting to extend his reach to Australia, and there had been a series of invasion scares in the first half of the 19th century. Such fears were fuelled by increasingly regular visits by Russian warships to Australian waters, notably the Pacific cruise of a Russian naval fleet in 1854, the year Britain and France entered the Crimean War.

Turkey had gone to war with Russia the previous year, when Russian forces invaded what is now Romania, then under Turkish control. Fearful that Russian expansion would continue its march into Afghanistan and India, upsetting the balance of power, Britain and France entered the fray, which was mostly fought on the Crimean Peninsula and would end in 1856 with Russia defeated.

While a mere handful of Australians (Australian members of British regiments) fought in the Crimean War, public support in the colonies for Britain's participation in the conflict was at fever pitch. Invasion hysteria, fanned by anti-Russian propaganda, conjured up images of Russian barbarians attacking and occupying Australian cities.

Typical of the enduring rivalry between Sydney and Melbourne, there was debate over which city the invaders would prefer to pillage. Some Melburnians, boasting that the Victorian gold rush had made their city the richest in the world, were hopeful the Russians would be content to plunder the gold from the city's banks and go away. Other less optimistic souls suspected their worst fears had been realised when their sleep was shattered one night by explosions and rockets' red glare, and rushed down to Hobson's Bay to defend their fair city.

'It threw the city and its suburbs into a state of great excitement,' *The Argus* reported. 'The military in the barracks were under arms for some hours, waiting intelligence and orders, if necessary, to proceed to the scene of action. Thousands of people were hurrying from all directions down the road to Sandridge, determined to see what was up, and by no means inclined to turn tail upon the Russians, even if they were there. Should it ever happen that an enemy should enter our port, the people, if armed, would fight like tigers.'

As it turned out, no Australian tiger had to face the Russian bear. The explosions and rockets were fireworks and guns from a British ship celebrating its release from quarantine. The newspaper added that the excitement was heightened by some 'young rascals' moving among the crowd, pretending to be newsboys selling an extra edition of *The Argus*, shouting, 'Full particulars of the battle of Melbourne!'[5]

Although such worries were unfounded, insecurity became ingrained in colonial society. Clinging to the edges of a continent on the far side of the world, Australians were all too aware of their vulnerability. Life as they knew it could change overnight. All it would take was for a hostile man-of-war to sail through the heads.

The 1860s brought another rush to foreign killing fields. During the Maori Wars in New Zealand, the Victorian colonial navy sent the sloop-of-war *Victoria* – five years later it will be nestled nervously in Hobson's Bay, moored near the *Shenandoah* – to support the conflict. The first Australian warship deployed to a foreign war, the *Victoria* carried out shore bombardments and coastal patrols, and suffered one casualty – a sailor shot dead by friendly fire.

In 1863 and 1864, more than 2,400 Australians, mostly from Victoria, enlisted in militia to fight the Maori. The conflict also involved British regiments based in Australia.

The 1863 Waikato War, fought on the North Island of New Zealand, was the largest campaign in a series of battles history would call the New Zealand Wars. Second only to the American Civil War in the size of opposing forces, it involved 14,000 imperial and colonial troops, and some 4,000 warriors from a confederation of Maori tribes. The Maoris, determined to turn back the tide of land-hungry Europeans driving them from their territories, faced off against an invading force equally determined to prosecute the case for Manifest Destiny.

In August of 1863 – while, in America, Union forces under Ulysses S. Grant were laying siege to Vicksburg, Mississippi – recruiters in Australia for the Waikato War were promising land in New Zealand in exchange for service. For three years' service, plus pay, recruits would be granted from 50 to 400 acres – depending on rank – of land taken from the Maori. The recruiters were all but trampled in the rush as, in New South Wales, Victoria, Queensland and Tasmania, would-be farmers took up the offer. Even though many of them – luckless diggers from the oldfields, townsmen and assorted misfits and adventurers – couldn't milk a cow to save themselves, the lure of acres for bullets was irresistible. Off they sailed to a foreign war, more as mercenaries than loyal volunteers, and often leaving their wives and families destitute.

Nine months, 1,000 Maori and 700 British and colonial lives later, the Waikato War ended. For the victorious imperial forces it was a Pyrrhic victory. Four million acres of land were seized from the Maori tribes as the price of rebellion, but all that did was to provoke another war, then another and another, and a dispute over land title that would continue – albeit peacefully – into the 21st century.

Of the Australians who fought in the New Zealand Wars, 31 were killed in action. Medals were awarded to veterans who had been under fire, and, arguably, the most decorated Australian was Captain John Phelps, of Sydney, who had served in both the Crimean and New Zealand wars.

Of some 1,500 Australians who settled on confiscated Maori land, most failed to make a go of it. The land offered was of poor quality and the New Zealand Government's promises of support were never honoured. It was the first and last time Australians would be offered acres for bullets.

*

For most Australians who fought for the Union in the American Civil War, there is little or no flesh upon the bones of history; most are merely names on a muster roll or a headstone; footnotes in the fortunes of war. Yet there are standout stories to be found, such as that of George Robert Scott.

Born in the Sydney suburb of Punchbowl, in 1846, Scott was the son of a cabinet-maker who, drawn by the California gold rush, took his family to America, joining the thousands of Australians there hoping to strike it rich.

George Scott was just 15 when the Civil War began. A year later, in July 1862, he joined the Union Army, enlisting in the 3rd California Volunteer Infantry. But although Scott had signed on for three years, he deserted after only seven months. In those seven months, Private Scott never once set eyes on a grey uniform or heard the rebel yell. His company was posted to Fort Gaston, in the redwood forests of Northern California, as far from the action as it was possible to be, and ordered to fight not Confederates but Native Americans. Scott saw action in a skirmish at Light Prairie, near Fort Gaston, after which his company was posted to Camp Union, California. It was there, on 21 February 1863, that he stole away and was listed as a deserter.

We can only guess why this 17-year-old soldier decided to risk shame and execution, but it may be because of his regiment's involvement, a few weeks earlier, in an incident known as the Bear Creek Massacre. On 29 January 1863, in the early hours of a cold winter morning, a detachment of California Volunteers, under Colonel Patrick Edward Connor, attacked the village of Shoshone chief Bear Hunter. Connor, whose several requests to be transferred to the 'real war' in the east had been denied, was determined to win military glory by suppressing Indian resistance to invasion by white settlers into what is now Idaho. Crossing the creek, the soldiers charged the village, firing indiscriminately. Bear Hunter and his warriors put up a courageous defence but soon lay dead in the snow, and while the fight could have ended there, Connor let his men run amok. Women were raped and killed, children and infants were bludgeoned to death, lodges were torched and people found sheltering inside were shot and killed, many of them at point-blank range. Almost 500 Shoshone men, women and children died that day. The California Volunteers' casualties were 14 killed and 49 wounded.

For his role in the massacre, Colonel Connor was decorated and promoted to General. George Scott, meanwhile, made his way safely back home to Australia. He settled in Kempsey, in northern New South Wales, where he married twice, fathered five children, and spent the rest of his days as the respected proprietor of the local newspaper, *The Macleay Chronicle*.

Another George Scott who fought in the Civil War is better known to history as the bushranger Captain Moonlite (his spelling). The son of an Anglican minister, cultured, handsome and homosexual, Moonlite wasn't your average bushranger. Born in Rathriland, Ireland, and educated in London, where he qualified as an engineer, he served with Garibaldi's redshirts in Italy, then with the Waikato Militia during the New Zealand Wars. Wounded in action but dishonourably discharged for malingering, he headed for the California goldfields, joined the Union Army after the Civil War broke out, and – legend has it – turned a dishonest dollar selling confiscated cotton on the black market.

In 1868, Scott turned up in Australia, where, after a short period as a lay preacher in Ballarat, Victoria, he turned to robbery under arms, reinventing himself as Captain Moonlite, leader of an outlaw gang which included his lover, James Nesbitt.

In 1879, during a hold-up at a sheep station near Wagga Wagga, in southern New South Wales, Nesbitt and another gang member were shot and killed in a gun battle with police. A police trooper, Constable Bowen, was also killed, shot down by Moonlite, who was then captured while grieving over Nesbitt's body. Convicted of Bowen's murder, Moonlite went to the gallows in January 1880, wearing a ring woven from a lock of his lover's hair. His request to be buried alongside Nesbitt, at Gundagai, was denied.

There's a postscript, however. The location of Moonlite's unmarked grave, in Sydney's Rookwood Cemetery, was unknown until discovered in 1984 by researcher Roy Parker while searching for graves of American Civil War veterans. In 1995, the bushranger's dying wish was honoured at last. His remains were exhumed from Sydney and taken to Gundagai, to be buried alongside James Nesbitt.

Of all the tales of Australians who fought for the North, the most intriguing is surely that of Morris Mason Farrar. Born in Sydney, in 1844, to an American father and an Irish mother, he migrated to the United States and settled in Fitchburg, Massachusetts. In 1862, at 18 years old, Morris Farrar joined the Union Army, enlisting as a private in the 53rd Massachusetts Volunteer Infantry for service in the Civil War.

Deployed to Louisiana, the 53rd engaged Confederate General Richard Taylor's Army of Western Louisiana at the Battle of Fort Bisland, pushed the enemy back after five hours under heavy fire, and was the first Union regiment to plant its flag on the ramparts. The 53rd lost one officer and 13 privates, killed and wounded, in the battle, but Private Morris Farrar wasn't one of them. Luck was with him.

In pursuit of the retreating Confederates, the men of the 53rd again found themselves under heavy fire during the attack on Port Hudson. Once more, they drove the rebels back, but the surrender of Port Hudson was won at the cost of seven officers and 79 men killed and wounded. Private Morris Farrar wasn't among them. Luck was still with him.

By the time the 53rd, having done its duty, was ordered back to Massachusetts, met by cheering crowds and mustered out of service, it had lost almost half its 300 officers and men. Private Morris Farrar's luck had held out. Again, he was not among the casualties.

The 1865 Massachusetts census listed Farrar as born in New South Wales, Australia, and his occupation as soldier, living in the family home in Fitchburg with his mother, Rosa, and 11-year-old sister, Harriet. The 1870 census found him still in Fitchburg, working at a woollen mill, married to Irish-born Catherine Tierney and with a one-year-old daughter, Alice.

It seems civilian life simply didn't suit Morris Farrar. Two years later, he gave up his job sharpening tools, kissed his wife and daughter goodbye and leapt into the saddle and into history. On 23 January 1872, he enlisted in the US Seventh Cavalry, Company E, and, in June of 1876, rode with US General George Armstrong Custer into eastern Montana Territory to suppress Native American resistance to white invasion – an expedition that would end at Little Bighorn.

The Battle of the Little Bighorn, commonly known as Custer's Last Stand, has often been portrayed as a short, sharp engagement but was in fact three separate battles fought over two days between the Seventh Cavalry and combined forces of the Lakota, Northern Cheyenne and Arapaho tribes. Custer himself and five of the 12 companies of his command – 264 men – were annihilated in the second engagement, on 25 June.

Cut off at the end of a long ridge after fighting a running battle, Custer and his men stood exposed on what would be called Last Stand Hill, with relentless gunfire from the south-east making it impossible to secure a defensive position. According to Native American accounts, a charge from the north-east led by the Lakota leader Crazy Horse caused the troops to panic, some throwing down their weapons as the warriors charged in for the kill. Witnessing Crazy Horse's charge, a Northern Cheyenne leader reputedly cried, 'I have never seen anything so brave!'[6]

History records that Custer and all the troopers with him on that fateful hill died that day. There were no survivors. The five companies wiped out included Company E, Morris Farrar's company, but Farrar was not among the dead. For unclear reasons he was not with the unfortunate Company E that day but with companies D, H and K, under the command of Captain Fred Benteen.

Earlier that day, about 12 miles from the Little Bighorn River, on discovering the position of a large Indian encampment, Custer had divided his force into three. Major Marcus Reno was to attack from the upper end of the village, Custer from further downstream, while Benteen was sent to scout the hills on the left flank. Custer, grossly underestimating the number of warriors in the village – it contained at least 7,000 men – decided to attack at once rather than wait for the main army under General Alfred Terry to arrive. Two hours later, as Benteen's battalion approached the river, having encountered no resistance, trumpeter John Martin rode up at a gallop with a hastily scribbled message from Custer to Benteen: 'Come on. Big village. Be quick.

Bring packs.'[7] Controversially, instead of rushing off at once to Custer's aid, Benteen, who was known to dislike Custer intensely, calmly tucked the note into his pocket and spent 20 minutes watering the horses at a ford. It was only when distant gunfire was heard that he mounted up and led his men into battle – not to assist Custer, however, but Major Reno, who was under heavy fire across the river on a bluff that is now called Reno Hill.

Some idea of what Private Farrar experienced when Benteen arrived at Reno's position can be gained from an account by George Herendon, one of Reno's scouts, given shortly after the battle: 'Captain Benteen saw a large mass of Indians gathered on his front to charge, and ordered his men to charge on foot and scatter them. Benteen led the charge and was upon the Indians before they knew what they were about and killed a great many. They were evidently much surprised at this offensive movement, and I think in desperate fighting Benteen is one of the bravest men I ever saw in a fight. All the time he was going about through the bullets, encouraging the soldiers to stand up to their work and not let the Indians whip them; he went among the horses and pack mules and drove out the men who were skulking there, compelling them to go into the line and do their duty. He never sheltered his own person once during the battle, and I do not see how he escaped being killed.'[8]

Before General Terry's cavalry arrived to save the day, 47 men of Reno's and Benteen's commands had been killed. Morris Farrar was not one of them.

The army scout George Herendon was clearly as impressed by Captain Benteen's leadership and courage under fire as the Cheyenne leader was of Crazy Horse's bravery. But while Crazy Horse would be immortalised as a great warrior and military tactician, both Benteen and Reno would be forever haunted by accusations of cowardice. Why, when the fight at Reno Hill was all but finished, and the sound of heavy gunfire to the north-east told them Custer was in deep trouble just a 15-minute ride away, did they stand idly by and not press on to join forces with him?

At an 1879 court of inquiry, Benteen said he found it impossible to obey Custer's orders because to do so would have been suicide. We can only guess whether Private Morris Farrar, 7th Cavalry, Coy. E, would agree. He never told his story. The only Australian-born participant in the most famous battle of the American West passed away peacefully in his bed in Philadelphia in 1899. Lucky to the last.

Chapter 5

The very model of a Southern gentleman

By his own admission, the irascible captain of the *Shenandoah* was an incorrigible child. In his memoirs, he confesses that in his birthplace of Pittsboro, a hamlet in Chatham County, in the southern state of North Carolina, 'All the deviltry committed in and out of that hamlet the mothers of my playmates laid at my door and would exclaim, "I'll bet it was James Iredell."'[1]

James Iredell Waddell, born in 1824, makes no mention of his parents, Francis and Elizabeth, in his memoirs, revealing only that as a young boy he was adopted by his paternal grandmother. Intriguingly, he was not orphaned. His mother lived until 1869, his father until 1881.

At 13 years old, when his grandmother fell ill, he was sent to live with his maternal grandfather in Orange County, North Carolina. It was this grandfather who had named him James Iredell, after the eminent US Supreme Court Justice of that name.

At 17, for reasons he does not disclose, the teenager who had never seen the sea joined the US Navy as a midshipman. He reported for duty to Commodore William B. Shubrick aboard the warship *Pennsylvania*, in Norfolk, Virginia. Having never seen a boat, let alone a 120-gun man-of-war, he was mightily impressed.

Commodore Shubrick told him, 'Young gentleman, you must remember that you are now a servant of the people. They are taxed for your support, and you should at all times be respectful to the people. They can dismantle the Navy whenever they choose to exercise the power.'[2] Waddell would reflect on these words in later years, when the old ideals of service to the people were compromised; made complicated and dangerous by fickle winds of change and the whims of politics.

After graduating from the Annapolis Naval Academy in 1841, his career took him to the Gulf of Mexico for three years during the Mexican–American war provoked by the US annexation of Texas. He went on to serve in Brazil, during which time he was promoted to Second Lieutenant, thence in Panama, the Mediterranean, and China, where he saw action during the Second Opium War, of 1856–1860, so called because British demands for opening all of China to foreign merchants included legalising the opium trade. In that conflict, the US Navy provided fire support to British and French ground forces attacking Chinese positions.

Contemporaries described Lieutenant Waddell as a tall, strong, broad-shouldered and handsome man with a quick temper and a somewhat aloof air belying a kind heart. He spoke only when he had something to say and chose his words carefully. Of noble bearing, gracious and courtly in the finest traditions of Dixie, he walked with a slight limp – a wound acquired not in battle but in a duel fought with a fellow officer over the honour of a lady. Here, then, was the quintessential Southern gentleman.

In China, Waddell served on the *Saginaw*, a California-built vessel he considered inferior. 'The laurel of California is fit only for furniture,' he wrote. 'The *Saginaw* was built of laurel, and she was never considered seaworthy.'[3] Waddell's assessment of the *Saginaw* would one day inspire his most daring plan of attack.

By 1861, he was married – to Anne Sellman Inglehart of Annapolis, Maryland – had a two-year-old daughter, Annie, and was stationed in Hong Kong. It was there word reached him that war was likely to break out between the states.

'I was detached from the *Saginaw*, and ordered to the *John Adams*,' he would write in his memoirs. 'I was pleased to receive the order, I had determined if the North made war on the South to go south and assist those people. I hoped there would be peace between the sections, war would intensify hatred, without even a hope of ever restoring good fellowship, it mattered not which were victorious. I still hoped for a better feeling to prevail.'[4]

A better feeling did not prevail, and when the *John Adams*, en route to New York, reached the island of St Helena in November, Waddell was saddened to learn that the dogs of war, let loose in April after the Confederate attack on Fort Sumter, were now in full cry.

The first major battle of the war had been fought and won, by the South, on 21 July, on a bloody field in Virginia, just 25 miles (40km) south-west of the Union capital. The Northerners, who named battlefields after geographical features, called it Bull Run, after the river of that name. The Southerners, who named battles for localities, called it Manassas, after the nearby town.

On that field, the rebel general Thomas Jackson earned a nickname and a place in American folklore. With the Confederate line about to break under a fierce Union attack, the sight of Jackson 'standing like a stone wall' rallied the rebel troops to launch a successful counter-attack.[5]

On that day, Union casualties were 460 killed, 1,124 wounded and 1,312 missing in action or taken prisoner. On the Confederate side, the toll was 387 killed, 1,582 wounded and 13 missing in action. It was the biggest and bloodiest battle fought on American soil thus far, yet there were longer casualty lists to come and much more blood to flow. On the same field, over three days the following August, Confederate forces under General Robert E. Lee would again win the day, but the casualty count for the Second Battle of Bull Run or Second Manassas would be 14,000 for the Union and 8,000 for the Confederacy. Each battle to follow would take a heavier toll until, in the end, that grim tally would rise to 596,670 killed, wounded or missing for the North, and 490,309 for the South.

Lieutenant Waddell, like many Southerners serving in the US Navy, was shaken by the news of First Manassas. Accepting the sad fact that the war was likely to be longer and more terrible than he had imagined, and mindful that, like most men of his era, his first loyalty lay with his home state – he considered himself a Carolinian first, a US citizen second – he saw no alternative but to quit the service. By late 1861, some 370 serving commissioned officers, warrant officers and midshipmen had resigned or been discharged from the US Navy and joined the Confederate Navy, mostly retaining their Union rank.

Observing the formalities, Waddell wrote to the Secretary of the Navy resigning his commission: 'The people of the State of North Carolina having withdrawn their allegiance to the Government, and the State from the Confederacy of the United States; and owing to these circumstances, and for reasons to be hereafter mentioned, I return to his Excellency the President of the United States the commission which appointed me a Lieutenant in the Navy, with other public documents, asking acceptance thereof.'[6]

Making it clear this decision had not been taken lightly, he added, 'In thus separating myself from associations which I have cherished for 20 years, I wish it to be understood that no doctrine of the right of secession, no wish for disunion of the States impelled me, but simply because my home is the home of my people in the South, and I cannot bear arms against it or them.'[7]

When the *John Adams* arrived at New York, Waddell was visited by an old friend and roommate from naval college, Lieutenant Watson Smith, who surprised him with an offer of a senior command in the US Navy. When Waddell politely declined the offer, Smith said coldly, 'I shall not respect friendship on the field.'

Waddell replied, 'I shall be pleased to meet you, since you shall not respect friendship on the field.'[8]

The two former friends never faced each other in battle, and Watson Smith was killed in the war.

Having had no reply from the Secretary of the Navy, and assuming he had perhaps not made his position plain enough, Waddell wrote another letter of resignation – this time to President Lincoln himself – repeating his assertion that 'it is impossible that I could bear arms against the South in this war'.[9]

There was no reply, and so he waited, expecting to be arrested any day. At last, a letter came from the Navy Department accepting his resignation. 'By order of the President,' it informed him, blunt and to the point, 'your name has, this day, been stricken from the rolls.'[10]

In a seemingly chivalrous gesture, former US Navy officers were entitled to claim pay owing from their prewar service, but there was a catch, as Waddell would discover.

The catch was that the money would only be paid 'if you will address a communication with the Department, engaging upon your word of honour, to take no part in the war now being waged against the Government'.[11]

Waddell would not, could not, take such an oath, and the money was never paid.

His problem now was to make his way south from a Yankee port. A friend told him that if he went to a certain stall at the Baltimore markets – the first stall on the right at the southern end of the market – and asked a certain fat butcher the price of beef, a passage south would be arranged for him.

Having satisfied himself that his wife and child were as far from harm's way as possible – the risks in such a wartime journey being considerable – he and an unnamed companion paid the butcher $100 and boarded a schooner bound for Virginia. On learning that a Union cavalry force was sniffing about for rebels fleeing the North, Waddell and his friend disembarked at a creek on the south shore of the Potomac River. Hoping to get help from sympathetic locals to find a way overland to Richmond, they knocked at the door of a nearby house.

As Waddell tells it, 'An old man of kind demeanour opened the door and said, "Friend or foe?"

'"Friends," I replied.

'"Come in friends."

'I entered. The old man's wife sat at one corner of the fireplace, and a lad of 16 years sat at the other corner, dressed in a Confederate grey uniform, infantry.

'I was in the act of stating my mission, when turning to address the old man, he said, "That boy is my grandson. He was in the battle of Bull Run and was sent home to die," and a big crystal tear rolled down his furrowed cheeks.'

'"We are old and alone. They can't hurt us. Our sons, all of them are gone. Some to return no more."'[12]

Despite his grief, the old man helped the two rebels reach a village where they hired a wagon to take them to the Rappahannock River ferry. After crossing, they took a train to Richmond, where they applied for commissions in the Confederate States Navy.

The Confederate Navy, when established in 1861, had only 14 seaworthy ships compared with more than 90 US Navy vessels. Four years on, even though the rebel fleet had swelled to about 100, including submarines – one such, the *Hunley*, was the first submarine to sink an enemy ship in wartime – the Confederacy was still hopelessly outgunned for traditional naval warfare.

Some among the Confederate Navy top brass, convinced the war at sea would never be won by lumbering men-of-war pounding away at each other with heavy cannon, favoured guerrilla tactics: disrupting Union commerce worldwide by attacking its merchant fleet, and breaking the Union blockade of Southern ports by enticing US Navy ships to give chase to rebel raiders. It would be a game of hit and run; of catch us if you can. And it would be a game the raiders could win. Others remained unconvinced, believing what was needed was armoured ships with superior firepower.

James Waddell received his commission as a lieutenant on 27 March 1862, and was ordered to an 'ironclad ram' under construction and near completion in the New Orleans shipyards.

Ironclad warships were the floating fortresses of the age. Powered by steam, they were protected by armour plates and designed to ram opposing ships. At the start of the Civil War, the Union had many more warships than the Confederacy but none was armour-plated. The South did all in its power to compensate for its smaller fleet, buying ironclads from overseas, building iron-clads and also converting wooden ships in Southern shipyards. The Union followed suit and rushed to armour-plate its ships.

The first battle between ironclads was fought between USS *Monitor* and CSS *Virginia* in March 1862 – just a few weeks before Waddell received his commission and his orders. The outcome, although inconclusive, proved to the South that iron-clads were its best hope of breaking the Union blockade. To the navies of the world, watching with interest, it proved that the age of the wooden warship was over.

Lieutenant Waddell never got the chance to go to war on a floating fortress. He arrived in New Orleans to find the ironclad nowhere near completion, and a Union fleet steaming towards the city. He had no choice but to destroy the ship to prevent it falling into enemy hands.

James Waddell set fire to the ironclad ram. It was the first of many ships he would put to the torch, but the irony was that the first was one of his own.

Chapter 6

Into the breach

Come listen all you gals and boys,
I's jist from Tuckyhoe.
I'm going to sing a little song,
My name's Jim Crow.
Weel about and turn about, and do jis so,
Eb'ry time I weel about and jump Jim Crow.[1]

On Monday 16 February 1863, the world-famous Christie Minstrels were performing at the Theatre Royal in Bourke St, Melbourne. It was a sell-out; the hit of the season. Australians just couldn't get enough of 'nigger minstrel' shows featuring white men in blackface, whether on stage, on the street outside pubs or on steamers carrying crowds to race meetings.

The song and dance routine 'Jim Crow' – a crude caricature of a black man, and in time a term for racial segregation laws and attitudes in the post-war South – had been a crowd favourite in Australia since first performed at Sydney's Royal Victoria Theatre in 1838. The minstrel shows it inspired would continue to re-inforce racial stereotypes well into the 20th century, but on that particular Monday the colonists had other distractions.

The hottest table-talk topic, and the big story in Australian newspapers in February of 1863, was outrage over a popular proposal in England to reintroduce the transportation of convicts to the Australian colonies.

Transportation had officially ended in the eastern states 10 years earlier, and would continue on a limited basis in Western Australia until 1868. The last convict ship sent to eastern Australia was the *Adelaide*, out of London, bound for Melbourne, in 1849. Aboard were 303 male convicts who, on arrival, were to be granted conditional pardons, allowing them to live as free settlers.

When the *Adelaide* sailed into Port Phillip Bay, however, it was met by crowds on the docks, howling in protest, and the colonial authorities refused permission for the ship to land. The *Adelaide* sailed on to Sydney, arriving on Christmas Eve 1849. There, too, it was met by angry crowds but managed to get its convicts safely ashore.

Tub-thumping editorials condemned the 1863 plan to reintroduce transportation as monstrously unjust, a dangerous folly and an affront to law-abiding colonists. *The Sydney Morning Herald* thundered, 'A few daring robbers who have seized people in the streets of London, and seemed to defy the control of the police and the penalties of justice, have awakened that periodical alarm which now and then seizes the English mind, and affects the penal administration of Great Britain.

'There can be no doubt whatever that the prevailing feeling of the English public is a simple desire to get rid of criminals, and to restore a sense of security to householders and travellers. They are supremely indifferent to the moral reformation of people who cut your purse or your throat. Thus, whenever any panic seizes the popular mind, the general cry is in favour of transportation.'[2]

South of the Murray, Melbourne's *Argus* observed, with a typically parochial slant, 'At this moment, New South Wales is almost at the mercy of her convict population. Mail robberies are of daily occurrence, and on more than one occasion the gold escort has been stopped and pillaged by armed bands, composed, it is believed, of convicts or the descendants of such men. The influence old settlers of this kind have over the young in their neighbourhood is well known. It is openly stated that the leaders in the latest outrages on the Sydney side of the border would have long ago been in the hands of the police but for the shelter and assistance afforded to them by settlers and their descendants having the taint of the chain gang upon them.

'There are other lands where prisons may be built, and islands where convicts may be employed, and where they would not be brought into contact with free settlers. *The Times* proposes Labrador, and the Falkland Islands have been suggested.'[3]

In South Australia, which had never experienced transportation, the press raised the spectre of the rise of a race of super-criminals: 'Amalgamating with the natives, the result would be the appearance of a class of men combining the cunning and endurance of the Aborigines with the worst features of the European criminal.

'Before an influx of garrotting bushrangers, our handful of police would be utterly powerless, and for England to save London by throwing its criminals into Australia would be equivalent to sending an infant to the rescue when a giant had failed.'[4]

It was never a serious proposal and it never happened, but for a while the good folk of colonial Australia got to wallow in moral outrage and dystopian fantasies.

*

Monday 16 February 1863 was a day James and Anne Waddell would never forget. That morning, at their home in Annapolis, Maryland, their little daughter Annie died of scarlet fever. Annie Harwood Waddell passed away a week short of her fourth birthday. She was the only child the Waddells would ever have.

Annie's father was not with her at the last. Ordered to England to take command of one of two ironclads being built in Liverpool, he was in Halifax, Nova Scotia, waiting for safe passage to England, when he received the sad news. He sent for Anne, who somehow made it through the Union blockade to Halifax, and together they sailed for England and took up residence in Liverpool.

It is testament to Waddell's taciturn nature that his memoirs make no mention of this personal tragedy. Then again, perhaps he found the memory too painful to revive with pen and paper. He notes only that 'I was ordered to Europe for foreign service, and I reached England in May, 1863.'[5]

In Scotland, meanwhile, at Glasgow's Stephenson & Co. ship-yard, a cargo ship was under construction. Owned by London merchants Gladstone & Co., shipbrokers Robinson & Co., and Jersey mariner and shipbuilder Captain Jean Pinel, she was intended for the China tea trade. The *Sea King* was a 1,160-ton, fully rigged, three-masted ship with 21 square sails, and auxiliary power from a 200 horsepower A & J Inglis steam engine, driving a screw that could be lowered into the water for extra propulsion or lifted when under sail alone. She was 230 feet in length, with a beam of 32 and a half feet and a draught of 20 feet. Composite-built of iron frame with teak planking below the waterline and elm planking above, the *Sea King* was sleek and built for speed.

Launched on 17 August 1863, her trial run, from Glasgow to London, was a near disaster; enough to cause superstitious sailors, wondering what fate the sea gods might have in mind for the *Sea King*, to declare her a lucky ship, but a lucky ship that trouble was sure to follow.

John Pinel, who accompanied his father Jean on the journey, recorded in his journal, 'We had a very rough voyage and put in to Loch Ryan in the south of Scotland. From there we made a fresh start and ran into a heavy gale in the Irish Sea.

'Our cargo consisted of pig iron taken for ballast and a quantity of gunpowder in kegs stowed on top of the iron. The cargo shifted during the gale and some of the powder kegs were buried under the iron, with great danger of an explosion should the iron shift again and crush the kegs.

'Water was poured on the iron to minimise the chance of this and fortunately no further trouble occurred; the weather moderated and we had fine weather for the rest of the passage.'[6]

In that fine weather, to the delight of her designers and owners, the *Sea King* showed she could make an impressive 12 knots (14 mph or 22.5 kph).

When, later that year in New Zealand, hostilities again broke out between Maori tribes and government forces, the British Government, which at that time had no steam transport ships, chartered the *Sea King* and other merchantmen to carry troops to Auckland. During that maiden voyage, she visited Australia, calling in at Sydney for 11 days, Newcastle for a day to load coal, then on to Wuhan, China, before returning to Liverpool with a cargo of tea.

At 10 Rumford Place, Liverpool, a bald man with thick mutton-chop sideburns and piercing eyes had been anxiously awaiting the return of the *Sea King*. James Dunwoody Bulloch was the Confederacy's chief agent in Britain. His mission involved organising blockade runners, providing arms and other vital supplies to the South, and outwitting Yankee diplomats and spies. And he was very good at his job.

Scion of a prominent slaveholding Georgian family connected to the Roosevelts – one of his nephews was Theodore 'Teddy' Roosevelt, a future US president – Bulloch had served in the US Navy and on merchantmen, was experienced in commerce and had a natural talent for espionage. He also had an eye for the main chance, and he was sure that the main chance for the South in the war at sea lay with privateers: privately owned armed raiders licensed by the Confederate Government to target the enemy's commercial fleet, and, in particular, Yankee whalers.

Back in 1861, in response to President Lincoln's call for the raising of an army to put down the rebellion, and for a naval blockade of Southern ports, Jefferson Davis, President of the Confederacy, issued the following proclamation: 'Whereas, Abraham Lincoln, the President of the United States has, by proclamation, announced the intention of invading this Confederacy with an armed force for the purpose of capturing its fortresses, and thereby subverting its independence and subjecting the free people thereof to the dominion of a foreign power; and, whereas, it has thus become the duty of this government to repel the threatened invasion, and to defend the rights and liberties of the people by all the means which the laws of nations and the usages of civilized warfare place at its disposal.

'Now, therefore, I, Jefferson Davis, President of the Confederate States of America, do issue this my proclamation, inviting all those who may desire, by service in private armed vessels on the high seas, to aid this government in resisting so wanton and wicked an aggression, to make application for commissions or letters of marque and reprisal to be issued under the seal of these Confederate States.'[7]

Letters of marque and reprisal authorised privateers to wage war and to cross international borders to take action. Whether for love of country or lust for booty or some measure of both, privateers could capture and destroy ships of an enemy's merchant fleet, claiming the value of the ships' cargoes as prize money.

Lincoln promptly countered by declaring that privateers would be considered pirates. And the penalty for piracy was death by hanging.

There was nothing new about attacking the commercial marine of an enemy. It had been employed throughout the ages as an effective means of damaging an enemy's economy, and thus its capacity to wage war. Americans had used it to devastating effect on the British during the Revolutionary War and the War of 1812.

The practice of privateering had been outlawed in Europe in 1856 by the Declaration of Paris, which branded privateers as pirates, but the United States had not signed that treaty. The United States offered to ratify the treaty after the Civil War began, but the request was denied. Britain rejected the offer as a hypocritical reversal of America's recently declared policy to employ privateers in naval warfare. Now that it faced the threat of Confederate privateers wreaking havoc on its own merchant fleet, Washington had turned an about-face, threatening to hang privateers as pirates.

While the North reacted to news of Jeff Davis's letters of marque and reprisal with rising panic, the South considered ways of turning a profit for privateering, and Richmond was soon besieged with applications for letters of marque from ship owners on almost every Confederate port on the Atlantic and Gulf coasts.

It did prove profitable for a while, with 50 or so Yankee merchantmen captured in the first few months of the war. By 1862, however, many European ports had been closed to privateers and their prizes, and the US Navy was exacting a heavy toll on Confederate cruisers.

After the loss, in quick succession, of the raiders *Savannah*, *Beauregard* and *Jefferson Davis*, and the fall of New Orleans and other vital ports, Southern entrepreneurs turned instead to outfitting blockade runners and supplying the fledgling Confederate Navy. Privateering with wooden sailing ships was simply not effective enough. What was needed were fast, armed, propeller-driven steamers, and since the Confederacy's few shipyards were either inadequate for the task or under Yankee control, the plan was to build or buy such vessels in foreign shipyards.

If, as anticipated, steam-powered raiders decimated the slower, cumbersome ships of the Yankee merchant fleet, insurance rates in the Union would skyrocket, Northern ship owners would rush to register their vessels under foreign flags, and US Navy warships blockading Southern ports would be diverted to hunt for commercial raiders. And that's exactly what happened.

Not wishing to be seen to be taking sides, the treaty nations, including Britain, France and Spain, refused to treat Confederate privateers as pirates.

The British Government, while proclaiming Britain and its colonies to be neutral, recognised the Confederacy as a belligerent power and declared the Union blockade of Southern ports lawful. Accordingly, Britain despatched rules of neutrality to be strictly observed by all its colonies. Under these rules, no warship,

privateer or other armed vessel belonging to either side in the conflict visiting a British port would be allowed to leave port within
24 hours after an enemy vessel left port. Belligerent vessels would
have to leave port and put to sea within 24 hours of arriving in a
British port, unless delayed by bad weather or need of provisions.
In such cases, ships would be required to leave as soon as they
were able, and could take on only enough supplies to enable them
to reach their country of origin or some nearer destination.

None of this British boondoggle bothered James Dunwoody
Bulloch. There were ways and means to run this bureaucratic blockade, and he knew them all. Bulloch's mission, on the orders of the
Confederacy's Secretary of the Navy, Stephen P. Mallory, was to
create a fleet of steam-propelled raiders with 'the greatest chance for
success against the enemy's commerce'.[8] Given the urgency, his brief
was to buy foreign ships suitable for the purpose, and at the same
time arrange for the building of new raiders in British shipyards.

Building, purchasing and illegally arming ships for war under
the noses of the British Government, as well as US diplomats and
their agents, was never going to be easy. Pitted against Bulloch
were the cold, calculating US Ambassador Francis Adams – son
and grandson of past presidents John Quincy Adams and John
Adams – and the US Consul in Liverpool, Thomas H. Dudley.
The cunning and fiercely anti-Southern Dudley, in particular,
would prove a dangerous adversary.

Bankrolled by Liverpool cotton trader Charles Kuhn Prioleau, a
Southerner who was the Confederacy's unofficial banker in England,
Bulloch contracted with a Mersey shipwright to build a 185-foot
wooden ship to be outfitted as the Confederacy's first raider. The
ship, named the *Oreto*, was launched in December 1861. The trick
now was to get her to sea without arousing suspicion. Bulloch

achieved this by renaming her the *Palermo*, registered in the name of a compliant Italian merchant in Liverpool. The *Palermo* steamed out of Liverpool with the British Government and the Yankee agents none the wiser, then headed for the Caribbean where, at Nassau, she was armed and renamed the *Florida*.

At the same time, at shipyards on the opposite side of the Mersey, another ship was under construction for Bulloch's front-men. Tagged vessel number 290, it was named the *Enrica* but was destined to become the *Alabama*, the most notorious Confederate raider before the *Shenandoah*. Changing tactic from the ruse he used to get the *Florida* out of port, Bulloch got the *Alabama* away to sea on the pretence of a trial run.

Perhaps it was because these raiders got away so easily that Bulloch pushed his luck too far. Ordered by Mallory to turn his efforts to building ironclad rams – supposedly the best hope of breaking the Union blockade – he commissioned the construction of two rams, one of which was to be commanded by James Waddell.

There was no way of keeping the building of such powerful warships a secret. Each steam-driven ship was 220-feet long, clad with iron and with teak a foot thick. They had a top speed of 10 and a half knots, and blistering firepower from revolving turrets. The battleships of their day, they had the potential to win the war for the South, so it was hardly surprising that the United States lurched into panic mode.

US Ambassador Adams went so far as to threaten war with Britain if the ironclads were allowed to sail into Confederate hands, and the threat had the desired effect. In October 1863, the ships were seized by the British, leaving Bulloch with no ships capable of entering enemy ports, and Waddell without a command. He had no choice but to cool his heels and await new orders.

When Waddell arrived in England in May 1863, news from home had at first been encouraging. Confederate victories at Fredericksburg and Chancellorsville eased the frustration of waiting to join the fight. But then, in July of 1863, came Gettysburg, the crushing defeat that ended General Lee's second invasion of the North and sent his Army of Northern Virginia limping back to Richmond. Gettysburg would later be called the turning point of the war; the battle where the cause was lost; but all that the South knew for sure at that moment was that tens of thousands of men lay dead and wounded on a muddy field in Pennsylvania, and that Robert E. Lee was not invincible.

Lee himself saw the defeat not as a disaster but as a setback. He wrote to his daughter-in-law Charlotte that his grief was over the casualties. 'The loss of our gallant officers and men throughout the army causes me to weep tears of blood and to wish that I could never hear the sound of a gun again,' he told her. 'My only consolation is that they are the happier and we that are left are to be pitied.'[9]

On Thursday 24 September 1863, one of Lee's soldiers who survived Gettysburg, 21-year-old Sergeant Eli Pinson Landers, of Lawrenceville, Georgia, wrote home to his mother from Chattanooga, Tennessee:

Dear Mother,
I tell you it was a trying case for me to pass so near home and not call but I pondered the matter. I thought sufficiently and thought it was my duty to stick to the company, deny myself, forsake home for the present and cleave to the cause of our bleeding country to drive the oppressors from our soil

which threatens our own door. I thought we was badly needed or we would not a been sent for. I knew it would not be much pleasure for me to be at home without leave.

I may never see you nor my home again but if I never do I can't help it. I expect to be a man of honour to our country at the risk of my life. I don't want to be a disgrace to myself nor my relations. It is unknown who will get killed in this fight. It may be me and if I do get killed if there is any chance I want my body taken up and laid in the dust round old Sweetwater [Lake] and I want a tombstone put at my head with my name and my company and regiment, the day I enlisted and the name and date of all the battles I have ever been in. I have spoke to some of the company to see to this matter if they should live and me not. I reckon what little I've got will pay expenses. This is my request if it is possible.

Now don't think I've give up to being killed but you know it is an uncertain thing as we are expecting to be called to attention soon so I will hasten through. Don't be uneasy about me.

Your affectionate son,
E.P.

On Friday 16 October 1863, Eli Landers, a veteran of 11 major battles, twice wounded, died of typhoid fever in camp at Rome, Georgia – 80 miles (130km) from home.

For James Iredell Waddell, consolation for the failing fortunes of the South would come late in 1864 with an order from Bulloch to make ready to take command of a new raider to replace the *Alabama*, sent by Yankee cannon fire to the bottom of the ocean.

For two years, under the command of the dashing and charismatic Raphael Semmes, the *Alabama* had raided from the Atlantic to the Pacific, capturing 65 Union merchantmen and notably sinking USS *Hatteras* off the coast of Galveston, Texas.

The *Alabama* could even be in two places at once, if two conflicting newspaper reports were to be believed. On 16 February 1863, Melbourne's *Argus* told its readers: 'Captain Simpson of the barque *Selim*, bound for India from Melbourne, sighted a black man-of-war steamer off the Cocos Islands, 3,000km northwest of Perth.

'When she sighted the *Selim*, she bore away from her under canvas, and when sufficiently near to land put out the English flag, rounded to under small canvas, and showed what the captain of the *Selim* says has been described to him as, and which he had no doubt of being, the Confederate flag.'[10]

Was it the *Alabama*? The description of the ship, and its tactic of flying a false flag to avoid identification and lure its prey, fit those of a Confederate raider. On the same day, however, the anti-abolition and anti-Lincoln Northern newspaper *Patriot & Union* reported that the *Alabama* was in Kingston, Jamaica, after being 'severely riddled' in its battle with USS *Hatteras*. Semmes and his ship's company had been in Kingston since 20 January bringing with them 165 prisoners – the officers and crew of the defeated Yankee warship. The report continued, 'Captain Semmes had a reception at the Commercial Exchange, at Kingston, which was given to him by the merchants of that city. He was lustily cheered.

'The American consul had chartered the ship *Borodino* to bring the crew of the *Hatteras* to the United States. A portion of the crew of the *Alabama* had been before the magistrate for creating a row in a drinking saloon.'[11]

The depredations of the Confederate raiders sparked a diplomatic duel between Washington and Westminster. The United States was concerned that Britain's recognition of the Confederacy as a belligerent power might be the first step to recognising the Confederate States of America as a sovereign nation. US Secretary of State William H. Seward summed up the case for the Union: 'The United States claim that in this war they are a whole sovereign nation, and entitled to the same respect as such they accord to Great Britain. Great Britain does not treat them as such a sovereign; and hence all the evils that disturb their intercourse and endanger their friendship.'[12]

The British, in turn, reminded Seward that Britain claimed to be a whole sovereign nation when France recognised the independence of the United States during the Revolutionary War.

Seward also complained about British subjects enlisting in the Confederate service, prompting Britain's Foreign Secretary (later prime minister) Earl Russell to reply: 'If thousands of British subjects are to be found fighting in the ranks of the Federals, on the invitation of the United States authorities, it is no breach of neutrality that some hundreds should be found in the ships and armies of the Confederates upon a similar invitation on their part.'[13]

As the trans-Atlantic war of words wore on, with neither side giving ground, at the sharp end of the shooting war, Raphael Semmes' luck ran out on 19 June 1864, when, off the coast of Cherbourg, France, the *Alabama* engaged the Union warship *Kearsarge*. Semmes opened fire but, outgunned and unaware that the hull of the *Kearsarge* had been iron-plated, was forced to strike his colours after an hour-long battle. Sinking fast after an 11-inch (28cm) shell tore her open below the waterline, the *Alabama* waved a white flag of surrender.

As his ship went down by the stern, Semmes threw his sword into the sea, denying the victor the satisfaction of a formal surrender. He also denied the *Kearsarge*'s skipper, Captain John Acrum Winslow, the pleasure of his company. While boats from the Union warship were busy plucking the Confederate raider's crew from the sea, Semmes was rescued by a private British yacht, the *Deerhound*, and sailed off for England and the chance to fight another day.

The North declared the Battle of Cherbourg a famous victory, and medals were struck in its honour. The South immortalised it in a sea shanty, 'Roll, *Alabama*, Roll', written, according to tradition, by Frank Townsend, a sailor who served on the *Alabama*. The closing lyrics go:

> *From the Western Isles she sailed forth*
> *To destroy all commerce of the North.*
> *Down to Cherbourg came she straight one day*
> *For to take her toll in prize money.*
> *There many a sailor lad met his doom*
> *When the ship Kearsarge hove in view*
> *And a shot from the forward pivot that day*
> *It shot the Alabama's stern away.*
> *In the three-mile limit in sixty-five,*
> *The Alabama sunk to her grave.*

Such was Raphael Semmes' fame worldwide that a deal of the excitement when the *Shenandoah* arrived in Melbourne the next year was due to a rumour that Semmes was aboard. Yet while this captain who did not go down with his ship was hailed a hero, the one brave officer who gave his life to save the lives of others was forgotten.

When the order came to abandon ship, the *Alabama*'s surgeon, Dr David Llewellyn, continued attending to the wounded and helping them into overcrowded lifeboats. A fellow officer shouted to him to board the last lifeboat but he refused, replying that he would not risk causing the boat to capsize with so many wounded aboard.

As the *Alabama* went down, Dr Llewellyn, who could not swim, jumped into the sea and was drowned.

In 1984, 120 years after she was sunk by the *Kearsage*, the wreck of the *Alabama* was found off the coast of Cherbourg by the French Navy minesweeper *Circe*.

The vessel James Bulloch had in mind to replace the *Alabama* was the *Sea King*. He had sent Charles Prioleau's son-in-law, Richard Wright, to cast an eye over her, and Wright's glowing report that she was one of the fastest ships afloat convinced him the sleek merchantman would make an ideal Confederate cruiser.

At the same time, Bulloch's nemesis, US Consul Thomas Dudley – who had planted spies in the Liverpool shipyards – had reached the same conclusion. With the *Sea King* identified as a likely privateer, his agents were keeping a close eye on it.

Bulloch, suspecting as much, arranged to buy the ship in Richard Wright's name, and hatched a plan to refit it, arm it, man it and get it out to sea, all without arousing suspicion.

On 7 October, while Bulloch prepared to sool his next attack dog on a vulnerable enemy, his first commerce raider, the *Florida*, came to grief in Brazil. While at anchor in a neutral port, and when her captain, Charles Manigault Morris and most of his crew were ashore, she was boarded and seized by the men of a Yankee warship, USS *Wachusett*. When the Brazilian Government protested that the hostile act in a neutral harbour was illegal, the *Wachusett*'s commander, Napoleon Collins, was court-martialled and found guilty of violating Brazil's sovereignty. Still, the US Navy chose not to punish but promote him.

The *Florida*, after taking 37 prizes, was gone, like the *Alabama* before it. It was all up to the new ship now, and to Jimmy Bulloch's talent for distracting the enemy with smoke and mirrors.

Unlike her predecessors, which had set out to damage the Yankee merchant fleet in general, the new ship had a specific target. It would target the most lucrative branch of the enemy's commercial marine – the whaling fleet.

Bulloch had hatched the idea after a conversation with Lieutenant John Mercer Brooke, a Confederate naval officer who, when serving in the US navy before the war, had been a member of a scientific expedition that cruised the Arctic whaling grounds. Reasoning that where you found whales you were sure to find whalers, he obtained a set of whaling charts and planned the expedition.

The ideal ship for such a mission would need to be able to carry enough supplies to operate in remote areas for extended periods, and be equipped with a plant for condensing steam into drinking water. She would need to be a fully rigged ship, fast and manoeuvrable under sail but also have auxiliary steam power to keep her moving when the wind fails, and to get her out of trouble in a hurry. So as not to impede her when under sail, she must have a retractable propeller. And she must have sufficient strength and deck space for armaments.

As the perfect ship for the enterprise, the *Sea King*, steamed out of Liverpool, supposedly on a routine trip to Bombay with a cargo of coal, Dudley's agents, watching through telescopes, spied nothing suspicious on deck – no gun mountings, teak planking or iron cladding, just the fittings of a typical merchantman.

That evening, 27 men separately made their way through cold and misty streets to Princess Dock, Liverpool. All were commissioned officers and petty officers of the Confederate Navy, recruited by Bulloch and smuggled into England weeks before. Some knew each other, having served on the *Alabama* or on other ships during or before the war, but all stayed silent, pretending to be strangers.

One of the men, Cornelius Hunt, later recalled, 'It was curious, too, as I plodded my solitary way down the wet, slippery street, to see men accoutred like myself, and bound as I well knew upon the same mission, without venturing to exchange with them a word of greeting, but the injunctions of secrecy were peremptory and too much was at stake for orders to be lightly disregarded.'[14]

An hour earlier, at the hotels, boarding houses and apartments where they had been staying, keeping as low a profile as possible, a Confederate agent had passed on orders to go immediately to the dock. None of them had been told why, but all knew the waiting and wondering was about to end.

Among the officers waiting on the dock were bona fide Southern aristocrats.

Lieutenant Sydney Smith Lee Jnr, 28, born and bred on a grand Virginia plantation, was the second son of Confederate Navy

Commander Sydney Smith Lee, the nephew of Commanding General Robert E. Lee and the grandson of Revolutionary War hero Henry 'Light Horse Harry' Lee.

His elder brother Fitzhugh Lee was a Confederate Army general. Of his younger brothers, John Mason Lee was an army major (who would be with his uncle Robert at the surrender at Appomattox); Henry Carter Lee was adjutant-general to Confederate cavalry General Williams Carter Wickham; and Daniel Murray Lee was a captain on his brother Fitzhugh's staff.

Another Virginian, Midshipman John Mason, was a great-nephew of Founding Father George Mason. Known as the Father of the United States Bill of Rights, George Mason was one of the largest slaveholders in Virginia (along with George Washington) yet publicly condemned the institution as immoral.

Midshipman Mason, related by marriage to Robert E. Lee, was a cousin of James Mason, one of the two Confederate envoys captured in the 1861 Trent Affair, which almost sparked war between the United States and Britain (see Chapter 12).

Lower on the social ladder but no less the Southern gentleman, First Lieutenant Francis Thornton Chew, 24, a descendant of George Washington, was born in Tennessee and raised in Missouri. A graduate of the United States Naval Academy at Annapolis, he joined the US Navy in 1859 and, on the outbreak of war, resigned his commission and joined the Confederate Navy as an acting midshipman. Chew, who had previously only served on river gunboats, had never been to sea before joining the *Shenandoah*.

Before the war, Paymaster William Breedlove Smith, of Louisiana, was a lawyer with the firm of Thomas J. Semmes, a cousin to Captain Raphael Semmes. After joining the Confederate

Navy on the outbreak of war in 1861, Smith served firstly on CSS *Sumter*, then as captain's clerk under Raphael Semmes on the *Alabama* from 1863 until her sinking in 1864. He was then ordered to the *Shenandoah*.

Second Lieutenant Dabney 'Dab' Minor Scales, 24, was born in Virginia but raised in Mississippi. A midshipman in the US Navy, he resigned in 1861 when Mississippi seceded from the Union, and was granted a commission with the same rank in the Confederate Navy. Before joining the *Shenandoah*, Scales served on several Confederate warships, including the *Savannah*, the *Charleston* and the *Arkansas*.

First Lieutenant John Grimball, 25, of Charleston, South Carolina, was a graduate of the US Naval Academy. He was a midshipman when his state seceded, and resigned to join the Confederate Navy, with the same rank. Before joining the *Shenandoah*, he served on the *Arkansas* and the *Baltic*.

The officers and men gathered on Princess Dock boarded a waiting tug that took them to the cargo steamer *Laurel*, where they were hustled aboard to find the man who would be their commander, James Waddell, waiting for them.

The man appointed the *Shenandoah*'s Executive Officer, William Conway Whittle Jnr, was not among them. James Bulloch had other plans for him.

Whittle, of Norfolk, Virginia, was 25 years old. The son of a Confederate Navy Commodore, he enjoyed a privileged childhood at 'The Anchorage' – the Whittles' stately home in Buchanan, Virginia – and was a devout, Bible-quoting Episcopalian.

Whittle joined the United States Navy as a midshipman in

1854, and in 1861 resigned to join the Confederate Navy. He served on York River shore batteries and on CSS *Nashville*, and in 1862, after being promoted to First Lieutenant, on CSS *Louisiana*. Captured in April of that year, at the fall of New Orleans, Whittle was imprisoned at Fort Warren, in Boston harbour. Four months later, after being released in a prisoner exchange, he served on the *Richmond Station*, then on CSS *Chattahoochee*, before being sent to England in 1863, where the following year he was appointed Executive Officer of the *Shenandoah*.

Lieutenant Whittle's fiancée Elizabeth 'Pattie' Page was from an old Virginia family, related by marriage to Robert E. Lee. Her family, like the Whittles, had a longstanding connection with the Episcopalian church. It seems the upper strata of Southern society moved in tight, concentric circles.

James Bulloch had taken every precaution – down to the smallest detail – to preserve secrecy. After all, the success of the mission depended on it. His orders to William Whittle were to catch a 5pm train to London on 6 October, go to Wood's Hotel in High Holborn and book a room under the name W.C. Brown.

The next morning, at 11am precisely, he was to go to the hotel restaurant and take a seat in a prominent position, with a white handkerchief poking through the buttonhole of his coat, and a newspaper in his hands. A man would approach him and ask if his name was Brown. He would reply that it was, then accompany the man to his room, and hand him a letter of introduction from Bulloch. The man, a Confederate agent, would then arrange for him to meet with Captain Corbett, master of the *Sea King*, to devise a way of smuggling him aboard.

Early on 7 October, Whittle and the agent made their way to the docks where Whittle, 'at an unsuspicious distance viewed the ship, and later, at a safe rendezvous, was introduced to her captain, Corbett'.[15]

Bulloch had instructed Whittle to tell Captain Corbett that 'I desire him to carry you to Madeira, and explain how he is to communicate with the *Laurel*. It is important that the *Sea King* should not be reported, and you will request Captain Corbett not to exchange signals with passing ships or at any rate not to show his number.

'When you reach Madeira and the *Laurel* joins company, you will report to Lieutenant-Commanding Waddell, and thereafter act under his instructions.'[16]

Bulloch had also sent orders to James Waddell, informing him: 'You will sail from this port [Liverpool] on Saturday, the 8th instant, in the screw-steamer *Laurel*, under the command of First Lieutenant J.F. Ramsay, taking with you all the officers detailed for your command except First Lieutenant Whittle, who will take passage in the ship with Captain Corbett, with the view of learning her qualities and devising the best and speediest manner of making such alterations and additions in her internal arrangements as may be necessary, and to observe the character and disposition of her crew.'[17]

Lieutenant Whittle recalls, 'On the early morn of 8 October, 1864, I crawled over her side, at the forerigging, and the ship in a few moments left the dock and went down the Thames. To everybody on board except Captain Corbett, who was in our confidence, I was Mr Brown, a super-cargo, representing the owners of the coal with which she was laden. We were fully instructed to proceed to Madeira, where we were to call, a fact only known on board to Captain Corbett and myself, and not to exchange signals with passing Captain Corbett's assistance, I possessed myself of much information that served a good purpose afterwards. No-one on board suspected anything out of the usual course.'[18]

That same day, the *Laurel* slipped her lines and pointed seaward. To Yankee eyes, she seemed, like the *Sea King*, to be just another merchantman, her only visible ordnance being the two 12-pounder signal guns carried by all merchant ships. But hidden between her decks were four eight-inch smooth-bore guns, and two rifled Whitworth 32-pounder guns, with ammunition and other equipment necessary to refit a merchantman as a man-of-war.

The officers' baggage had already been taken aboard in boxes, each marked with a diamond and a number known to each man, and, on boarding, each was given a receipt, in a fictitious name, for £32 for passage to Havana.

Cornelius Hunt's fake receipt read, 'Received from Mr Elias Smith, thirty-two pounds, for his passage in the cabin of Steamer *Laurel*, from this port to Havana.' Signed 'Henry Lafone.'[19]

Of course, the ship wasn't really going to Havana. Both the *Laurel* and the *Sea King* were bound for Madeira, to rendezvous 11 days later. There, in the lee of a barren island, the *Laurel* would transfer its cargo to the *Sea King*, and the *Sea King* would be reborn as the *Shenandoah*.

Chapter 7

First prize

As the *Sea King* rode at anchor on a smooth sea in a light breeze, with the *Laurel* lashed alongside, Captain Waddell's officers assembled on deck.

Joining lieutenants Whittle, Grimball, Chew, Scales and Smith Lee, Paymaster Breedlove Smith and Midshipman Mason were Master's Mate Cornelius Hunt, Surgeon Charles Lining, Assistant Surgeon Fred McNulty and Sailing Master Irvine Bulloch, younger brother of James Bulloch and former sailing master on the *Alabama*. Other *Alabama* veterans reunited were master's mate John Minor, sailmaker Henry Alcott, boatswain George Harwood and chief engineer Matthew O'Brien.

The Union Jack was hauled down and the Stainless Banner hoisted, marking the commissioning of the vessel as a ship of the Confederate States Navy, renamed CSS *Shenandoah*. The recommissioning relieved the fears of superstitious sailors, who believe it is bad luck to rename a ship without an official ceremony. The traditional alternative is to write the original name on a piece of paper, fold the paper and place it in a wooden box. The box is then burnt, and the ashes thrown into the sea on an outgoing tide.

It took 13 hours of hard labour to haul coal, water and other supplies across from the *Laurel*, along with the cannons, muskets, pistols, powder and shot.

'All was confusion and chaos,' Lieutenant Whittle tells us. 'Everything had to be unpacked and stored for safety. No gun mounted, no breeching or tackle bolts driven, no portholes cut [for the guns], no magazine for powder or shell room for shells provided. All was hurriedly transferred and in a lumbering, confused mass was on board. Every particle of work, of bringing order out of chaos and providing for efficiently putting in a condition for service, and of converting this ship into an armed cruiser at sea, admits wind and storm, if encountered, stared us in the face.'[1]

Captain Waddell, accustomed to stepping aboard ships already in shipshape, was appalled. Not only was the ship vulnerable to enemy attack in such a condition, but she desperately needed more manpower to finish the work, and then to sail her. To that end, he ordered all sailors from both vessels to assemble on the quarterdeck of the *Shenandoah*.

Waddell went down to his cabin and reappeared on deck in full uniform, wearing the dress sword and sidearm of a captain in the Confederate Navy, and addressed the men.

Waddell writes, 'I informed them of the changed character of the *Sea King*, read my commission to them, pictured to them a brilliant, dashing cruise, and asked them to join the service of the Confederate States and assist an oppressed and brave people in their resistance to a powerful and arrogant northern government.'[2]

But if he'd hoped his speech would stir the blood like Shakespeare's Henry V at Agincourt, he was sorely disappointed.

Only 19 men accepted his offer, leaving him with a complement of only 43 to sail a ship that required 150.

Captain Corbett told Captain Waddell that, in his opinion, taking to the ocean so seriously shorthanded would be foolhardy. Waddell, swayed by the view of such an experienced seaman, advised Lieutenant Whittle he thought it wise to sail to Teneriffe, and from there arrange for James Bulloch to have a crew sent out to join them.

Whittle counselled against this. 'Don't confer, Sir, with parties who are not going with us,' he said. 'Call your young officers together and learn from their assurances what they can and will do.'

The Captain did so, and put the question to his officers – Should they take the ship to Teneriffe or take the ocean? The response was unanimous: 'Take the ocean!'[3]

And so the die was cast. The men who refused to join the *Shenandoah* were sent aboard the *Laurel*, which, after exchanging guns of salute, steamed away.

The 43-man complement of the new raider included 24 officers and 19 men, only 10 of whom were deckhands. The rest were stokers, stewards and a cabin boy. In an age when it was seen as an affront to the natural order for an officer and gentleman to engage in manual labour, the officers were obliged to help sail the ship, even stripping off their jackets to help raise the anchor.

Waddell dashed off a letter to James Bulloch, expressing his disappointment at the poor response to his call for volunteers.

Bulloch later commented, 'Under the circumstances, I was not surprised that the tone of his report was somewhat desponding; but there was no evidence of a wish to be out of the work – only a fear that he might not be able to accomplish all that was expected of him.'[4]

'Never before was ship beset by difficulties apparently so insurmountable,' Assistant Surgeon Fred McNulty remarked.

'Although liable at any hour to meet the challenge shot of the enemy, we entered upon our duties without fear. There was work for every man to do and every man put his heart in his task. Then, when after days of toil with blistered hands, all was stored properly below, and while the carpenter and his mates cut portholes for the guns, the captain took his place at the wheel, and officers and men, regardless of rank, barefooted and with trousers rolled up, scrubbed and holy-stoned the decks.'[5]

Lieutenant Whittle, while sharing McNulty's pride in a job well done, felt a pang of homesickness. Although only 24, he was the oldest of the officers (apart from the 41-year-old captain) and keenly felt the distance between himself and his family back in Virginia. 'Notwithstanding my being so busy, I have time to feel blue, as I can't get my usual letters from my own dear ones. Oh, how much would I give to know how they are.'[6]

With not nearly enough hands on deck, the skipper decided to steam by day and sail by night, yet, for all his problems, his mood soon lifted. 'The little adventurer entered upon her watchful career, throwing to the breeze the flag of the South, and demanding for her a place among her sister nations upon that vast expanse of water.

'Lieutenant Chew effaced the words *Sea King* from the stern of the *Shenandoah*. Our flag unfolded itself gracefully to the freshening breeze, and declared the majesty of the country it represented amid the cheers of a handful of brave-hearted men who stood upon our deck and acclamations from the *Laurel* that was steaming away for the land we love to tell the tale to those who would rejoice that another cruiser was afloat and who would share the triumphs or reverses which might befall her.'[7]

When news of the rebels' ruse got back to England, leaving US Ambassador Adams incandescent with rage, a pro-Confederacy British newspaper crowed, 'We have much pleasure in being able to state that, at almost the same time when the *Florida* was treacherously seized in Bahia harbour, the Confederate flag was hoisted on a new cruiser at least the equal of the *Florida*.

'Having received her crew and armament on the high seas, far beyond any neutral jurisdiction, there can fortunately be no pretence of accusing her of violation of municipal law or international operations.

'The *Florida* is gone – long live the *Shenandoah*!'[8]

For the new raider, first blood was mere days away. On the afternoon of 30 October, the *Shenandoah* spied in the distance a barque – in other words a sailing ship with three or more masts, having square sails on the foremasts and the aftermast rigged fore-and-aft. Guessing the ship to be a Yankee, the *Shenandoah* gave chase, and by dusk was within seven miles (11km) of her and closing fast. The next morning, to the Confederates' surprise, their quarry, which yesterday was dead ahead, was now to windward. The *Shenandoah* took in sail, lowered the propeller, got up steam and, when in signalling range, raised the Union Jack. Over the coming months, she occasionally displayed the French and other flags apart from the Union Jack when flying false colours, and her crew sometimes wore blue shirts over their grey uniforms to avoid suspicion.

When the unsuspecting barque replied by hoisting the Stars and Stripes, the raider moved within firing range, ran up the Stainless Banner then fired a warning shot.

'The stranger showed chase, but quickly changed his mind when a hustling shot across his bows said, "Do come and see us," – the first of 50 pressing invitations,' Assistant Surgeon Fred McNulty recalls.[9]

Outgunned and out-manoeuvred, the barque hove to and the Confederates boarded her. She was a Yankee, sure enough – the 573-ton American barque *Alina*, out of Searsport, Maine, a new ship on only her second voyage, bound for Buenos Aires from Newport, Wales, with a cargo of railroad iron.

The *Alina*'s master, Captain Staples, was told his ship was a prize of the Confederate States of America, and he was ordered to collect his papers and personal property and come aboard the *Shenandoah*, along with his officers and crew.

The *Alina* was a valuable prize, estimated to be worth $95,000 in gold. Captain Waddell was delighted, as was his executive officer, who recorded in his journal, 'We stripped her of everything we wanted, which well may be imagined was an immense deal particularly as she was our first prize.'[10]

From the *Alina*, Waddell's crew removed blocks for the gun tackles, cotton canvas for sails, and other provisions lacking on the *Shenandoah*. The officers helped themselves to cutlery, crockery, basins and jugs for the mess, and the skipper commandeered a chronometer, and a spring mattress to make his bunk more comfortable.

In Waddell's opinion, Yankee shipwrights were the best in the business, and the *Alina* – a beautiful and well-equipped vessel – was a credit to their craft. This assessment did not cause him any regret for sending her to Davy Jones's locker, however. Concerned that setting her afire risked a red glow in the sky that could alert any Yankee cruisers lurking nearby, he opted to scuttle the *Alina*, ordering the ship's carpenter to drill holes in her hull below the water line.

Master's Mate Cornelius Hunt writes, 'The *Alina* was condemned, and it fell to my lot to return with the Captain to say goodbye to his ship and bring away his clothing and any other little personal property he might wish to preserve.

'That he felt his misfortune keenly was evident, although he manfully strove to conceal it under a cool, nonchalant exterior.'[11]

Informed of what was about to happen to his ship, Captain Staples turned to Hunt and said, 'I tell you what, matey, I've a daughter at home that that craft was named for, and it goes against me cursedly to see her destroyed.'

Hunt replied that he and his fellow officers meant him no harm, but, in carrying out their orders to prey upon US merchantmen, individuals were bound to suffer.

'I know it's only the fortunes of war, and I must take my chances with the rest,' said the captain, 'but it's damn hard.' And he hoped the day might come when he'd have his revenge.[12] Lieutenant Whittle describes what happened next:

'At 4.45pm she went down stern first under all plain sail and the sight was grand and awful. You might go to sea for many a day and would not see a vessel sink. She had been gradually sinking for some time and had gotten to the water's edge. She was in this position a man going down for the first time and struggling to prevent it. Finally, at 4.45 a sea swept over her, she settled aft, her stern sank very rapidly and her bow went straight into the air and turned a regular somersault as she went down. [We] could distinctly hear the cracking and breaking of the spars of the sails and as the bow went under a beautiful jet of water was thrown up high in the air.'[13]

Cornelius Hunt, who, like Whittle, had never before seen a ship sink, was appalled by the sight. Watching the barque go down, he felt 'a curious heart-heaviness that none but the sailor can understand'. He likened it to witnessing 'the sinking away of a soul into the oceans of eternity'.[14]

The captain and officers of the *Alina* declined an offer to join the rebels but signed paroles. After declaring under oath that they would not go to sea again until the war was over, and would not take up arms against the Confederacy, they were accommodated in the wardroom and given the freedom of the ship. The captain admitted he did not expect to be treated so kindly by an enemy, but initially refused all offers of refreshment and remained aloof. However, after a while he thawed somewhat in the company of Cornelius Hunt, whom he regaled with rollicking tales of his adventures at sea.

Of the *Alina*'s crew, only two, German sailors Herman Wicke and Charles Behnck, agreed to enlist in the Confederate Navy. The rest were clapped in irons and confined in the topgallant forecastle, which they shared with the *Shenandoah*'s crew, the sheep and the chickens.

Curiously, contradicting the accounts of other officers, Fred McNulty insists no captured crewmen were ever put in irons on board the *Shenandoah*. 'I will not stop to enumerate in detail, but rise to indignantly deny as a base lie that Captain Waddell ever put a man in irons because he would not join our ship,' McNulty writes. 'James I. Waddell was a gentleman, and would never stoop to such conduct. Certainly there must be discipline on board ship, and at times when there were too many prisoners we had to see that they did not rise and take possession of the vessel.'[15]

The sailors Wicke and Behnck would later claim they had signed up under duress – in fear of their lives. Captain Waddell insisted otherwise – that their captors had enlightened them as to the righteousness of the Confederate cause.

The *Shenandoah* continued southward for days of alternating rain squalls and tropical sunshine, while her crew, still short-handed but in good spirits, looked forward eagerly to the next cry of 'Sail ho!'

The cry came on 5 November, when the rebels chased, captured and burnt the schooner *Charter Oak*, out of Boston and bound for San Francisco. Her cargo, valued at $15,000, included coal, furniture and canned tomatoes.

While the rebels helped themselves to the canned tomatoes, the *Charter Oak*'s master, Captain Gilmer, came aboard the *Shenandoah* with his wife and her widowed sister with her young son, Frank. Waddell showed them Southern hospitality.

'The widow had lost her husband at Harper's Ferry. He had been a sergeant in the Federal army. We all felt a compassion for these poor women, and we had no idea of retaliating upon them for the injuries which General Hunter, Sheridan, Sherman and their kind had inflicted upon our unhappy countrywomen.'[16]

Waddell let Captain Gilmer and his family occupy his stern cabin, and, in a further demonstration of chivalry Dixie-style, when $200 in cash was found aboard the *Charter Oak*, and Gilmer swore it was all the money he had, Waddell presented the cash to Mrs Gilmer on behalf of the Confederacy, on condition that she give none of it to her husband.

The crew of the *Charter Oak* were shown no such compassion. They all refused to sign on and were sent in irons to join the men of the *Alina*, and the sheep and chickens, in the forecastle.

Three days on, the raider's third prize, the barque D. *Godfrey*, out of Boston, bound for Valparaiso, was sent to the bottom of the sea along with most of her cargo of beef and pork, much to Waddell's regret. The *Shenandoah* was by now so full of booty that she had room for only 22 barrels of each. Six of the captured crew signed on, boosting the ship's complement to 35, still nowhere near the 150 required.

Another three days later, Waddell offered the Danish brig *Anna Jane* a barrel of beef from the D. *Godfrey* and the chronometer from the *Alina* in exchange for taking aboard some of the Confederates' prisoners. The Danes accepted the offer.

Through the South Atlantic to the Cape of Good Hope, the tally of prize ships rose almost daily: the brigantine *Susan*, out of New York, from which vessel two men and a boy joined the *Shenandoah*; the barque *Adelaide*, of Baltimore; the clipper ship *Kate Prince*, of Portsmouth; and the schooner *Lizzie M. Stacey*, out of Boston. Four of her seven crew joined the *Shenandoah*.

Of the captured ships, most were set afire, two were scuttled and two were ransomed. To ransom a captured ship, a raider set a price on her based on the value of her cargo, to be paid to the Confederacy at the end of the war. Unsurprisingly, no ransoms were ever paid. The ships ransomed were the *Adelaide*, upon proof that she was owned by a Southern sympathiser, and the *Kate Prince*. All the prisoners were put aboard the *Kate Prince*, including Captain Gilmer of the *Charter Oak*, Mrs Gilmer and her sister Mrs Gage, all of whom thanked the rebels for their hospitality as they parted company.

The schooner *Lizzie M. Stacey*, out of Boston, bound for Honolulu, fell prey to the black raider on 13 November. Of her crew of seven, four joined the *Shenandoah*. Enlistments from ships captured thus far had increased the ship's complement to 62 – still well short of the ideal of 150, but noticeably boosting efficiency.

True to maritime tradition when 'crossing the line', King Neptune came aboard the *Shenandoah* on 15 November as she crossed the equator. In time-honoured fashion, men crossing into the Southern Hemisphere for the first time were summoned on deck that evening for the initiation ceremony.

Neptune, a harpoon in his hand and a rope doormat for a hat, appeared from over the bow, followed by a motley retinue in assorted outlandish costumes.

Lieutenant Frank Chew, first of Neptune's new subjects to face the consequences, is asked, 'Where are you from?' Chew knows better than to answer, for opening your mouth to speak will get it filled with a revolting concoction of grease, soap and molasses. It is, of course, a no-win situation, so the penalty for not opening your mouth is having your face lathered with the same noxious mix, shaved with a long wooden razor by the barber, then almost drowned by a torrent of water from the pump. First Officer Whittle had presumed that, although he'd never crossed the line before, his rank would spare him the indignity, but the men had other ideas. Like Chew and others, he was treated to a lather, shave and drenching.

On Assistant Surgeon Fred McNulty's turn, when asked 'Where are you from?' he replied 'Ireland', whereupon the concoction was shoved into his mouth. Unlike the rest of the initiates, who took it all in good spirits, McNulty hauled off and punched the barber, sending him sprawling onto the deck. His shipmates, except for the barber, laughed it off as all part of the fun, but it would not be the last time on this cruise McNulty would let his quick temper get the better of him.

On 4 December, the Confederates captured their first whaler, the *Edward*, out of New Bedford. When the *Shenandoah* overhauled the *Edward*, it still had a harpooned whale attached to it. Fred McNulty, who found the sight amusing, wrote, 'It was the case of the big fish eating up the little one, and we were the largest in the pond just then.'[17]

Lieutenant Frank Chew, after demonstrating an unfortunate tendency to be accident-prone, soon found himself on the wrong side of the Captain. On 15 December, when on watch during a heavy swell, he lost his balance and was almost lost overboard, Waddell was not amused. The next day, Chew found he had been replaced on watch by Master's Mate Joshua Minor.

Miffed at being replaced on watch by a man of lesser rank, Chew sought advice from Surgeon Lining, who sympathised but at the same time sowed seeds of discontent, telling Chew it was wrong of the Captain to undermine his authority with the petty officers and crew. Chew, awash with reckless youth and injured pride, dashed off a letter of resignation, which he handed to Lieutenant Whittle to deliver to the Captain.

When, to Whittle's surprise, Waddell readily accepted Chew's resignation, Whittle proposed a compromise. Chew would return to duty as if nothing had happened, but in rough weather

Whittle would join him on watch. Again, to Whittle's surprise, the Captain agreed.

It was going to be a white Christmas – far too white.

'I was instructed to pass the meridian of the Cape of Good Hope by the first of January 1865,' Waddell writes, 'and at noon of the 17th of December, the *Shenandoah* was east of that meridian, with a west wind following fast. The speed of the ship varied with the strength of the wind.'[18]

In open ocean, 5,000 miles (8,000km) from Australia, the *Shenandoah* had reached its farthest latitude south, between Madagascar and Antarctica – a world of floes and icebergs, scoured by the Roaring Forties.

For those among the crew entranced by the sight of towering bergs, the novelty soon wore off when they lurched too close for comfort.

Midshipman John Mason, away from home at Christmas for only the second time, lonely and feeling the cold seep into his bones, managed to look on the bright side. 'I suppose we will find delightful weather in Australia,' he wrote in his journal.[19]

On Christmas Eve, the wind whipped up to gale force, sheets of freezing rain and sleet came in torrents, blown sideways by the wall of wind, and white-capped waves washed over the decks. A terrifying whistling sound roared through the rigging, and suddenly there was no ocean, no sky. This was a white squall – a rare but fearsome thing and the cause of many a shipwreck. Some said white squalls could occur only in the tropics. Some said there was no such thing; that it was a myth, but sailors knew the truth of it.

Coming off watch, chilled to the core and wishing himself

safe and sound in Dixie, Lieutenant Whittle warmed himself with thoughts of his beloved Pattie. He wrote in his journal, 'Oh, how much would I not give now to be on shore, with our dear country at peace, and a certain little angel sitting by me as my wife. I would certainly be the happiest man in the world.'[20]

That night, the wind shifted to the west, and the weather grew even worse. Whittle ordered the canvas to be reduced to storm sails only, and for braces to be set on the starboard yardarms, allowing the ship to be able to sail at different angles to the wind. Still, it seemed the fate of the ship depended less on good seamanship than on the whims of the elements.

At midnight, as heavy seas slammed the *Shenandoah* from side to side, listing precariously to port, then to starboard, then to port again, men on deck hauling on the braces and manning the pumps clung desperately to lifelines. The ship plunged into deep troughs then surged upward to perch for one heart-stopping moment on the crest of a wave taller than the foreyard, before crashing down into the next trough.

Below decks, officers in the wardroom raised glasses to toast the season, while in the topgallant forecastle, sailors savoured the extra ration of grog allowed them. But while the men of the *Shenandoah* drank to peace on earth, the ocean showed no goodwill towards men. At about 6am on Christmas Day, a massive wave smashed through a skylight to flood the engine room, then the wardroom – where officers present leapt atop the furniture – then washed into the cabins. We can only guess what happened in the crew quarters, which were liable to sea spray even in the best of weather.

Like all long and narrow vessels, the *Shenandoah* had a tendency to roll deep, exacerbated by the large quantity of coal in her hold. And the higher the sea, the deeper the roll.

Waddell writes, 'She rolled so heavily that sea after sea tumbled in over her railing and her preparations for freeing herself were so indifferent that water was several inches deep, flooding all the compartments on that deck.'[21]

In a Christmas miracle of sorts, the captain of the maintop, William West, was washed overboard, then picked up by another wave that dropped him back on deck unharmed.

Christmas dinner for the officers included goose, pork, potatoes, corned beef, mince pies and plum pudding, washed down with sherry. For the crew, dinner for the festive occasion came courtesy of the biggest pig in the pen.

'A Christmas dinner had been prepared of the captured supplies,' Waddell recalls, 'but it was quite impossible to sit long enough to enjoy it, except under difficulties. Most of the dishes left the table for the deck, and notwithstanding the disappointment at the loss of a good dinner, there was still enough life among us left to record it as an incident in the sailor's life.

'Should I ever again make a trip to Australia, I would go very little south of the howling forties.'[22]

Master's Mate Cornelius Hunt was more to the point: 'My solemn advice to the world at large is, never go off the Cape of Good Hope in a cruiser to enjoy Christmas.'[23]

The Captain, who, like most on board, seemed determined to make the best of a bad situation, had only one complaint: 'The decks were leaking dreadfully, and the bedding was more or less wet. A wet watch is uncomfortable enough, but to nod in a chair or be forced to turn in to a wet bed is even worse, as we found.'[24]

On 27 December, the *Shenandoah* reached the remote South Atlantic island of Tristan da Cunha. The tall but tiny island, named for the 16th-century Portuguese explorer who discovered it, had been a British naval station during the Napoleonic Wars, and was still a British protectorate, but was now home to just seven families, farming beef cattle, sheep and poultry. The rebels found deep water on one side suitable for loading stores, but the water there was so choked with seaweed that it was difficult to get through, and risked clogging the propeller. They landed 26 prisoners, leaving them a three-month supply of provisions, and pressed on.

It proved lucky for the Confederates that their stay on the island was brief. Only 12 hours after they left the harbour, the Yankee man-of-war *Iroquois* arrived. The *Iroquois* took the marooned prisoners aboard, weighed anchor and, unaware that the *Shenandoah* was headed for Melbourne, steamed off for Cape Town – which the Yankees knew to have been a favourite port of the *Alabama* – hoping the *Shenandoah* might be bound there too.

Two days later, in calm weather, the Confederates sighted the island of St Paul rising out of the sea. Anchoring outside the island's harbour, a party went ashore to explore. Among them was Fred McNulty, who noted, 'Entering its basin in a yawl, we found that the waters must be over an extinct crater, as they were hot enough to boil penguin eggs. These birds rose like clouds before us.'[25]

Flying penguins? Had McNulty made the ornithological discovery of the century?

He continues: 'Here we found, to our surprise, three Frenchmen. They were employed curing fish, while their vessel was off for another catch. Besides their rude quarters, we were taken to the residence of the owner of the island, who lived in France, and were astonished to find here, far from all the world, apartments displaying all that luxury, wealth and culture suggested, including a library of nearly 1,000 volumes. No bolt or key unlocked this; it was all open as the Garden of Eden to our first parents. On our departure the hospitable Frenchmen presented us with a supply of cured fish and half a barrel of penguin eggs.'[26]

On 29 December, with the wind still howling and the ship buffeted by a cross-sea, the *Shenandoah* spied her eighth and last victim before arriving in Melbourne. She was the American barque *Delphine*, out of Bangor, Maine, bound for Akyab, Arabia, to load a cargo of rice for the Union armies. The Confederates put a shot across her bows and set about their dread business. By now, they had it down to a fine art.

The captain of the *Delphine*, William Nichols, when told his vessel was a prize of the Confederacy and would be burnt, begged Waddell to spare the ship, claiming his wife, Lillias, was too ill to be transferred to the *Shenandoah* in such rough seas. 'It may cause the death of my wife to remove her,' he told Waddell, 'The report of the gun has made her very ill.'[27]

Waddell was not convinced. He sent his surgeon, Charles Lining, to examine the lady, and when Lining pronounced her fit to be transferred, Waddell told Captain Nichols that while he regretted causing his wife such inconvenience, she would be in no danger. He assures him that the boat sent to fetch the ladies has six good oarsmen who would bring them safely to the *Shenandoah*.

Captain Nichols knew it was useless to object further, and soon the boat returned with the unsinkable Mrs Nichols, her young son Phineas, her maid, and as many of her possessions as the boat could carry, including a canary in a cage. The sea being rough, a bosun's chair was lowered to the boat from the yardarm, and Mrs Nichols confidently climbed on and ordered the men to hoist away.

Cornelius Hunt quipped, 'If a bandbox containing her best bonnet had been added to her baggage, it would have been complete.'[28]

Fred McNulty declared Lillias Nichols 'as plump and healthy a specimen of the sex as the Pine Tree State [Maine] ever produced.

'Laughing heartily, when asked if she were ill, she said "No." She was a brave, cultivated woman, and I was real sorry the ruse failed, as I wanted to see the ship spared.'[29]

When safely aboard the *Shenandoah*, the lady berated her husband for failing to save his ship, then sought out the Confederate commander. Waddell recounts, 'When in the act of leaving my cabin, into which they were invited, Mrs Nichols asked in a stentorian voice if I was captain, what I intended to do with them, and where would they be landed.

'"On St Paul [Island], madam, if you like."

'"Oh, no, never. I would rather remain with you."

'I was surprised to see in the sick lady a tall, finely proportioned woman of twenty-six years, in robust health, evidently possessing a will and voice of her own.'[30]

Lillias Nichols was pretty, elegant, and an incorrigible flirt. As a prisoner on the *Shenandoah*, she would spend much of her time in the wardroom chatting and playing checkers and backgammon with the officers, who were clearly charmed by her. It seems the commander was rather taken with her, too, and in the days to come the two would often seek each other's company.

An officer and a few men remained on the *Delphine* to set her afire. The sea was heaving and night was falling as the first flames flicked from the companionway, then rapidly spread throughout the vessel, bursting from doors, windows and hatchways, then licking at the spars until the yards, sails and halyards were ablaze and the sea around the ship had a lurid glow. Captain Nichols, pacing the deck and watching his ship destroyed, was a pitiable sight. A part-owner of the vessel, he was forced to witness a lifetime of wealth and work go up in smoke.

Lieutenant Chew, in a clumsy attempt to relieve Captain Nichols' distress, suggested he consider how small things can have big consequences. If, for example, at daylight he had altered course by just a quarter of a point, the *Shenandoah* would not have caught sight of the *Delphine* and he would not be standing there now, watching her sink. Nichols, unsurprisingly, found no comfort in that. Tersely, he replied, 'That shows how darned little you know about it, for this morning at daylight I just did changed my course by a quarter of a point, and that's what fetched me here!'[31]

So entranced were the Confederates by what Hunt called 'a holocaust to the God of War',[32] they failed to notice that the men sent to torch the *Delphine* had not yet returned. When they realised the men were missing, concerns were raised that in the heavy seas the boat might have been swamped on its way back. Even in the glow of the burning ship, the *Shenandoah*'s watch could find no sign of it.

Lanterns were run up the rigging so the men could find their ship, and all eyes on deck scanned the dark ocean until, after what seemed an eternity, someone spotted them – rising on the crest of a massive wave.

A voice called, 'Ahoy there! Throw us a line!' A rope cast through the spray reached its mark, and there were whoops of joy and sighs of relief all round. Trouble continued to follow the *Shenandoah*, but she was still a lucky ship.

Captain Nichols eventually admitted to Waddell that he had lied about his wife's illness. It was a deceit intended to save his ship; a desperate attempt he hoped a fellow captain would understand. Waddell did indeed understand, and appreciated Nichols' frank confession. What he would not appreciate, on arriving in Melbourne, was discovering that Lillias Nichols' coquettish attentions had been a greater deceit.

On New Year's Day 1865, Cornelius Hunt was just about to be relieved from watch when the ship's bell struck 12. He recalls, 'The weather was fine, with a light, variable wind blowing, and the stars threw their silver shimmer over the quiet water. Everyone on board, save the officers of the deck, the quartermaster, the lookout, and the man at the wheel, were wrapped in slumber.

'Many thousand miles from home and friends, with the broad Atlantic all around us, and our adventurous career just begun, we did not forget the day, and at eight o'clock in the morning we unfurled our banner to the breeze, and there at our peak it waved, the emblem of a young nation which for four years had struggled, God only knows with what self-denying patience and resolution, for liberty.'[33]

Chapter 8

The grey and the good

William Blanchard, the US Consul in Melbourne, is fit to be tied as he stomps into his office on the corner of Little Collins St and Chancery Lane. It's the morning of 26 January 1865, and the arrival yesterday of an enemy cruiser, and the rapturous welcome the rebels received, sent his blood pressure soaring and gave him a restless night. He's still in a foul mood this morning, but his mood's about to improve – for a while, anyway.

Blanchard is surprised to find a dozen people in his office, waiting to see him. They are Captain William Nichols and his wife Lillias, their son Phineas and their maid, two officers and six crewmen, all taken prisoner by the *Shenandoah* in December after the capture of the *Delphine*.

Blanchard begins taking depositions from the former prisoners, who tell him they had been released the previous day, as soon as the ship arrived.

Captain Nichols doesn't have a lot to say. He tells the consul he's constrained by the oath he took, on signing his parole, not to reveal any information that could disadvantage the raider or the Confederate cause, such as details of the ship's armaments.

Lillias Nichols, on the other hand, is more than happy to spill the beans. If her mood had genuinely mellowed while a captive of the Confederacy – which is doubtful – it changed for the worse when boarding the boat to take the Nichols family and their luggage ashore. Lieutenant Whittle noticed among Lillias' possessions taken from the *Delphine* a copy of the anti-slavery novel *Uncle Tom's Cabin* – a bestseller worldwide but loathed in the South. Whittle grabbed the book and tossed it overboard. Outraged, Lillias cried out that she hoped the *Shenandoah* would be set afire some day soon.

Uncle Tom's Cabin wasn't the only book belonging to Lillias Nichols that fell into enemy hands. In August 1943, on reading a newspaper article on the visit of the *Shenandoah*, Ada Wheeler, of St Kilda, wrote to the paper that she had in her possession two old leather-bound volumes of the works of the 18th-century English novelist Henry Fielding. The books had been presented to her father, and an inscription in the flyleaf read, 'D.D. Wheeler, from I.S. Bulloch, CSS *Shenandoah*. Taken from the Yankee barque *Delphine*, captured by the above ship on Dec 29, 1864.'

At the consulate, Lillias tells Blanchard everything she knows about the *Shenandoah*, above and below decks; her Whitworth guns and other armaments, her 79 officers and crew, and most particularly her opinion of the ship's bluff, recalcitrant captain.

From Lillias and from the six crewmen, Blanchard learns of the raider's strengths, but, more importantly, her major weakness – because it's unsafe for all the guns on one side to be fired at the same time, the ship cannot fire a broadside.

'Never was a courtesy more completely thrown away upon an enemy,' says Master's Mate Cornelius Hunt of Captain and Lillias Nichols, apparently surprised that someone whose ship you had looted and sunk might take it personally.

'They not only utterly failed to appreciate, in any degree, the manner in which they were treated while they were with us, but indulged in the most scandalous romance at our expense after they got on shore. This was all well enough no doubt, but if our friend of the *Delphine* had fallen into our hands a second time, we, knowing the reputation he had given us, would have taught him by experience ere we parted company, something of the dark side of the picture which a prisoner of war has occasion to inspect.'[1]

Mindful that a mail ship is leaving for England that day, Blanchard dashes off a letter to Ambassador Adams in London, informing him that the former *Sea King*, reborn as a Confederate cruiser, is in port, flagrantly flouting neutrality laws. He makes a copy for the US Consulate in Hong Kong, adding a suggestion that the consul request that one of the US Navy warships there be despatched to Melbourne posthaste, to catch the Confederates unaware.

While Blanchard is still scribbling, a note is delivered from the colony's Commissioner of Customs, James Francis, belatedly informing him that the master of the *Shenandoah* has asked permission to land prisoners – the Nichols and others from the *Delphine* – in the port. Waddell will later claim the prisoners 'left the ship without my knowledge in shore boats soon after my arrival in this port'.[2]

Francis wants to know if the consul will take care of the prisoners. Indeed he will. They have spent the day loudly blowing the whistle on Waddell, and this is music to Blanchard's ears.

He pens another letter, to Governor Darling this time, outlaying the testimony of Captain Nichols, Lillias and the six singing sailors. He argues that because the former British merchantman has not been naturalised by entering a Confederate port, the vessel is legally stateless and therefore not entitled to assistance in a neutral port. In other words, the *Shenandoah* is a pirate ship and should be seized as such.

'Here was a dilemma for the Governor,' McNulty writes. 'The United States consul was demanding of him that we be ordered out of the harbour, and we, as recognised belligerents, were demanding to stay. He "darst" and he "darsn't" as the gamins [street urchins] say.'[3]

Too bad for Blanchard, though; the Governor has already granted Waddell permission to land his prisoners and to repair and resupply his ship.

Blanchard is enraged and frustrated by Governor Darling's decision but probably not surprised. Sir Charles Henry Darling is the personification of the maxim that it's not what you know but who you know. While neither the first nor the last gormless English aristocrat to be appointed governor of a British colony, he is nonetheless a classic example of the triumph of nepotism over merit. His qualifications for the job include having been assistant private secretary to his uncle Sir Ralph Darling – a heartless tyrant and history's most hated governor of New South Wales – and having served without distinction as governor of Newfoundland, then of Jamaica, thanks to family connections with Lord Thomas Elgin – famed for stealing shiploads of ancient statues from Greece, notably the Parthenon's Marbles that to this day bear his name.

In 1863, Darling was appointed Governor of Victoria, one of the highest paid governorships in the empire, and wasted no time proving to Whitehall that it was not money well spent. By 1865, his heavy-handed meddling in political affairs – a governor was expected to be an independent arbiter in local politics – has created constitutional chaos, earned him the rebuke of the British Government, and will eventually lead to him being declared temperamentally unfit for office and recalled to London.

It's widely believed that the Governor is merely a mouthpiece for his Minister for Justice, Archibald Michie, and his Attorney-General, George Higinbotham, both of whom are known to be sympathetic to rebel causes.

English-born Michie was a lawyer and journalist before entering politics. When practising law in London, he was an associate of the radical philosopher John Stuart Mill, who abhorred slavery but supported secession. Mill believed the right to secede 'is merely saying that the question of government ought to be decided by the governed'.[4]

Michie, a gifted and persuasive orator, was one of the barristers who in 1855 successfully defended the Eureka Stockade rebels.

Higinbotham, a Dubliner, and grandson of a former US consul in that city, is, like Michie, a lawyer and journalist turned politician. A past editor of Melbourne's *Argus* – a newspaper with unabashed Confederate sympathies – he is a fierce advocate for self-government; for freedom from interference by centralised powers.

These are Governor Darling's chief advisors, and their advice, in the case of the *Shenandoah*, is to deny the US consul's request that the ship be seized as a pirate.

And so, the sightseers keep coming. 'All day long and until far into the evening,' Cornelius Hunt writes, 'all eager to say that they had visited the famous "rebel pirate".'[5]

When many visitors ask whether or not the rebels rescue the crews from captured vessels before burning or scuttling the ships, Hunt is taken aback, shocked that anyone could consider Southerners capable of such barbarism. 'But not withstanding this hard character they were ready to ascribe to us, they vied with each other in showing us every courtesy in their power, and the ladies in particular were well pleased when they could secure the attendance of a grey uniform to escort them on their tour of inspection.'[6]

The Captain is rushing to keep a 12.30pm appointment. In company with ship's officers Grimball, Scales and Lining, he is riding to Toorak, about 10 miles (16km) from the city, for a meeting with Governor Darling. Dressed to impress, in full dress uniform with caps and swords, they arrive at the Governor's mansion at 12.30 precisely, only to find that Darling is not there.

To Captain Waddell, a stickler for punctuality, this is unfor-givable; a gross insult to himself and his men. Declaring it unbecoming of Southern officers and gentlemen to sit cooling their heels in the waiting room of a tardy bureaucrat, he leaves his card and they ride off. A few minutes into the journey, they pass the Governor in his carriage, returning to his residence. Waddell stubbornly refuses to turn back, and rides back to the city with his compatriots.

Come the weekend, the Confederates are under siege by curious Victorians. On Saturday, the Hobson's Bay Railway brings 5,000 visitors to Sandridge, and more than 7,000 on Sunday. The three steamers that ferry visitors to and from the ship on Sunday are overcrowded, and the *Shenandoah* is so packed with people that the last couple of boatloads on Sunday are unable to get on board.

One boatload of visitors gets a taste of what the *Shenandoah*'s victims experience. A small yacht, with two men and a woman aboard, is rounding the raider's stern, about to tie on, when a strong wind gust catches the yacht and it capsizes. A nearby boat rescues the trio; the men choose to come aboard the *Shenandoah* regardless, and inspect the vessel dripping wet. The woman refuses to join them, however, and, in high dudgeon, demands that her rescuers take herself, her injured pride and her sodden crinoline back to shore.

On one of the many small craft bumping alongside is an old man, so desperate to come aboard that he climbs the spar of his yacht, leaps into the mizzen chains and scrambles up onto the deck. The officer of the deck is so taken aback by the impudence of this uninvited guest that he can't decide whether to welcome him aboard or throw him over the side.

The old man announces himself as 'the only genuine Confederate in the country'.[7]

As such, he says, he is entitled to the hospitality of any vessel that flies the Stars and Bars. The officer, doubting his sanity but admiring his audacity, allows him to stay.

Invitations to dinners and balls are thrust at the officers from all directions, and each is given a free return pass from Sandridge to Melbourne on the Hobson's Bay railway for as long they're in port.

Hunt writes: 'Whenever and wherever an officer appeared on shore, he was forthwith surrounded by a little conclave of sympathetic admirers, and had we accepted a tithe of the invitations we received to indulge in spiritous comforts, we should all of us, from the Captain down to the toughest old shellback in the forecastle, have been shockingly inebriated during the whole period of our sojourn.'[8]

Melbourne's pro-Northern newspaper, *The Age*, is less than impressed by the carnival atmosphere, and considers the *Shenandoah* 'a marauding craft' and her officers and crew 'a gang of respectable pirates'. The editorial sneers, 'The appearance in these waters of a Confederate cruiser has created no small commotion. There is some fear lest the habitual idol-worshippers, who are always ready to fall on their knees, should commit some extravagance which would compromise the whole community. We fully expect to hear of a proposal for a testimonial or a public dinner to the officers.'[9] When Melbourne's afternoon paper, the *Herald*, echoes *The Age*'s view, *The Bendigo Advertiser* wades in:

We observe that the *Herald* endorses the remarks of the *Age* in reference to the *Shenandoah*. So far as condemning the fussy and forward conduct of those who are so anxious to lionise the officers and crew of this vessel, we quite endorse the opinions of our contemporaries. But the cause of the Confederates has won the sympathy of most generous minds, and an expression of this sympathy in a becoming way is not at all improper. We are amused at the remarks of the two journals in reference to the *Shenandoah*'s being merely a buccaneer, because its mission is to injure and cripple the commerce of the United States. We beg to ask these detractors what else is the Federal navy doing when it is blockading Charleston and the ports of the Southern States?

The termination of the career of the *Alabama* is sufficient to answer to this, and some of the officers of that vessel are aboard the *Shenandoah*. We are inclined to ascribe this deprecation of the *Shenandoah* and the Confederate cause to the very sorry motive – a desire to please the Americans in Melbourne, the chief of whom are Northerners, and of course very bitter against the South.[10]

And as if to snub the nose at the anti-Confederate press and those who share such sentiments, an invitation is extended to the officers of the *Shenandoah* to attend a banquet in their honour at the exclusive Melbourne Club. Boasting a membership that reads like Who's Who in Australia, the gentlemen's club, according to some, is a bastion of the great and the good. Others regard it as a sanctuary for stuffed shirts in overstuffed club chairs.

Captain Waddell and five of his officers not on duty meet at Scott's Hotel, and, punctual as ever, arrive at the club at 7pm on the dot. Waddell writes, 'The doors of the Melbourne Club were hospitably opened to the officers of the *Shenandoah*. They were royally entertained and received by a society composed to a considerable extent of government officials, including judges of the courts.

'The entertainment was a courtesy which the club always extends to strangers, and the presence of the company was an expression of sympathy for a gallant people engaged in resisting a wicked aggression.'

He adds, 'Although there was a general sympathy in the community for the Confederate cause as kindly exhibited in many ways in the hospitalities shown to the officers of the *Shenandoah*, it was equally true there were sympathies warmly disposed towards the Federals.'[11]

At least two prominent Melbourne families have direct American connections, on both sides of the conflict.

The Irvine family are related to John Mitchell, an Irish rebel transported to Van Diemen's Land after the 1848 uprising. Mitchell escaped to the United States and settled in Richmond, Virginia. His three sons are serving in the Confederate Army. Mitchell's nephew, William Hill Irvine, just seven years old in 1865, will grown up to be premier and chief justice of Victoria.

Thomas Lalor, one of the four brothers of Eureka Rebellion leader Peter Lalor, fought for the Union with the 6th Wisconsin Infantry – most of the family migrated to America in the 1840s – and was killed at the Battle of the Wilderness in May 1864. Two other Lalor brothers are believed to have fought in the war – on opposing sides – although that claim is not verified.

In 1865, Eureka leader Peter Lalor, once a wanted man with a £400 price on his head, is a respected parliamentarian and a member of the Melbourne Club. It's not known whether or not he attended the dinner for the *Shenandoah* officers. Having lost a brother to rebel gunfire just a few months earlier, it's doubtful, although all members of parliament are said to have been present.

In the club's elegant dining room, the Confederates are seated in pride of place at the president's table, flanked by about 60 members and guests. The Confederates banquet being the most exciting thing to happen at the staid old institution since 1839 – when two members came to blows over a card game – more than 100 local notables applied to attend, but the organisers have weeded out those deemed not quite notable enough.

Among the most notable of the notables is Sir Redmond Barry, first chief justice of Victoria and secretary of the club. His Honour is also a notorious rake in the habit of scandalising polite society by promenading with his mistress and their illegitimate children. Famously, he was the judge at the 1855 Eureka rebels' trials. Infamously, in 1880, he will send to the gallows an outlaw who, in the year of the *Shenandoah*, is still a boy with a sash awarded for bravery.

The plates are laden with fine fare, and the wine flows like water, but all are on their best behaviour, if more than a little mellow, by the time the club president, wealthy merchant and politician James Graham, rises to propose two toasts: firstly, to the Queen; then to the *Shenandoah* and her officers, followed by a hearty 'three cheers'. The rebels' hosts gleefully inform them that cheering is strictly against club rules and that this is the first time official dispensation has been given to allow it. Such a privilege!

Captain Waddell, seated at the president's right hand, rises to respond but is quietly told the club rules prohibit speechifying of any kind. The three cheers were a special treat, but even a polite 'Thank you' is out of the question.

The formalities over, all retire to the smoking and billiard rooms for port, cigars and good-natured banter. Lieutenant John Mason is deep in conversation with a Doctor Barker, who kindly offers to pick him up the next morning at Scott's Hotel in his dogcart and drive him to the Yarra Bend Lunatic Asylum, at Kew, to look at the inmates. The doctor invites Captain Waddell and Smith Lee, too, and both accept.

Mason is fascinated by Doctor Barker's theories on hanging. Barker claims the conventional method of adjusting the rope, whereby the knot is placed behind the ear, is not as effective as placing the knot behind the neck. He tells Mason he has tested his theory by experimenting on condemned criminals in England, and that his method invariably snaps the neck, causing instantaneous death, whereas the traditional method often leaves the subject choking at the end of a rope for up to 10 minutes. Such is Melburnian small talk in 1865.

At the end of the evening, the Confederates bid a fond farewell to their hosts and, having missed that last train back to the port, beg the Captain's permission to spend the night in town. The Captain takes his leave of the junior officers, who, after a few more drinks at pubs along the way, and a good time had by all, turn in at the Albion Hotel.

Next morning, Mason and Smith Lee return to Scott's Hotel to meet Dr Barker and Captain Waddell. The doctor is right on time, but the otherwise obsessively punctual captain fails to materialise. After waiting a while, the others leave without him.

Lunch with the hanging doctor and his family is the prelude to a pleasant drive to the asylum, about three miles (5km) out of town. There, they are surprised to find not a large foreboding institution but separate stone cottages with flower and vegetable gardens tended by patients, under the watchful eyes of attendants. Why, it could almost be a plantation in the South, had the field hands not been picking flowers instead of picking cotton.

The asylum houses some 960 patients, including intellectually disabled children. The visitors are introduced to the star attraction of what is effectively a human zoo – an old woman who believes she is the Empress of Victoria.

Annie Baxter Dawbin, a guest at Dr Barker's for lunch with the Confederates, notes in her diary, 'Mrs Barker came here in the morning and asked me to go to her house to lunch, as some of the officers of the *Shenandoah* were to be there. Accordingly, I went at one o'clock and met Messrs Lee [nephew of the Confederate Commander-in-Chief Robert E. Lee] and Mason, Captain Brewer, Police Magistrate of Ginchen Bay, and Captain Murchison. The two officers were very gentlemanly Southerners, nice-looking, and quite charming in their manners.

'Dr Barker drove them to the Yarra Bend Asylum after lunch, but before doing so, he drove from the next street a Miss Clarke, who, when she got off the dogcart, never said a word of thanks to Mr Lee who had politely got down to help her from the vehicle. What must foreigners think of us English, when we behave so rudely?'[12]

After a fine day's entertainment courtesy of the mentally ill, it's back to Dr Barker's for drinks, thence to Scott's Hotel for more of the same. In the company of 20 or so well-wishers, the officers are treated to yet another banquet with drinks on the house, and are toasting the Confederacy when an uninvited guest joins them. The man, not identified in any of the officers' journals, launches into a tirade of abuse, damning the rebels and the Southern cause, and, according to Cornelius Hunt, 'making use of such language as gentlemen seldom submit to in silence'.[13]

Roused to defend the honour of the Confederacy, Assistant Surgeon McNulty springs to his feet and punches the man squarely between the eyes, felling him. With that, all hell breaks loose. Fists are flying, guns and knives are drawn, shots are fired, glasses, bottles and decanters are hurled amid a cacophony of shouts, curses and breaking glass.

No-one is seriously injured in the brawl, but Hunt tells us that, 'for a few moments there was a scene of excitement and confusion as I have seldom witnessed; but the *Shenandoah* men were victorious, drove their antagonists from the field, and then marched off to the theatre in a body, to conclude the evening in a less exhilarating time'.[14]

The theatre Hunt refers to is the Theatre Royal, where McNulty tells us that 'Barry Sullivan, then playing Othello, gave us an especial night, when, with true British gusto, the [playbills] read: "Under the distinguished patronage of the Confederate Steamship *Shenandoah*."'[15]

It's not known if any hint of irony influenced the choice of play, in which the lead character is played by a white actor in blackface. The celebrated English actor Barry Sullivan is touring Australia after performing in the same play, in Richmond, Virginia, and Philadelphia, Pennsylvania, with John Wilkes Booth.

A member of a famous theatrical family, Booth is presently playing Romeo in Shakespeare's *Romeo and Juliet*, at Ford's Theater in Washington. Critics have praised his performance, with one describing it as 'the most satisfactory of all renderings of that fine character, particularly in the death scene'.[16]

Booth, a Confederate sympathiser vehemently opposed to the abolition of slavery, will give the performance of his life at Ford's Theater on Good Friday, 14 April 1865. During the play *Our American Cousin*, attended by Abraham and Mary Lincoln, Booth will slip into the presidential box and shoot Lincoln in the back of the head. The assassin will escape and flee south until, after 12 days on the run, fate and a Yankee bullet catch up with him.

The *Shenandoah* will capture many whalers in her career, one such being the *Euphrates*, out of New Bedford, but the *Euphrates*' sister ship, the *Tigris*, will not be one of them. And that's a pity, because a shot across the bow of the *Tigris* would have exploded one of the most unlikely conspiracy theories of the war – that Lincoln's assassin, John Wilkes Booth, was not shot and killed on 26 April 1865, while on the run in northern Virginia, but escaped to Australia.

So that story goes, Booth inexplicably escaped capture and headed north to the Yankee heartland, rather than south to Dixie, and at New Bedford shipped aboard the *Tigris*. Presumably, he boarded under a false identity, since Yankees were hardly likely to welcome aboard the man who killed their President. Unless, of course, the *Tigris* was manned by Confederate agents cunningly disguised as New England Yankees, having mastered the tricky dialect.

The *Tigris* sailed to South Australia, where Booth was smuggled ashore under cover of darkness at a whaling station on

Kangaroo Island. He settled in Hahndorf, a township of mostly German migrants, in the Adelaide Hills, under the name Jack Holmes, and lived happily ever after.

The only supposedly supporting evidence for this theory is that Booth's mother's maiden name was Holmes, and that his father's second wife's first name was Adelaide. Actually, Adelaide was his father's first wife's second middle name, not that it makes much difference.

At Melbourne's Theatre Royal, after pushing through a large crowd that has gathered outside in hopes of catching a glimpse of the visiting celebrity rebels, the *Shenandoah* officers take their seats in the royal box, looking down upon a packed house staring back up at them, as Barry Sullivan frets and struts upon the stage.

During intermission, a band plays 'Dixie', at which some among the audience begin to cheer and others to jeer. The Confederates, irritated by the Yankee sympathisers' booing and hissing, and still smarting from the bar-room brawl, are inclined to get up and leave. However, it's a triple bill tonight, so for the sake of propriety they sit through the remainder of the program – 18th-century melodrama *The Wonder: A Woman Keeps a Secret*, and the black comedy *Robert Macaire* – before beating a hasty retreat.

The officers return to their ship where Lieutenant Mason, for whom too much of a good thing is barely enough, immediately applies for further shore leave but is refused. Captain Waddell tells him he has already spent a day longer ashore than was allowed, and confines him aboard ship. Mason, who has several more assignations lined up, is not a happy midshipman.

Still, he gets a better reception on returning to duty than did gunner John Guy, who, after being refused shore leave, stole one of the ship's boats and rowed off. Guy rowed back to the ship the next morning, pulled alongside, and was clambering up the ladder when Sailing Master Irvine Bulloch told him he could not come aboard because he was considered a deserter. When Guy refused to obey the order and continued to climb the ladder, Bulloch kicked him back into the boat.

While the men of the *Shenandoah* are making merry in Australia, the great drama being played out in America is nearing its climax. In Washington, the US Congress has passed the 13th Amendment, abolishing slavery. In Richmond, the Confederate Congress has appointed the commander of the Army of Northern Virginia, Robert E. Lee, as commander-in-chief of all Confederate forces. It is not so much a vote of confidence in Lee as a consensus that President Jefferson Davis – ailing both physically and mentally – is not up to the task.

The last Confederate port, at Wilmington, North Carolina, has fallen, cutting off supplies of food and war materiel to the people and armies of the South. In Richmond, the Confederate capital, sugar is selling for $10 a pound, coffee for $12 a pound and flour for $1,250 a barrel, and prices are set to soar even higher now that the Union blockade is a complete stranglehold. On the once grand plantations, most of the slaves have escaped or have been run off by the enemy, and the few who remain are selling for up to $6,000 – six times as much as before the war.

As General Sherman's army sweeps northward from Savannah, Georgia, in an unrestrained orgy of arson and pillage – leaving desolation and destitution in its wake – representatives of North and South meet in the salon of a steamer in Hampton Roads to negotiate a truce. For the North, President Lincoln himself has come, along with Secretary of State Seward. For the South, President Davis is represented by Vice-President Andrew Stephens, accompanied by former US Supreme Court justice John Campbell.

The so-called peace conference is a failure. While the Southerners have come with the vain hope of a negotiated peace, Lincoln makes it plain that he will accept nothing less than unconditional surrender, with slavery abolished, as the terms of peace. With compromise out of the question, it's back to the barricades.

Meanwhile in Melbourne, in a polite exchange of letters on more mundane matters, Customs Commissioner Francis asks Captain Waddell to provide a list of the immediate needs of his officers and crew. Waddell requests daily supplies of fresh meat, vegetables and bread, and stores of brandy, rum, champagne, port, sherry, beer, porter, molasses, lime juice and lightweight material for summer clothing for the men.

A diver's inspection of the *Shenandoah* reveals that 'the lining of the outer sternback is entirely gone and will have to be replaced'.[17] 'Sternback' is not found in any glossary of nautical terms but is probably an outmoded term referring to the stern tube containing the propeller shaft, and associated bearings, in a hybrid sailer–steamer such as the *Shenandoah*.

The *Shenandoah* is towed across the bay by tug to Enoch Chambers' slipway at Williamstown, so that her propeller shaft can be inspected and repaired. The work is expected to take about 10 days.

And still the sightseers keep coming, which inspires the slipway company to charge them sixpence each, with all the money raised going to local charities. Thinking along similar lines, Cornelius Hunt jokes, 'Indeed, so great was the curiosity we excited, that had we been content to stay for six months in Melbourne, and charged an admission fee of one dollar to visitors, I believe we could have paid a large instalment upon the Confederate debt.'[18]

But there's work to be done, and the decision is made to allow no more visitors on board. The sightseers crawling all over the decks are replaced by workmen caulking the decks with pitch and oakum. The heaviest stores and furnishings are hoisted into lighters hauled alongside, to lessen the load as much as possible before setting the ship upon the slip. And so the refit begins, with gangs of men working in shifts, day and night.

Captain Waddell is seldom seen soaking up the city's hospitality with his officers. Perhaps mindful of the fate of the *Florida* – captured while her master was ashore – he sticks close by his ship. He has serious concerns about her safety, and complains to Melbourne's Superintendent of Police, Thomas Lyttleton, that agents of US Consul Blanchard have threatened to blow it up while in port. He requests police protection for the *Shenandoah*, and Lyttleton complies by ordering the water police to keep an eye on it.

Waddell also claims Blanchard's agents have induced several members of his crew to desert, presumably by offering men bribes to jump ship. And he's less than impressed with a certain customs official who 'did not have sufficient intelligence to recognise the distinction between a national and piratical vessel, who, for many days kept watch over the *Shenandoah* with his assistants, under disguise of friendly visits to her officers'.[19]

Waddell says he explained the difference to the customs officer, who troubled him no further. Apparently, the difference between a warship and a pirate ship – a distinction legal authorities in Australia, Britain and the United States consider blurry, to say the least – is perfectly clear in Waddell's mind.

The Captain's mood is darkening. He suspects there are forces at work here that will stop at nothing to derail his mission and destroy his ship. And although he'll never receive confirmation, he's absolutely right.

Wary of undue attention from Yankee agents and sympathisers, Waddell orders that three sentries must be posted aboard ship at all times, directed to hail three times any vessel that comes too close, then, if no satisfactory reply is received, to open fire on her. This does not happen, but the Confederates remain blissfully unaware how close they come to destruction.

When the *Shenandoah* was still at Sandridge, before being towed across the bay to the Williamstown slipway, anchored nearby was a Yankee merchantman, the *Mustang*, out of New York. The captain and crew of the *Mustang*, which had arrived in Melbourne a month earlier, were incensed by the presence of the rebel raider in port, and hatched a plot to blow her to smithereens. The Yankee ship's master, Captain Sears, arranged with local collaborators for a bomb to be made. The device contained 250 pounds (115kg) of gunpowder and was designed to be detonated by a cocked revolver with a line attached to the trigger. The aim was to blow a large hole in the *Shenandoah*'s hull and send her to the bottom of Hobson's Bay.

One night, dark figures boarded a boat from the *Mustang*, rowed silently to where the *Shenandoah* lay at anchor and pulled alongside. After attaching the bomb to the raider's hull, the saboteurs rowed a safe distance away and tugged on the line.

Nothing happened.

Chapter 9

Buttons and beaux

There's a fair chance that somewhere in Victoria, perhaps in an old box of keepsakes, is an heirloom passed down from a great-great-grandmother or distant aunt. This old curiosity is a gilt button bearing the emblem of an anchor and two crossed cannons, above the initials C.S.N. And oh, if that button could speak, what a tale it could tell.

As repairs to the *Shenandoah* continue at Williamstown, life on the slips is somewhat tedious after the mad social whirl of the previous week. Lieutenant Mason, permitted shore leave again, heads for the city to indulge in whatever is going by way of diversion. But it's a Sunday, and all Melbourne has to offer is attendance at church. At St Peter's Church of England, near Parliament House, he and Lieutenant 'Dab' Scales are shown to a pew by two young women. The women are polite and friendly but decidedly plain, and the rebels sit bored and restless for more than an hour, suffering a mind-numbing sermon and the stares of a congregation apparently amazed to see pirates in the house of God. After the final Amen, they seek sanctuary in the Albion Hotel, where they find Assistant Surgeon Fred McNulty propping up the bar. Unlike his fellow officers, McNulty has sought solace not in the Holy Spirit but in spirituous liquor. After a bottle or two of 'very nice colonial wine', the trio retires to an upstairs parlour to smoke cigars. Writes Mason:

Whilst we were chatting quietly in the sitting room, who should make his appearance but the Steward of the *Delphine* [captured on 29 December], a Yankee-looking fellow, who hails from Missouri and claims to be a good Southerner, but at the same time he wanted to be paroled, which our captain very properly refused to do. He walked into the room dressed in shiny slop clothes [loose-fitting sailors' clothing], accompanied by an individual of the same stamp, apparently. The blackguard spoke to us with as much freedom as if we were old friends of his.

As soon as I saw that he was decidedly inclined to be communicative in spite of the cold reception we gave him, I walked up to the window and commenced reading the signs on the other side of the street with the greatest possible diligence, and Mr Yankee did not venture to accost me. But Scales and McNulty, who kept their seats, were not so fortunate, for they had the pleasure of being introduced to this fellow's companion, and it was only after some skilful manoeuvring and very broad hints that they succeeded in getting rid of them.[1]

Mercifully, just as it seems the Confederates' colonial honeymoon might be over, a deputation from the gold-mining town of Ballarat arrives to invite the ship's officers to a ball to be held in their honour. The event is being organised by William Eaves, a grains trader, and E.J. Brayton, the agent for Cobb & Co coaches. Americans of Southern persuasion, both are now prominent citizens of Ballarat.

The Ballarat press enthuses, 'The Confederate cause is certainly in the ascendant just now, if it never was before, and as it seems to have the suffrages of the fair sex – some of the Melbourne ladies wear the Confederate button – it is not to be wondered at that the men follow in the wake.

'The Ballarat ball to the officers is expected to be a grand affair. In addition to the leading citizens of Ballarat, many of the notabilities of Melbourne will be invited to meet the officers.'[2]

Six officers not on duty – Hunt, Grimball, Bulloch, Lining, Scales and Smith, are granted the Captain's permission to attend. In the early evening of Thursday 9 February, dressed in their best, they board a train for the two-hour trip to Ballarat. Sharing their carriage is an officer of the Victorian militia, an elderly Chinese man and an American who is a Southerner but supports the North. During the journey, the militiaman and the American pass the time by baiting and abusing the old Chinese man, much to the Confederates' amusement.

Australians and Americans share a fear and loathing of the Chinese, an antipathy born on the goldfields in both countries when Chinese arrived in large numbers; and in both countries is expressed in official discrimination, and unofficially by persecution and murder.

In New South Wales, when the gold rush began, the press accused Chinese diggers of unspecified 'unnatural crimes'.[3] The Victorian press condemned them as 'a social evil that would contaminate and degrade the superior European race'.[4] The widespread perception among white miners is that their Anglo-Saxon Eldorado is being overrun by 'Celestials' – so called because China is known as the Celestial Empire, its emperor styling himself the Son of Heaven.

In Australia, the general public has come to share this perception, whipped up by the colonial authorities into yet another invasion scare. In Victoria, an 1855 parliamentary inquiry into conditions on the goldfields stated, 'The question of the influx of such large numbers of a pagan and inferior race is a very serious one, and comprises an unpleasant possibility of the future, that a comparative handful of colonists may be buried in a countless throng of Chinamen.'[5]

White miners soon came to realise that violence against the Chinese would go unpunished. You could bash them, drive them from their claims, burn down their camps, even kill them, and officialdom would either turn a blind eye or give you a nod and a wink. 'You must have killed a Chinaman,' becomes a common Australian expression, meaning that it's not murder, merely bad luck.

When, in 1860, gold is discovered at Lambing Flat, in New South Wales, by an African-American known as Alexander the Yankee, European and Chinese diggers flock to the district. By December of that year, two Chinese miners had been killed, and 10 wounded. Others suffered the shame of having their 'queues', or 'pigtails', cut off. Wearing their hair in a long plait identified Chinese men as subjects of the Manchu Emperor, and signified manhood and dignity.

Attacks and other depredations continued on the goldfields, culminating in 1861 in the notorious Lambing Flat Riot, the worst incident of civil disorder in Australian history. Carrying a perversion of the Eureka flag – a banner bearing the Southern Cross with the inscription 'Roll up – No Chinese', a mob of up to 3,000 whites invaded the Chinese diggings, assaulting the diggers, burning and looting. An eyewitness reported seeing 'one

man who returned with eight pigtails attached to a flag, glori-
fying in the work that had been done. I also saw one tail, with
part of the scalp, the size of a man's hand attached, that had been
literally cut from some unfortunate creature.'[6]

Police sent in to restore order were attacked at night by a force
of about 1,000 miners, who retreated only after a fire-fight and a
mounted charge by troopers wielding sabres.

In the aftermath, the ringleaders of the riot were arrested and
jailed, and the Chinese returned to the diggings, but the bad
blood remained.

By 1865, even though most of the Chinese miners have
returned to China – as they had always intended to do – the
irrational fear and loathing of 'Celestials' remains undimin-
ished. In time, the ugly seed planted in the colonial goldfields
will germinate into the racist imperative of a new nation. It will
be called the Immigration Restriction Act, better known as the
White Australia Policy.

At Ballarat, the Confederates are met by well-wishers and escorted
to Craig's Hotel. It seems the whole town has turned out to greet
them, and on a triumphal arch across the main street, flowers
spell out 'Welcome to Ballarat'.

The following day's agenda begins with a tour of the Black Hill
Quartz Mining Company's operation, followed by a 420-foot
(130m) descent into a shaft of the Band of Hope mine. Surgeon
Lining's journal entry reads:

It was a horrid sensation that of going down, and certain death
if any accident had happened, for if the fall had not killed us, the

chain falling on us certainly would. After we had gone a certain distance, suddenly a flood of water came in upon us, putting out the cigars of the smokers and wetting us more or less.

On getting to the main shaft they put us into small cars and trolled us about a thousand feet or more when we came to another shaft which went upwards, and we were in the bed of an ancient river and consequently where the gold was found. We followed this gallery to where they were digging and I myself dug a little to see if I could find a nugget, but was unsuccessful, only seeing a few sparkling pieces of sand, which they told me was gold. At this spot the air was so bad that we could hardly keep our candles lit, and our breathing was a little oppressed, not as much so as I expected. There was a curious smell they said was the foul air.

Altogether it was a most interesting visit and one I would not have missed for a great deal, but I should never go down another shaft – we suffered a good deal from the heat.

Later that evening, back at his hotel, Lining has a tight squeeze of another kind. 'The ball was to commence at 10pm. For, I think, this first time in my life, I was the last dressed and they had to wait for me, all owing to the button holes of my waistcoat being too small.'

Buttoned up at last, he goes downstairs to find he and his comrades are expected to escort 'three to four rather old ladies' to the ball.[7]

Lining's evening is set to improve considerably, however.

Tripping the light fantastic at Craig's Hotel tonight are braces of middle-aged misters and missuses, but, happily, a surfeit of misses. As usual, the Confederates are spoilt for choice.

*

Preparing for a ball in the Victorian Age is an organisational challenge, and there are strict rules to follow. Interested parties meet to choose a Committee of Arrangements, tasked with securing a venue, booking an orchestra, sending out invitations and providing refreshments. Etiquette dictates that food and drink must never be served in the ballroom, so a separate refreshment room offers guests tea and coffee, biscuits, cakes, ices, cracker-bonbons, cold tongue and sandwiches.

Ladies dressing for a ball must select the design and colour of their attire according to marital status and the dictates of propriety. For a married woman, a white or lightly tinted silk dress in a shimmering pattern is suitable, trimmed with tulle and flowers. Unmarried women are similarly obliged to select light materials for their gowns, although in fabrics other than silk, but with a wider choice of colours – light blue, maize or apple green for blondes; richer colours for brunettes and redheads. In the hair, single flowers, wreaths or small feathers are acceptable – although a tall woman should avoid any head-dress that might make her appear taller than the gentleman dancing with her. Jewellery should be minimal; one bracelet is quite enough, since one does not wish to appear gaudy or common.

For all ladies, the hoop dress is quite the thing, with a low neckline and short sleeves, worn with short white gloves or lace mittens, matching satin shoes or boots, and that most essential accessory for flirting – a fan.

A married woman must arrive at a ball on the arm of her husband; an unmarried woman accompanied by her mother or a chaperone. And it's fashionable to arrive an hour late.

Gentlemen not in military uniform should dress for a ball in a black dress coat with matching trousers and waistcoat – low-cut to display an embroidered shirt front with gold studs – black or white cravat or tie, patent leather boots with low heels, white kid gloves and a white linen handkerchief. Hair should be neither unkempt nor too curly; jewellery restricted to studs, cuff-links and a watch chain; and perfume avoided so as not to seem effeminate.

The last word on ballroom etiquette for gentlemen comes from Thomas Hillgrove, the author of *Hillgrove's Ballroom Guide*, who warns, 'The practice of chewing tobacco and spitting on the floor is not only nauseous to ladies, but is injurious to their dresses. They who possess self-respect, will surely not be guilty of such conduct.'[8]

The ball begins with an order to strike up the band, whereby gentlemen escort ladies to seats and fetch dance programs for them before introducing friends and notable guests – such as the dashing officers of a Confederate warship – who write their names in the ladies' dance programs.

Dances are categorised as 'round' and 'square', or 'set'. 'Round' dances, performed by individual couples, such as the waltz, polka, schottische and two-step, are popular but also practical, because the number of turns involved keeps women's hoop skirts out of the way. 'Square' dances, performed by couples in formation, include the Virginia Reel, Pop Goes the Weasel, and the ballroom favourite, the Quadrille.

Etiquette dictates that gentlemen ask the ladies to dance, and that ladies carry a dance program on which is written the name of the gentleman they're going to dance with next, and the number of the dance. Ladies try to save dances for the men they particularly fancy, although, strictly speaking, to dance with the same man more than three times is regarded as rather unseemly. Unfortunately, history does not record how many times the names Hunt, Lining, Grimball, Bulloch and Smith appeared on those dance programs.

Both ladies and gentlemen are expected to dance with as many different people as possible, including single and married people. For a lady to refuse an offer to dance is most improper unless she is tired or has already promised to dance with another man. It is also improper for a lady who has enjoyed a large number of dances with eligible gentlemen to boast of that fact, especially to a wallflower.

Lining's pick for belle of the ball is the daughter of Major Wallace, a retired officer of the British Raj in India. Bulloch has his eye on a girl from Geelong, Smith has had his hand squeezed by a pretty young thing, which seems promising, and all agree as to who are the two best looking women in the room. Both happen to be married, but the night is young.

Cornelius Hunt tells us, 'It was a decidedly *recherché* affair. The wealth, beauty and fashion of Ballarat were out in full force, fully intent upon lionising and doing honour to a few of the unpretending supporters of a young government battling for existence with the lusty Giant of the Western world. Every attention that kindness and courtesy could suggest was shown us, and more than one heart beat quicker at such convincing evidence of the existence of sympathy in this country of the Antipodes, for the service in which we were engaged.

'Many a grey uniform coat lost its gilt buttons that night, but we saw them again ere we bade a final adieu to Australia, suspended from watchguards depending from the necks of bright-eyed women, and we appreciated the compliment thus paid not to us, but to our country. God bless the gentle women of Melbourne and Ballarat!'[9]

The Confederates dance on until four in the morning then, after the ladies have reluctantly taken their leave, drink and chat until breakfast time, catch an hour of sleep, then bathe and take a stroll around town.

The morning paper deems the ball a glittering success and describes the guests of honour in gushing terms: 'They are all quite young men, and have a quiet gentlemanly demeanour, which seems to be the antithesis alike of the traditional Yankee and of the swaggering buccaneer.'[10]

Before leaving Ballarat, Lining calls on Major Wallace and his lovely daughter, while Bulloch manages to find and lock lips with the girl from Geelong.

And when the Confederates board the 7pm train for Melbourne, a certain pair of married ladies is there to see them off.

Chapter 10

The trouble with Charley

US Consul Blanchard is beside himself. His efforts to have the *Shenandoah* seized as a pirate having failed, what he sorely needs is proof that the Confederates are secretly recruiting men in a blatant infringement of the British Foreign Enlistment Act. Much to his relief, such evidence presents itself in the shape of a ship's cook named Charley.

Two deserters from the *Shenandoah*, John Williams and Herman Wicke – both of whom joined the crew after their ships had been captured and sunk – tell the consul that when they jumped ship on 12 February, the *Shenandoah*'s cook was a man called Charley, who had come aboard in Melbourne.

John Williams, a free African-American who had served in the US Navy, is one of the sailors from the *D. Godfrey* – captured the previous November – who had joined the crew of the *Shenandoah*. He claims he resisted joining until Captain Waddell told him it would go hard with him if he did not join the ship because coloured people were the cause of the war. When he offered to work but would not enlist in the Confederate Navy, Waddell threatened to lock him in the coal hold, then, when he still refused, offered him a month's pay in advance. Williams says he told the captain that as a US Navy veteran and loyal citizen of the United States he could not accept, whereupon Waddell sent him to the galley to work as a cook.

In the months to follow, Waddell continued to ask Williams to join and Williams persisted in his refusal. So Lieutenant Whittle tried other means of persuasion. It is part of Whittle's role as first officer to order punishments for breeches of discipline, and it's a role he seems to relish.

In all navies, mutiny, treason and sodomy are hanging offences, but the death sentence is rarely imposed, particularly for sodomy. The most common offences, which warrant corporal punishment, include disobeying a command, neglect of duty, quarrelling, fighting, insolence to a superior officer, and drunkenness.

In the British Navy, flogging with the 'cat-o'-nine-tails', a whip of nine knotted ropes, has long been the favoured method of punishment, and will remain so until banned in 1881. Adult males can be sentenced to receive up to a dozen lashes on the bare upper back, while boys – males under 18 – for unspecified reasons, are lashed on the bare bottom.

Flogging in the United States Navy was abolished in 1850, however, and the Confederate Navy did not see fit to reinstate it. American naval officers, both blue and grey, have sought other means of imposing discipline aboard ship. These include branding, confinement in irons, sweatboxes or straitjackets, and continuous dousing with sea water.

Lieutenant Whittle's favourite punishments are 'gagging' and 'tricing up'. A seaman ordered to be gagged is bound in chains with an iron rod placed between his teeth like a horse's bit. If gagging is both humiliating and painful, tricing is even more so. It involves binding a man's hands in front of him, then hauling him up by a rope until his feet barely touch the deck. Whittle, a devout Christian who often quotes the Bible to justify brutality, is fond of tricing men higher and higher, inflicting more and more pain, if their contrition is not to his satisfaction.

Whittle justifies his actions thus: 'With such a mixture of nation-alities the most rigid discipline had to be, and was, maintained, and the happiness of all was promoted by prompt punishment of all offenders. This, of course, devolved on me. Justice was tempered with humane and kind treatment, and to the general good and as necessary to success.'[1]

John Williams tells Blanchard he was triced up seven times by Whittle but remained unbroken. On one such occasion, when he and a sailor named John Flood were brought before Whittle charged with fighting, Flood, a Yankee but a white man, went unpunished while he, a Yankee but a black man, was triced up.

Whittle's journal confirms this claim. He writes, 'I justified Flood and triced up Williams. Here was a Negro against a Yankee. I had trouble in bringing him to his bearings but he finally came down.'[2]

John Williams' sweet revenge is to drop the Confederates right in it. His affidavit reads:

I, John Williams, of Boston, Massachusetts, do make oath and say that I was taken from the barque *D. Godfrey*, the seventh day of November, 1864, as a prisoner, and put aboard the steam-ship *Shenandoah*, now in Hobson's Bay; that I served as a cook under compulsion and punishment on board said *Shenandoah*, from the day of my punishment until Monday, sixth day of February, 1865; that on Monday last I swam ashore to obtain the protection of the United States consul; that when I left the said *Shenandoah* on Monday last there were 15 or 20 men concealed in various parts of the ship, who came on board since the *Shenandoah* arrived in Hobson's Bay, and said men told me they came on board said *Shenandoah* to join ship; that I cooked for said concealed men for several days before I left; that three other men, in the uniform of the crew of the *Shenandoah*, are at work on board said *Shenandoah* – two of them in the galley, and one of them in the engine room; that said three other men in uniform joined said *Shenandoah* in this port; that I can point out all the men who have joined said *Shenandoah* in this port.[3]

Consul Blanchard immediately delivers the affidavit to Governor Darling, who flicks it to Attorney-General – and Confederate sympathiser – George Higinbotham, who flicks it to the Crown Solicitor's office, which flicks it to Detective Superintendent Charles Nicholson, who flicks it to the redoubtable Detective D.S. Kennedy.

After two days of sniffing around, Kennedy reports to Nicholson that Captain Waddell intends to ship 40 hands from Melbourne, and that the recruits will sign articles of enlistment when outside the Heads. Three Melbourne boarding housekeepers, McGrath, Finlay and O'Brien, are vetting prospective recruits, offering wages of £6 a month plus an £8 bounty. A Sandridge shipwright, Peter Kerr, was overheard by Kennedy telling others, presumably in a pub, that Captain Waddell offered him £10 a month to join the ship as a carpenter. Kennedy also heard that a Sandridge waterman named McLaren has joined the ship or is soon to do so.

Detective Superintendent Nicholson flicks Kennedy's report to Police Commissioner Frederick Standish – who will one day win a place in history for bungling repeated attempts to capture the Kelly Gang. Standish, in turn, flicks the report to Victoria's Premier, James McCulloch, who flicks it back to the Dixie-whistling Attorney-General, George Higinbotham, who files it in his in-tray, on the bottom of the pile.

While the Victorian Government is busy duck-shoving, Governor Darling surprises everyone – including himself, most likely – by taking immediate and drastic action. He orders that all work stop on repairs to the *Shenandoah*; a magistrate duly issues a warrant for the arrest of Charley; and a phalanx of high officials is despatched to Williamstown to serve the warrant on the commander of the raider, accompanied by some 50 armed police and followed by a parade of curious citizens. But Captain Waddell isn't there.

As he tells it, 'I was on shore, and Lieutenant Grimball was in charge of the *Shenandoah*. Superintendent Lyttleton and Inspector Beam of the Victoria Police, with a magistrate's warrant to search for a person who was said to be a British subject, came on board. The cause of their visit was induced by deserters who had been employed by the American consul to give information that one Charley, an Englishman, had shipped on the *Shenandoah*.'[4]

When Grimball refuses to allow the ship to be searched, denying that any such man is aboard, and arguing that only the captain can permit such an intrusion, the officials and their police escort turn tail and march back whence they came.

They return the next day in greater force. Some 200 police and troops of the Royal Artillery take up positions at the Williamstown gun battery and on the wharves on each side of the *Shenandoah*.

Captain Waddell, calm and resolute, is waiting for them. Like Grimball, he refuses to allow a search of the vessel, implying that he would consider any search undertaken against his will to be an act of war. Coming from the commander of a warship with enough firepower to punch some sizeable holes in Melbourne's fine facades, if it cared to, the threat is taken seriously by the police, who suddenly find themselves on the back foot. When Waddell offers to have his master-at-arms search the ship for Charley and any stowaways, the compromise offer is meekly accepted.

In Lieutenant Whittle's words, 'At the request of the authorities I was ordered to have her thoroughly searched for any stowaways. I selected several of the best officers, who made a conscientious search.'[5]

Naturally, the search finds no sign of the elusive Charley or any other ring-ins, and Waddell gives his word as an officer and a gentleman that he has 'neither enlisted nor shipped any person for service in the Confederate cause since my arrival'.[6]

Within hours, Melbourne is abuzz with wild rumours: the ship and the shore battery are exchanging fire; the *Shenandoah* is about to shell the city; the ship has been blown up by Yankee saboteurs. A public protest meeting, hurriedly called at Melbourne's Criterion Hotel, attracts a large crowd of concerned citizens. Speaker after speaker condemns the authorities' actions as heavy-handed, and the meeting passes a resolution 'that the course adopted by the Government in seizing the *Shenandoah* was ill-advised, and likely to be subversive of our friendly relations with neighbouring neutral states'.[7]

True to form, *The Argus* fans the flames:

Although there is general sympathy in this community for the Confederate cause, as kindly exhibited in many ways in the hospitality shown to the officers of the *Shenandoah*, it is equally true that there are sympathisers and partisans as warmly disposed towards the Federals. The reception and shelter given to the *Shenandoah* have given serious offence to this party, and the abortive efforts to discredit the character of the officers and crew of this ship in connection with the cause for which they are in arms, have, as is openly asserted, been followed by the still more unworthy course of action of tampering with the allegiance of the crew. Be that as it may, Captain Waddell complains that 12 or 14 of his men have been induced to desert since the ship was taken onto the slip for repairs; and we are informed that he made a formal representation of the matter to the chief commissioner, and, it is also added, to the police magistrates at the city Police Court, but that Captain Standish intimated that it was beyond his province to interfere. It is now rumoured that one of these deserters has given false information to the police authorities that Captain Waddell has been enrolling men in this port for service on board the *Shenandoah* or in the Confederate cause.

We may add that Captain Waddell expressed himself with strong indignation against the insinuation that he had violated the hospitality shown to him by the enrolment of a single soul for the service in which he is engaged.[8]

Proving that when it comes to diplomatic double-talk, he can give as good as he gets, Waddell writes to inform the governor 'that execution of the warrant had not been refused, as no such person as the one specified was known to be on board, but permission to seize the ship had been refused as such proceedings would be contrary to the dignity of the Confederate flag'.[9]

This is, of course, a lie. And it's a lie revealed as all the more blatant when four men, including James Davidson, alias Charley, are caught leaving the ship late on the night of 15 February. Placed under arrest, Davidson, along with William Mackenzie, 22, Franklin Glover, 24, and 17-year-old Arthur Walmsley, appear the next day at Williamstown Police Court, charged with breeching the Foreign Enlistment Act.

James 'Charley' Davidson, 22 years old, is first in the dock, facing a packed courtroom and, on the bench, a magistrate and a justice of the peace. The rather ponderous charge is read: 'That being a natural-born subject of the Queen, you did unlawfully, knowingly, and without leave or license of her said Majesty for that purpose, and obtained under the sign manual of her Majesty, or signified by order in council or by proclamation of her Majesty, enter yourself and agree to enlist and enter yourself, to serve as a sailor, and to be employed and serve in and on board a certain vessel-of-war, fitted out, used, equipped, and intended to be used for warlike purposes in the service of a certain foreign power, province, or people, or part of a foreign power or people, exercising and assuming to exercise the powers of government, to wit, the Confederate States of America.'[10]

Davidson, who is undefended, might well be wondering if it is physically possible to 'enter yourself', when the prosecution calls its star witness, John Williams.

Williams repeats under oath the allegations made in his affidavit to US Consul Blanchard, adding that Davidson came on board the *Shenandoah* two days after it arrived in Melbourne; that Davidson had worn a Confederate uniform; and that he had been present when a Confederate officer, Sailing Master Bulloch, told Davidson to stay out of sight when visitors came aboard.

Davidson, without counsel and obliged to defend himself, asks the witness, 'Did I ever tell you my name?'

'Yes, in the galley,' Williams replies. 'I called you Bill, and then you told me your name was not Bill but Charley.'

'Are you sure that Mr Bulloch ever spoke to me?'

'Yes, and you asked me to lend you a razor to shave yourself, in order to disguise yourself. Before that you had full whiskers. You shaved them off.'

This is a cue for the magistrate, Mr Call, to indulge in a little judicial humour at the expense of the accused. Pointing to Davidson's chin, he asks, 'And he left that tuft. Was that to make him a Frenchman or an American?'

His Worship gets the intended response – much polite tittering in the court, and a guffaw or two.

Turning to the prisoner, Call asks, 'Have you no money or friends to provide for your defence?'

'No, Your Worship. I have neither money nor friends.'

'Has no-one been down to offer their services?'

'No, sir.'

As if things aren't looking dismal enough for Davidson, John Williams' testimony is corroborated by three other *Shenandoah* deserters. The arresting officer, Constable Alexander Minto of the water police, swears that while being taken to the police station, Davidson told him he had sold everything he had to join the *Shenandoah*.

Asked if he has any questions for these witnesses, Davidson remains silent. That concludes the case for the prosecution and, after a half-hour adjournment, Davidson is called in to hear his fate.

Asked if he has anything to say, he insists he has never used the name Charley, and accuses the prosecution witnesses of perjury. The magistrate and justice are not convinced and commit him for trial in the Supreme Court the following month. Mackenzie and Walmsley are committed to stand trial with him, but Glover claims to be an American citizen and is discharged. Undeterred by his brush with the law, he rushes off to join the *Shenandoah* as a sailmaker.

The public finds much amusement in the apparently over-the-top persecution of James Davidson, and the satirical magazine Melbourne *Punch* is inspired to publish new words to the old Scottish Jacobite song 'Wha Wadna Fecht for Charlie?' (Who Would Not Fight for Charlie?)

> *Charlie took a drap o' rum,*
> *Charlie as a cook enlisted.*
> *Charlie for the Shenandoah*
> *Went to battle, single-fisted.*
>
> *Wha wadna fight for Charlie?*
> *Scullion midst improper grease,*
> *Wha wadna capture Charlie*
> *With some fifty-strong police?*[11]

In fake letters to the editor, *Punch* also makes sport of the Confederates' effect on the women of Melbourne:

"'Oh! Mr Punch, I should so much like to go on board, and even be captured," gushes "Angelina Gushington".

"I have been in such a flutter ever since that darling *Shenandoah* has been here, and though I have been a dozen times to Melbourne on purpose, I cannot catch a glimpse of any of the officers.'"

And 'Tabitha Singlelife' simpers: "'I am in constant terror lest we should be murdered in our beds by those horrid American pirates. What can our stupid Government be thinking about to let such people come here? So nervous have I been that I have spent a small fortune in sal volatile [smelling salts]."'[12]

At the run-down boarding house at 125 Flinders Lane east, a man from nearby Carlton knocks at the door. The man's name is George Kennedy, and he has come about the newspaper ad placed by a Mr Powell: 'Wanted, two or three respectable young men to be generally useful to travel up to new country.'

The proprietor of the boarding house, a Mr Sigalsk, shows him in and introduces him to Mr Powell and another gentleman. Powell offers him a drink and, after some pleasantries, asks him if he knows how to operate big guns.

When Kennedy, who is a sergeant in the militia, answers yes, Powell tells him that the *Shenandoah* is in need of men of such experience, and, after plying him with more liquor, asks him to join the ship.

Kennedy agrees, and he, Powell, and the other man immediately set off for the docks. By the time they get there, however, Kennedy has sobered up enough to have second thoughts. He tells Powell he has changed his mind, and hurries off to report the incident to the police.

Kennedy tells his tale to a police sergeant then to a magistrate, adding that while he was with Powell, several other men arrived and accepted the offer, and that he believed these men were now aboard the *Shenandoah*.

The magistrate issues warrants for the arrest of Powell and his unnamed accomplice, but, curiously, there is no record of any arrests being made or even attempted. If the police did indeed bash at the door of 125 Flinders Lane east, which is doubtful, all they would have discovered about Mr Powell was that there was no such person.

Captain Waddell is sure the Victorians' show of force is all bluster, and decides to call their bluff. He knows that all an attacking force need do is knock away the props supporting the ship on the slipway and the *Shenandoah* would fall crashing from the slip and be ruined. Yet that hasn't happened, nor has it been threatened.

As for the guns trained on the ship: 'An officer came to the men on duty at the Williamstown battery, but as high ground intervened, the guns were of no use, as they did not command the government slip, nor were the guns at the pier put in use, which commanded that spot, why, I never learned.

'Stories were told to the effect that one of the government gun rafts was moved near to overawe any possible demonstration of strength by the *Shenandoah*. Why, the vessel lay on the slip as helpless as the Victorian Government could possibly desire.

'In the full belief that the ship would not be detained, I gave orders for her launch, and the tug *Black Eagle* was engaged for the purpose of being in readiness and near to. The manager of the slip explained he could not launch the ship, that he acted by order of the Government; whereupon I stated in a communication to the Government that a refusal to permit the launch of the ship amounted to her seizure, and I respectfully begged to be informed if such was known to his Excellency the Governor and met with his approval.'[13]

Waddell sends Lieutenant Grimball ashore to deliver this message and tells him not to return without an answer. He is gambling on Darling being too weak-willed to take the blame should Waddell make good his threat to 'regard officers and men as prisoners of the British Government, to haul down the flag, and proceed with my command to London by the next mail boat'.[14]

The gamble pays off. Within hours, Darling issues the following proclamation: 'The suspension of the permission given to Her Majesty's subjects to aid in the necessary repairs and supplies of the ship *Shenandoah*, dated the 14th instant, is relieved, in so far as launching the said vessel is concerned, which may be proceeded with accordingly.'[15]

On Saturday afternoon, 18 February, at high tide, the *Black Eagle* tows the *Shenandoah* off the dry dock at Williamstown and back across Hobson's Bay to Sandridge. As the tug nudges her out, a crowd gathers on the Williamstown wharf to see her off with waves and cheers.

Before anchoring at Sandridge, the *Shenandoah* is hauled alongside the merchantman *John Frazer*, out of Liverpool, to load 250 tons of coal, added to the 400 tons already on board. The presence in port of the *John Frazer* is no lucky coincidence but had been pre-arranged by James Bulloch – information Captain Waddell kept to himself.

As loading proceeds, the ship is vulnerable to attack, as she was in dry dock. So, should any Yankees in port or the Victorian authorities try to stop her leaving, all guns are loaded and ready to fire.

In the great game, the cards have not been kind to the colonial governor and the American consul, but for the Confederate commander it's a lay-down misère.

The memoirs of John Gurner, the son of Henry Gurner, Victoria's Crown Solicitor at the time of the *Shenandoah*'s visit, provide an insight into the prevalent attitudes of the day. After describing the arrival of the Confederate raider and its commander, 'a somewhat truculent officer who appeared to be a believer in bluster and bounce', Gurner continues:

> As between the combatants, there were in Victoria, as in England, a large number of sympathisers with the Confederate cause; and also, at the outset, a belief that they would succeed, as probably they would have done, owing to the military skill of their generals and their enthusiasm for their cause, but for the determination of President Lincoln and the fact that the prolongation of the contest enabled the wealth and the numbers of the North to prevail.
>
> It is not uncommon to assume that the War of Secession in the United States was one for and against slavery, but slavery was only one of a number of causes leading to the war. It was not the direct, nor the ostensible cause, but it obtained the principal place on President Lincoln's Proclamation of September, 1862, freeing the slaves if the Southern states had not returned to their allegiance by the 1st January following.
>
> Examining the history and constitution of the United States, there is much to be said in support of the legal and constitutional right of the Southern states to secede, and as regards their moral right to do so, there can be no question that it was as good as that exercised some 85 years before by those British colonies which seceded from Great Britain to form the United States of North America. But for many years after the war the mere suggestion of this in the United States in conversation would often cause a furious outburst of unreasonable passion.[16]

John Gurner's recollections include events of the night of 17 February 1865 – the night before the *Shenandoah* left port.

At about six o'clock that evening, his father Henry – who as Crown Solicitor would later share the blame for the failure to seize the *Shenandoah*, which cost Her Majesty's Government a fortune in compensation – was returning to his office from the Melbourne Club – which was directly across the street – when he ran into the US Consul, William Blanchard, his Vice-Consul, Samuel Lord, and a man named Forbes.

Forbes had just told Blanchard that a number of men at Sandridge were about to board a barque called the *Maria Ross*, which would take them out to sea to rendezvous with the *Shenandoah*. The men, all British subjects, would then transfer to the *Shenandoah* and join the Confederate service.

When Blanchard curtly demanded that Henry Gurner take Forbes's deposition immediately; that there wasn't a moment to lose, Gurner calmly told him that taking a deposition was a job for a magistrate, not a solicitor, even a Crown Solicitor. And besides, he was going home for dinner and didn't want to miss his train. Gurner bade them goodnight and sauntered away, leaving the consul incandescent with rage.

Blanchard, Lord and Forbes rushed off to report the urgent matter to, in succession: the Chief of Police, Captain Standish; Attorney-General Higinbotham, who told them to provide him with an affidavit; Chief Detective Nicholson, who said he couldn't act without a warrant; Metropolitan Police Magistrate Sturt, who told them he couldn't proceed on Forbes's uncorroborated evidence and suggested they try the Police Magistrate at Williamstown, who might be able to get corroborative evidence from the Water Police. Or not.

Blanchard and Lord were champing at the bit to set off for Williamstown, but Forbes, for reasons known only to himself, refused to go. In desperation, Blanchard took Forbes's deposition himself and sent Lord running back to the Attorney-General's office only to find he'd left for the day.

So had the *Maria Ross*. She had sailed at 5pm, an hour before the Consul accosted the Crown Solicitor. Blanchard finally managed to get the *Maria Ross* intercepted and searched before she reached the Heads, but there were no Confederate recruits on board. The ship was on her way to Portland to pick up a mob of sheep.

Chapter 11

A sailor's farewell

God's in his heaven, the captain is on the quarterdeck, and, to the whistle of the boatswain's pipe and the clanking of the windlass, the anchors are heaved onto the bow. It's eight o'clock on a sunny Sunday morning, 19 February 1865, and the *Shenandoah* is set to steam out towards the heads of Port Phillip Bay.

'Soon we were on the bright blue sea, standing away from the land to the westward,' Waddell writes. 'The pilot left us with his farewell and good wishes, but it was not like the farewell we exchanged with friends who from the ship's side, return to our own dear native shore with letters and last words of affectionate greeting to those we leave behind.'[1]

Cornelius Hunt describes the Australian sojourn as being like 'one continuous fete', but he suspects the incentive for some of the hospitality offered was purely financial: 'Every place of public amusement was not only open to us, but our presence was earnestly solicited by the managers thereof, probably because we were curiosities, and drew well.'

As for the price of fame: 'Balls, soirees and receptions followed in such rapid succession that the memory of one was lost in another, and, in brief, we were so persistently lionised that we were in serious danger of becoming vain, and taking the glory to ourselves instead of placing it to the credit of the cause for which we laboured.'[2]

As night falls, the raider is under sail and her captain is moved to wax poetic on the soft moonlight, the frosty air and:

> *The stars that oversprinkle*
> *All the heavens, seem to twinkle*
> *With a crystalline delight.*[3]

Waddell's orders, on departing Melbourne, are to head for the New Zealand whaling grounds, then continue north through the New Hebrides islands – now Vanuatu – to the Caroline Islands – a hunting ground for sperm whales – then on to intercept the North Pacific whaling ships bound for Hawaii to unload their catch; thence to the Arctic Ocean, where the harpooned harvest of New England whalers is a global industry, worth a sizable chunk of the Yankee dollar.

Whale oil is in high demand worldwide, especially for home and street lighting, and for lubricating machinery, but also provides ingredients in soap, paint and varnish. Baleen – the sheets of keratin through which baleen whales filter food – is used for buggy whips, fishing rods, hoop dresses, collar stays, typewriter springs, toys and 'whalebone' corsets. The teeth of toothed whales such as sperm whales and beluga whales are a popular alternative to ivory for piano keys, chess pieces and the handles of walking sticks. Spermaceti, a white, waxy substance produced by the sperm whale, makes almost smokeless candles that burn with a bright, clear flame, and is also used in the manufacture of cosmetics and ointments.

From New England whaling ports such as Nantucket and New Bedford, whaling ships set out for their hunting grounds to meet a demand which – in the 1860s – has reached its peak. The Yankee whalers don't know it yet, but a cruiser from Dixie is headed their way, steaming fast from Australia – where, coincidentally, some of the earliest American visitors were New England whalers, and where the whaling industry was founded in Sydney by a Massachusetts whaler, Captain Eber Bunker.

The cruiser *Shenandoah*, when it finds the fleet, intends to capture and destroy ships, ruin lives and blow a huge hole in the United States economy.

Although the depredations of the *Shenandoah* will all but cripple the New England whaling industry, the eventual demise of the industry was made inevitable a decade earlier, when a Canadian doctor and geologist named Abraham Gesner invented a product refined from shale oil or bitumen. The product was a liquid fuel that was cheaper and burned more efficiently than whale oil. Gesner, whose invention marked the beginning of the world's oil industry, named the product 'Kerosene'.

Washington has been following events in Melbourne with interest. US Consul Blanchard has kept Secretary of State Seward abreast of developments, and Seward, a committed abolitionist, shares the consul's surprise at the apparent widespread sympathy in Australia for the pro-slavery Confederacy.

Blanchard tells Seward that the fact that the *Shenandoah* is actually the British merchantman *Sea King* is proof that London is collaborating with the rebels.

'Instead of being assisted by the authorities,' he writes, 'I was only baffled and taught how certain proceedings could not be instituted.'[4]

The *Shenandoah* has left Australia amid rumours that Federal cruisers will be waiting to attack her.

Waddell is unimpressed. 'We felt no anxiety about Federal cruisers,' he writes, 'for we foresaw that they would in all probability be as unsuccessful in finding the *Shenandoah* as they had been in the search for the *Alabama*.'

Word reaches Melbourne that the Yankee warship *Iroquois* is hunting the *Shenandoah* off the Australian coast. But when the ship steams into Port Phillip Bay it turns out to be the paddle-wheeler *New Zealand*.

Another rumour doing the rounds almost as soon as the *Shenandoah* passes through the heads and fades into the mist, is that Captain Raphael Semmes, of *Alabama* fame, came aboard, under an alias, at 2am on the day she sailed.

Once again, Semmes is said to be in two places at once. In fact, he is in Richmond, Virginia, having just been promoted to Rear Admiral. After the sinking of the *Alabama*, he made his way home from England by way of Cuba.

Newspapers relay a rumour that the *Shenandoah* captured and burnt a Yankee ship just 12 miles (20km) outside Port Phillip Heads after leaving Melbourne: 'She was subsequently reported at one time to be laying under King's Island, in Bass' Straits, and at another time to be cruising under canvas off Wilson's Promontory. Woe betide all Yankees going to or coming from the Port of Melbourne whilst she is about.'[5]

In truth, since departing Melbourne, the *Shenandoah* will not see another sail, let alone sink another ship, until April.

April Fools' Day, to be exact.

There are tears of joy as the 55th Regiment of Massachusetts Volunteer Infantry marches into Charleston, South Carolina. Tears of joy not only among the hundreds of African-Americans lining the streets, cheering, singing and shaking the hands of passing soldiers, but tears of joy among the soldiers themselves.

All are aware that today, 21 February 1865, is an historic day. The fall of Charleston – the original Confederate capital and the birthplace of secession – is a symbolic event, but it's more than that. The first Union force to occupy the city, the 55th Massachusetts, is a black regiment, and is soon joined by the men of other black regiments, some of whom had been slaves in Charleston.

The Union troops are drawn to a particular address, Ryan's Mart, at 6 Chalmers Street – the last slave auction house in South Carolina.

The identity of the last slave sold in America is not known. Nor is it known where or by whom the last slave was bought. It is known, however, that slave traders remained active in the South right up until the end of the Civil War. In the interior of the Confederacy there were areas where Union forces had not yet reached, and where plantations with slave labour were operating almost as if the war had never happened.

The Agnew Plantation, in Tippah County, Mississippi, for example, still had more than 50 slaves until early 1865, when many of the men ran off to join the Union Army.

For prominent slave auction houses such as Browning & Moore, E.H. Stokes, Betts & Gregory, Dickenson & Hill, and others, it was business as usual.

Charleston's enclosed slave market, established in 1859 by Charleston's sheriff, Thomas Ryan, after public slave auctions were banned, includes an auction gallery, a four-storey 'barracoon' – a jail for slaves awaiting sale – and a 'dead house' – a morgue for slaves who, through disease or ill-treatment, never made it to the auction block.

The troops free the slaves in the barracoon, but rather than destroy the market, leave it standing as a reminder of an age of institutionalised inhumanity.

With the hectic, heady days of the Confederates' visit now behind them, Melburnians are beginning to wonder if their recent brush with fame was, in hindsight, a date with the devil.

'We may now speak of the Confederate war steamer *Shenandoah* as something that has come and gone,' *The Australasian* opines. 'With all the sympathy we may have had with her as the representative of those who are gallantly fighting against long odds, she, in the fulfilment of a warlike errand, was most unwelcome in our still peaceful port, and we are infinitely glad of her departure.

'During Friday night a large number of men found their way on board the *Shenandoah*, and did not return on shore again.

'The public have not yet heard the last of the alleged enlistments on board the Confederate steamer *Shenandoah*.'[6]

The return of cold, hard reality also rekindles invasion fears. *The Argus* – erstwhile advocate for all things Confederate – now asks 'what should we have done if the *Shenandoah*'s mission had been of a hostile character? What, in short, could be done to protect the city and port should Great Britain be forced into a war with a naval power? Experience has made it certain that the battery at the Heads is not to be relied upon to cripple an enemy. It would have been powerless to prevent the *Shenandoah*'s entrance to Port Phillip Bay.

'Once in Hobson's Bay, the chances are all in favour of the enemy. From where the *Shenandoah* anchored, the most distant parts of Melbourne could have been shelled.'[7]

Out of sight, out of favour.

Chapter 12

All Confederates now

As the *Shenandoah* rolls into international waters, the ship's complement suddenly increases by 42. From their cramped hiding places in the hollow bowsprit, the water tanks and the lower hold, the Australian recruits emerge and muster on deck.

Captain Waddell – who, when accused in Melbourne of breaching the foreign enlistment law was clearly standing on his dignity while lying through his teeth – welcomes them aboard. The ship's log maintains the fiction, noting, 'Forty-two men found on board; 26 shipped as sailors and six enlisted as marines.'[1]

In his memoirs, Waddell compounds the lie, claiming to have been taken by surprise at the appearance of the 42 'stowaways' – despite convincing evidence to the contrary by police, watermen, Williamstown residents, deserters and men who had wanted to join the ship but for various reasons did not make it aboard. In their journals and memoirs, ship's officers unconvincingly echo their captain's feigned surprise, all apparently preferring a thin veneer of honour to the unvarnished truth.

Perhaps they take their inspiration from Robert E. Lee, who asserted, 'True patriotism sometimes requires of men to act contrary, at one period, to that which it does at another, and the motive which impels them – the desire to do right – is precisely the same.'[2] It's doubtful, though, that Lee would agree with their interpretation of his maxim.

Lieutenant Chew would have us believe that the crew had somehow managed to smuggle the 42 men aboard under the very noses of their watchful superiors, who, being officers and gentlemen, would naturally have disapproved and sent the stowaways scurrying back to shore.

Embroidering the fiction, Master's Mate Cornelius Hunt tells us, 'Hundreds of men made application to join us here, but as we had no right to ship any in a neutral port, all were denied, reluctantly, as will be readily imagined when it is remembered how much we desired to augment our numbers.

'One day, I remember, an old lady came aboard with her little son. She was a Southern woman, she said, and her boy had been born in the Sunny South, and she desired Captain Waddell to take him as the only contribution she had to offer to her country, and educate him for the service. It was hard to deny such a request made in such a way, but it had to be done, and the woman with her little rebel went her way, sorrowful and disappointed.'[3]

Ingenuously, Hunt claims to have been offended by the melodramatic 'discovery' of the Australian recruits. 'Personally, I felt a good deal of annoyance over the affair, as it had been my watch a part of the preceding night, and strict orders had been given to prevent any sailors from coming on board except our own, as we were far from wishing to complicate ourselves in any way with the English Government.'[4]

Hunt claims it remains a mystery to him how so many men came aboard unseen. He says the Captain was equally outraged, and demanded that the recruits tell him their nationalities and what their intentions were. 'The old sea-dogs chuckled, rolled over their tobacco, hitched up their trousers, and with one accord, protested that they were natives of the Southern Confederacy, and had come on board thus surreptitiously for the purpose of joining us.'[5]

Presumably, Hunt expects his readers to believe that the recruits spent the hours in their hiding places rehearsing their lines and perfecting their 'down home' accents.

Surgeon Charles Lining notes, 'Large bets had been offered that our ship would never pass through the Heads in safety, consequently all our guns were loaded to prepare against any emergency. But nothing occurred, and at 11.45am we passed the Heads and were once more on the "rolling reef".

'Soon after discharging the pilot a funny sight was presented by the appearance of 42 stowaways, in every conceivable dress and look from the gentleman to the real sailor. We soon shipped them and much rejoiced to get their services. I got a steward from among them and so did Smith, and we all got some boys for the ward room.'[6]

Lieutenant Whittle seriously suggests that the 'stowaways' were smuggled aboard by Yankee agents to entrap the rebels into a violation of the neutrality laws, and, that when the men appeared on deck, he and his fellow officers suspected they were part of a plot. 'We shipped them all, but watched them closely,' he writes. 'They turned out to be good, faithful men.'[7]

Captain Waddell tells us, 'This increase placed on deck 72 men of different ratings, all adventurous and accustomed to a hard life. The first lieutenant, Mr Whittle, now saw a force under his

direction nearly sufficient to keep the *Shenandoah* in good condition. These men had smuggled themselves on board the steamer the
night before we left Hobson's Bay. A sergeant, a corporal and three
privates formed the nucleus for a marine guard, and their uniforms
were immediately ordered. We were supplied with a tailor.'[8]

The stowaway tailor now appointed sergeant of marines
is George Canning, who claims to have been aide-de-camp to
Confederate General Leonidas Polk; that he was invalided out of
the army after being shot in the right lung at the Battle of Shiloh
in 1862, and migrated to Australia. Canning's appointment as
sergeant of marines is no doubt due to his claimed Confederate
Army service.

Lieutenant Whittle, for one, is unconvinced by Canning's tale
of being wounded while fighting for Polk, and suspects that he
might instead have served on the staff of General Albert Sidney
Johnston, who was killed at Shiloh. However, there is no record
of a George Canning serving with either general or with any force
other than the Confederate Navy on the *Shenandoah*. And according to research by Kim Salisbury, a descendant of Canning's brother
Rafton, George Canning also claimed to have been wounded in the
Crimean War. Salisbury is sure both claims are untrue.

It's not uncommon in the 19th century for newcomers to the
colonies to rewrite their own histories or invent new identities.
Indeed, since the world is still wide and communications imper-
fect, it's not particularly difficult to do. There is no hard evidence
that George Canning had anything to hide, such as a criminal
record, yet he reinvented himself in grand style.

George Baltriune Canning, also known as George P. Canning
and Henry C. Canning, was born in or around 1837. While
the name Baltriune suggests a French connection, and Canning

sometimes claimed to have been born in France, his actual birth-place was the port of Rotherhithe, southeast London – near Greenland Dock, home of the Arctic whaling fleet. He is believed to have married in the United States and had two sons, the first of whom was born in France, in 1858, where Canning worked as a civil engineer, and the second in America.

Canning is accompanied on the *Shenandoah* by an African-American servant, Edward Weeks. It is not known how Weeks came to Australia or whether he had been a slave in the South. According to officers' accounts, Weeks was on board for the rest of the cruise, and Canning treated him badly. Weeks is not listed among the 42 volunteers.

Other newly minted marines include David Alexander, awarded the rank of corporal, and privates Henry Reily, Robert Brown and William Kenyon; the latter was recruited by the mysterious Mr Powell.

Confederate States marines are employed as gun crews on warships and on shore batteries guarding Southern ports, so Kenyon's artillery training in the Victorian naval reserve makes him well suited for the role. Marines also serve as guards, sharp-shooters, in landing forces and on boarding parties.

To formally enlist in the Confederate States Marine Corps, Kenyon, like the others, must raise his right hand and take an oath:

'I, William Kenyon, do solemnly swear that I will bear true faith and allegiance to the Confederate States of America and that I will serve them honestly and faithfully against all their enemies or oppressors whomsoever, and that I will observe and obey the orders of the President of the Confederate States and the orders of the officers appointed over me, according to the rules and Articles of War.'[9]

Soon, the Australian marines will be issued with uniforms of grey frock coats, dark blue trousers and forage caps, and with weapons – British Enfield rifles, swords and bayonets, .36 calibre Colt Navy revolvers and .42 calibre LeMat pistols.

Master's Mate Cornelius Hunt will later say of the new marines, 'Good men and true they proved, and very useful before our cruise was ended.'[10]

Williamstown sea dog and yarn-spinner 'Little Sam' Crook is among the new hands on deck. So, too, is sailmaker Franklin Glover, who was arrested with Charley but released after claiming American citizenship, which no-one bothered to check. With them is ship's carpenter Henry Sutherland, who, as the *Shenandoah* sailed out through the heads, gave the departing pilot a letter to deliver to his family, assuring them he liked the ship and was very comfortable on board.

Besides Crook, Glover and Sutherland, the names of seamen listed – some actual, some aliases – include John Collins, Thomas Foran, Lawrence Kerney, John McDonal, John Ramsdale, John Kilgower, Thomas Swanton, John Moss, James Fegan, John Simmes, John Hill, William Hutchinson, Thomas Evans, Charles Morton, George Gifford, Henry Canning (not to be confused with George Canning), James Ross, Thomas McLean, William Brice, William Green, William Burgess, Joseph Mullineaux, James Stranth, and a boy named John Williams.

Besides Marine Sergeant George Canning and Marine Corporal David Alexander, the petty officers recruited in Melbourne include: Robert Dunning, captain of the foretop; Thomas Strong, captain of the mizzen-top; Charles Cobbey, gunner's mate; John James, carpenter's mate; John Spring, captain of the hold; Ernest Burt, doctor's steward; James McLaren, master-at-arms; and William Smith, ship's cook, replacing the hapless Charley.

Completing the roll-up is Captain John Blacker, master of the steamer *Saxonia*. On 17 February, without notice or explanation, Blacker left his ship – then at anchor in Sandridge – taking with him his navigational instruments and personal effects. Now, he's standing on the deck of the *Shenandoah*, joining her as captain's clerk.

The 42 Australian recruits – as diverse a group as could be found anywhere – have become comrades with a common cause. For better or worse, they're all Confederates now.

The *Shenandoah* has three decks, a raised forecastle and a large poop deck over the captain's cabin, used by officers for scanning the horizon for ships, and for keeping an eye on the crew. On the quarterdeck, near the stern, is the wheelhouse, where the steersman keeps the ship on course, and off the wheelhouse is the tiny chart room, where the captain and his officers sit rustling charts and debating the finer points of navigation.

The space between the main and mizzen masts houses the steam engine, boiler rooms and coal bunkers. In this hot, poorly ventilated and dangerous area – where canvas partitions are strung to lessen the risk of fire from flammable coal dust – coal trimmers, coal heavers, oilers and firemen, under the supervision of the chief engineer, spend their days and nights below, feeding the furnaces, their faces black with soot and grease. The only times they get to see the sun or the stars are when the ship proceeds under sail alone. How they must bless a strong wind.

Beneath the half deck is a dining saloon, staterooms and the officers' cabins. Petty officers' quarters are between the fore and aft masts, as is the galley. The crew's berths are in the topgallant forecastle – the central triangular space at the bow of the ship, forward of the foremast. It's a cramped space with low headroom; berths are arranged in rows, and each ordinary sailor or marine private has a space he can call his own of just six feet by two feet (180cm × 60cm). A supposedly weathertight bulkhead at the aft end shields them from the worst of the elements but doesn't keep out the damp and the cold. And because the crew shares the space with the anchor-chain cables, it's often wet and dirty.

Unusually for vessels of its day, the ship has inside toilets. These facilities are for the use of officers only, however. The crew, as ever, must make do with a bucket. Such is life before the mast.

Still, there are compensations. Frank Chew plays a mean fiddle, and Sydney Smith Lee, who is remarkably light on his feet, can set the men dancing by the main hatch for hours, with the aid of a little whisky for social lubrication.

'The Bonnie Blue Flag' is a firm favourite of the Southerners on board. A stirring marching song about the first, unofficial, Confederate flag, it begins:

We are a band of brothers and native to the soil,
Fighting for our liberty with treasure, blood and toil.
And when our rights were threatened, the cry rose near and far,
Hurrah for the Bonnie Blue Flag that bears a single star.

Englishmen, Irishmen and Scots among the crew are fond of the sentimental 'Bold Privateer'.

It's oh my dearest Polly,
You and I must part.
I am going across the seas, love,

I give to you my heart.
So fare thee well my dear,
I am just a'going on board
Of the Bold Privateer.

Australian seamen are primed to belt out the rollicking sea shanty 'Bound for South Australia'.

In South Australia I was born,
Heave away, haul away.
In South Australia, round Cape Horn.
We're bound for South Australia.
Haul away you rolling kings,
Heave away, haul away.
Haul away, you'll hear me sing,
We're bound for South Australia.

Of course, every man jack knows 'Dixie'.

Oh, I wish I was in the land of cotton,
Old times there are not forgotten.
Look away, look away, look away Dixie Land.
In Dixie Land, where I was born in,
Early on one frosty mornin'.
Look away, look away, look away Dixie Land.
I wish I was in Dixie, Hooray! Hooray!
In Dixie Land I'll take my stand,
To live and die in Dixie.
Away, away, away down south in Dixie.
Away, away, away down south in Dixie.

And there may well be faraway looks and moist eyes around the capstan should someone give voice to an old folk song that captures a rebel's longing for home, particularly on a ship named for the Daughter of the Stars.

> *Oh Shenandoah,*
> *I long to see you,*
> *Away you rolling river.*
> *Oh Shenandoah,*
> *I long to hear you,*
> *Away, I'm bound away,*
> *'cross the wide Missouri.*

> *Oh Shenandoah,*
> *I love your daughter,*
> *Away you rolling river.*
> *For her I'd cross*
> *Your roaming waters,*
> *Away, I'm bound away,*
> *'cross the wide Missouri.*

The *Shenandoah* turns her prow north towards Middleton Reef, Lord Howe and Norfolk islands. All have whaling stations, but Waddell intends to give them a wide berth.

'They are contiguous to the coast of Australia and are in easy communication with Sydney. Our long delay in Melbourne gave the American consul ample time to warn American shipping of the danger to which it was exposed. If the ship had been favoured with a good wind, I should have visited the whaling grounds of each of those islands, but it was very certain the birds had taken shelter, and I would probably find them further north.'[11]

What Waddell finds further north is not whalers but wild weather. Above the Fiji Islands, the *Shenandoah* runs into a gale that batters and bruises her for four days and nights.

'In 23 years of service I had never seen such a succession of violent squalls,' Waddell writes. 'The vessel was enveloped in a salt mist and knocked by every angry sea. The machinery acted all right, and the ship's preparations for contending with adverse weather were so complete that wind and wave seemed now bent upon her destruction.'

He's mightily impressed by the way the *Shenandoah* handles the worst the Pacific can throw at her. 'I have never seen a vessel in a gale stand up better to it or receive less water on deck. Her easy motion and steadiness throughout that gale increased our admiration of her.'[12]

Calm seas follow, but so too does sweltering heat and heavy rain. With the trade winds proving elusive, Waddell orders steam and steers north to search for a good wind.

Off Tabiteuea, then known as Drummond's Island, in the Gilbert Islands – a haven for whalers and slave traders – islanders come out in canoes. Waddell describes them as docile, which is curious, given that as a former US Navy officer he must surely be aware of an infamous incident known as the Battle of Drummond's Island.

In 1841, sailors and marines from USS *Peacock* and USS *Flying Fish* – ships of the United States Exploring Expedition, better known as the Wilkes Expedition after its commander, Charles Wilkes – were ordered to explore the island and to investigate a rumour that the crew of a merchantman wrecked on a nearby reef had all been massacred except for a woman and child who were being held captive by the islanders.

Although the islanders claimed to know nothing of a massacre or a shipwrecked woman and child, items from the missing vessel were reportedly found in village huts; the Americans were forbidden to search the entire village.

When one of the sailors, John Anderson, was found to be missing, a search began, but was abandoned when the islanders, brandishing spears and other weapons, forced the Americans to return to their ship. At dawn the following day, with still no sign of the missing seaman, a landing party of about 80 marines and sailors, in seven boats, was despatched to rescue Anderson, with the *Peacock* and *Flying Fish* ready to provide covering fire from offshore.

It didn't go to plan. As the boats approached shore, some 700 warriors, anything but docile, rushed out of the jungle and waded out towards the invaders. The Americans retreated for some distance, then turned and opened fire. A series of close volleys cut down the first wave of advancing warriors and wounded many more. The rest fled into the jungle as the landing party made it to shore, but regrouped to skirmish with the Americans, who had set about burning the villages.

When the smoke cleared, 12 islanders were dead. There were no American casualties. The missing seaman was never found, and the rumour of a captive woman and child turned out to be exactly that.

It wasn't the first time this supposedly scientific expedition of naturalists, botanists and artists was mired in bloodshed. A year earlier, in Fiji, when two sailors were killed while bartering for food, Commander Wilkes' retribution was swift and severe. He ordered a massacre that left up to 80 Fijians dead. Wilkes was court-martialled on his return home, not for the mass murder of

Pacific Islanders but for mistreatment of his junior officers and excessive punishment of his sailors. He was acquitted.

Captain Waddell would be well aware that the same Charles Wilkes is now a commodore and his arch-nemesis. It was Wilkes who ordered his former flagship, USS *Wachussett*, to patrol the seas in pursuit of the Confederate raiders *Florida*, *Alabama* and Waddell's own *Shenandoah*. The *Wachussett* had captured the *Florida*, in Brazil, but the *Alabama* had eluded her, and, thus far, so had the *Shenandoah*.

Waddell might not have met Wilkes during his time in the old navy, but he must have known him by reputation. Arrogant, capricious and a harsh disciplinarian, Wilkes is believed to have been the model for Captain Ahab in Herman Melville's *Moby Dick*.

And it's tempting to imagine James Waddell, looking out from his quarterdeck at waves lapping the shores of Drummond's Island, quietly chuckling at the similarities between Wilkes' Civil War story and his own.

In 1861, Wilkes was at the centre of an international diplomatic crisis known as the Trent Affair – an incident that came close to igniting war between the United States and Britain. In November of that year, he was master of the *Wachussett*, the flagship of an American naval squadron on a visit to the British colony of Bermuda, chasing Confederate blockade runners. As Waddell would later do in Melbourne, Wilkes violated the neutrality laws, overstaying the time permitted in port while his gunboats blockaded St George harbour, preventing ships from leaving, and opened fire on a British mail ship, the *Merlin*. However, those were minor infringements compared with what he did next.

Word reached Wilkes that two Confederate envoys, James Mason and John Slidell, were en route to England aboard the

British packet *Trent*. The envoys' mission was to persuade the British Government – by cotton diplomacy – to recognise the Confederacy as a sovereign nation.

Wilkes ordered the steam frigate *San Jacinto* to intercept the *Trent* and arrest Mason and Slidell. On 8 November, the *San Jacinto* caught up with the mail ship, fired a shot across her bows, then boarded her and took the Southern diplomats prisoner. They were taken to Boston and confined at Fort Warren.

The proverbial hit the fan. The British, apoplectic over such an aggressive violation of neutrality, demanded an apology and the immediate release of the prisoners, at the same time flexing Britain's military muscle in Canada and in the Atlantic. The United States responded by threatening war with Britain if it recognised the Confederacy, and for some weeks, threats and counter-threats flew thick and fast between London and Washington. War seemed inevitable.

In Britain, Queen Victoria's consort, Prince Albert, was concerned that Her Majesty's Government's demands were too provocative. On 30 November, although gravely ill and within weeks of his death, he penned a memorandum to his wife the Queen, suggesting a less belligerent despatch be sent to Washington, giving the Americans a way to release the envoys without losing face.

Albert's draft, which was incorporated in an official despatch, reads, in part, 'The United States Government must be fully aware that the British Government could not allow its flag to be insulted, and the security of her mail communications to be placed in jeopardy, and Her Majesty's Government are unwilling to believe that the United States Government intended wantonly to put an insult upon this country and to add to their many distressing complications by forcing a question of dispute upon us, and that we are therefore glad to believe they would spontaneously offer such redress as alone could satisfy this country, viz: the restoration of the unfortunate passengers and a suitable apology.'[13]

The Queen later wrote in the margin, 'This draft was the last the beloved Prince ever wrote.'

When he brought it to her he said, 'I could hardly hold my pen.'[14]

President Lincoln, equally desperate to find a way to defuse the situation, grasped the proposition offered. While initially, like all Northerners, he had cheered and applauded when Wilkes was hailed as a hero and officially thanked by Congress for his courage and patriotism, Lincoln publicly denied any responsibility or support for Wilkes' actions and freed the envoys. The Southerners sailed safely to England where, after all the drama and tension wrought on both sides of the Atlantic, their mission failed.

Charles Wilkes, whose intemperance had almost started a war, now turned his attentions to tracking down the mercurial Captain James Iredell Waddell.

Chapter 13

The last of Charley

On Saint Patrick's Day, 17 March 1865, in a criminal sitting of the Supreme Court of Victoria, the sailor known as Charley to everyone but himself stands before his Honour Mr Justice Molesworth and a jury of his peers. James Davidson has been indicted on 24 counts, all relating to breeches of the Foreign Enlistment Act.

John Williams is called to reprise his Williamstown allegations, verse and chorus, as a witness for the prosecution, and is then cross-examined by Butler Cole Aspinall, counsel for the defence.

A firebrand radical, Aspinall made his name defending Eureka Stockade rebels charged with treason. Famously, he shamed the jury into acquitting the rebel John Joseph, an African-American, by asking, 'Surely, gentlemen of the jury, you won't hesitate to hang a trifling nigger to oblige the Attorney-General?' He is known for representing defendants in political cases for free, as he is doing for James Davidson.

Aspinall is also a member of the Melbourne Club, and attended the banquet for the officers of the *Shenandoah*.

'Who took you down to Williamstown?' Aspinall asks John Williams.

'A gentleman whose name I don't know,' Williams replies. 'We had no conversation about what I was to prove when I got there.'

'Did he say anything more than that he should like to sail on the *Shenandoah*?

'He said he should like to join the vessel. The defendant was dressed in the uniform of the Confederate States, but he did not wear full dress. He wore only the trousers and cap when he was cooking.'

'Were not the trousers an old cast-off pair given him by one of the sailors?

'No, the trousers were new.'

Changing tack, Aspinall asks, 'How are you living now?'

'By the United States consul,' Williams replies, then, apparently flustered, contradicts his earlier statement. 'The trousers were given to the defendant by one of the sailors,' he says.

Aspinall changes tack. 'Have you seen anyone on the subject of the prosecution?'

'I have seen the United States consul. I had a conversation with the person who drove me down to Williamstown about the trial.'

The next prosecution witness, Walter Madden, a seaman from the captured D. *Godfrey* who shipped with the *Shenandoah*, is asked by Aspinall if he is being paid by US consul Blanchard for giving evidence at the trial.

'I don't know,' Madden says.

'Are you to get money at all?'

'I believe so.'

'What leads you to suppose so?

'The consul said we were to get some money.'

'What are you to get for your evidence on this occasion?'

'Seven shillings a day, I suppose.'

'Who is to pay it?'

'The Government, I believe. The consul pays my board and lodging, but he says I am to pay for my own board after this. I have not got the money for attending the trial yet.'

'It depends on the Appropriation Act being passed whether you get it at all,' Aspinall quips, and the courtroom dissolves into laughter.[1]

Charles Behncke, an *Alina* crewman who joined the *Shenandoah* and jumped ship in Melbourne, also admits to being paid by the consul.

Police Superintendent Thomas Lyttleton tells the court that when he went on board the *Shenandoah* looking for Charley, he saw officers and men in uniforms that he understood to be those of the Confederate Navy.

Aspinall asks, 'I believe the uniform is something like that worn in Pentridge [prison]?

'It is something like it in colour but not in shape.'

'You were entrusted with the capture of the vessel, were you not?' Muffled laughter at this.

'No, I was entrusted with the slip.'

'I think they gave you the slip!' Much raucous laughter.[2]

With the case for the Crown closed, Aspinall submits there is no proof that the *Shenandoah* is a vessel of a belligerent power; that there being no proof of the commander's commission he might simply be a pirate; that there is no proof of the recognition of the Confederacy as a belligerent power; and – drawing a very long bow – that there is no proof of any war between the Northern and Southern states of America because the North has not recognised the South as a sovereign nation and considers the conflict a rebellion.

It's a brave effort by the defence counsel, but Judge Molesworth is unconvinced. He gives his reasons at length and in mind-numbing detail, then adjourns the court until the following day.

Next day, the judge rambles on for another hour or so then directs the jury to retire and consider its verdict. When the 12 good men and true return to the courtroom, James Davidson, alias Charley, is found guilty on the second count – that is, that he did 'unlawfully agree to enlist and enter himself to be employed and engaged in and on board a certain ship of war called the *Shenandoah*, in the service and for, under, and in the aid of certain foreign states styling themselves the Confederate States of America'. Judge Molesworth sentences him to 10 days' imprisonment – the lightest penalty the law allows.

Davidson's co-accused, William Mackenzie, pleads guilty and receives the same sentence. The Crown drops all charges against 17-year-old Arthur Walmsley, who had hoped that on the *Shenandoah* he could get to America to join his elder brother who had gone to fight in the war. The youth walks free to the sound of cheers and laughter from all in the courtroom, including the judge.

The delightfully acerbic editor of the *Creswick & Clunes Advertiser*, Francis Martin, sums up the case:

The Crown has obtained a conviction against the arch culprit 'Charley' for the crime of having attempted to serve the Confederate cause. The counts which charged him with enlisting, serving, etc, could not be sustained, but the jury appears to have no doubt of his attempting.

Cooking on board a fighting ship would probably, in the eyes of the law, be 'constructive fighting', so poor little Charley (for he is a diminutive chap) must be held to be guilty of intending to annihilate the whole northern marine, if he could.

As it was understood that the sentence would be a nominal one, Mackenzie, another of the prisoners, was advised to plead guilty of also 'attempting'. The third prisoner (a mere youth) was at the request of the Attorney-General set at liberty. Charley and Mackenzie were then sentenced, each to 10 days imprisonment which the Attorney-General admitted to be an ample punishment. So ended the great trial about the battle of the *Shenandoah*.[3]

Chapter 14

The captain and the king

They seek her here, they seek her there. And where might she strike next? Judging by a 30 March report, San Francisco newspaper *The Alta California* is unfamiliar with the maxim 'Loose lips sink ships'.

> We have today the unpleasant announcement of the arrival of the pirate *Shenandoah*, formerly the *Sea King*, at Melbourne. She is most probably bound for this coast. There is, of course, no danger to this city. It is so thoroughly fortified that the appearance off the bar of all the ships of war that England and France could bring together in these waters would occasion very little alarm; but we have but few vessels of war. The *Lancaster*, the only man-of-war of any force on this station, is now at Callao. The *Wateree*, originally intended for the defence of this port, sailed for Panama a few weeks ago. The *Saranac* is at Acapulco, and the *St. Mary's* is now on her way here.
>
> If the pirate should lie on and off the port, burning outward

The *Shenandoah* in Hobson's Bay, Melbourne, February 1865 (artist, Samuel Calvert).
Courtesy Photo Collection, State Library Victoria

This etching, bearing the legend 'Captain Waddell, of the Confederate War Steamer *Shenandoah*', appeared in a Melbourne publication around the time of the ship's arrival. *Courtesy Photo Collection, State Library Victoria*

'Ball Given to the Officers of the Confederate Steamer *Shenandoah* at Ballarat'.
Courtesy Photo Collection, State Library Victoria

Visitors flocked to the port, intent on seeing the 'man of war' for themselves.
When the *Shenandoah* was moved to a slipway in Williamstown for repairs,
it was decided to charge visitors sixpence each, and the money was donated to
local charities. In order to get on with the work, however, all sightseers were
soon banned. *Courtesy Photo Collection, State Library Victoria*

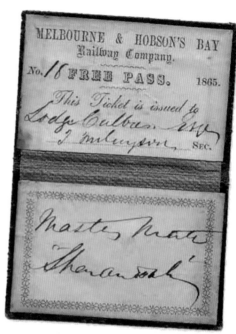

The visitors were presented with courtesy rail passes, so they could make their way from the port of Sandridge to inner-city Melbourne with ease.
Photo courtesy Barry Crompton

A single woman who found favour with one of the visitors might be presented with a button from the Confederate States Navy uniform. The design featured an anchor and crossed cannon device on a lined field with a rope border. The buttons were manufactured in London.

A small cannon salvaged from the *Shenandoah*. The raider's Achilles heel was that it was unsafe for all the guns on one side of the ship to be fired at once. *Photo courtesy Barry Crompton*

The Governor of Victoria, Sir Charles Darling, was briefly the meat in the sandwich. The US consul demanded the Confederate belligerents be ordered back out to sea; Captain Waddell insisted on his ship's rights according to internationally recognised rules of neutrality. The Governor agreed. *Courtesy Photo Collection, State Library Victoria*

The *Shenandoah*'s captain, Lieutenant Commander James Iredell Waddell (pictured circa 1864 wearing Confederate Navy uniform), was the quintessential Southern gentleman: tall, gracious of bearing, unfailingly punctual and courteous. He was also aloof and quick-tempered. *Photo courtesy US Naval Historical Center*

First Lieutenant John Grimball was one of six officers chosen by Waddell to attend the ball given in honour of the *Shenandoah* by the citizens of Ballarat. The event organisers were Americans who had made the gold-mining town their home. *Photo courtesy Liljenquist Family Collection of Civil War Photographs, Library of Congress*

The Bulloch brothers, James Dunwoody (left, in uniform) and Irvine Stephens, were from a family of wealthy Savannah planters. On the outbreak of the Civil War, James based himself in Liverpool, from where he organised, among other things, the purchase of the *Sea King*, which was renamed the *Shenandoah* and repurposed as a Confederate commerce raider. Irvine served on CSS *Alabama*.

The resting place of the *Shenandoah*'s enigmatic captain. After Waddell realised he had been prosecuting a war that had ended months earlier, he said, 'My life has been checkered from the dawn of my naval career.' *Photo courtesy Barry Crompton*

This etching depicts the *Shenandoah* off the coast of Alaska late in June 1865, discharging her sworn duty to wipe out the whaling marine of the enemy, which she did with deadly efficiency. The only problem was that Robert E. Lee had surrendered on 9 April 1865. *Courtesy Photo Collection, State Library Victoria*

and inward bound vessels, we would have only the *Saginaw* and the *Shubrick* to go out and give her battle. The *Comanche*, of course, is only intended for harbour defence, and it would not be judicious to send her across the bar. If the *Shenandoah* is bound in this direction, we shall probably hear from her first on the lower coast.

It is not a month ago since General McDowell wrote to the department at Washington, urging the necessity for more vessels of war in these waters. We ought to have a fleet in the Pacific equal, at least, to the combined fleets of England and France. The capture of all the Atlantic rebel ports has released a great many vessels from blockade duty, which might as well be cruising in this direction. General McDowell has not yet received a reply to his demand.[1]

If Captain Waddell had happened to find that particular newspaper report on a captured vessel, he surely would have been grateful for the intelligence. And as it happened, he did, and he was.

Two days out from the Gilbert Islands, the *Shenandoah* meets a friendly Hawaiian schooner, the *Pfeil*, trading in turtle shell. The skipper of the schooner tells Waddell that Chabrol Harbour, on Strong Island – now Kusaic, or Ualan Island – in the Caroline Islands group, north of New Guinea, is a regular rendezvous for whaling ships. He now has a fine trade wind and makes good time to the island under sail, and when close by, under steam. But when he gets there the harbour is empty.

Disappointed, Waddell makes sail for Ascension Island – now Pohnpei – in the Carolines. This time, he's in luck. He recalls, 'A little before midday the *Shenandoah* had approached sufficiently near to distinguish five sail at anchor close in with the land, and we began to think if they were not whale ships it would be a very good April Fool. The Honolulu schooner was the only sail we had seen from the 20th of February to April 1st, which was evidence that the South Pacific whaling fleet had taken flight. We were never on any occasion so long without seeing a sail, and sailing over almost unknown and strange seas produced a dullness and monotony intolerable.'[2]

As if on cue to relieve the monotony, just outside Lohd Pah harbour, on the southern side of Pohnpei, a small boat comes in sight, bearing one man. The man, an Englishman, comes aboard and introduces himself as Thomas Harrocke, a runaway convict from Sydney, New South Wales. He escaped from the penal colony many years ago – he doesn't say how – made it to these islands, where he married a native woman, and occasionally acts as the harbour pilot. Covered in tattoos and dressed in rags, Harrocke speaks with hesitation at first. Clearly, he hasn't conversed in his native tongue for some time.

Without revealing their identity, the Confederates ask Harrocke to direct them to a safe anchorage in the harbour. He obliges, and as the *Shenandoah* drops anchor, three of the ships in port hoist the Stars and Stripes, and a fourth raises the flag of the Kingdom of Hawaii. All four are whalers and, for the Confederates, all are sitting ducks.

Four boats are launched from the *Shenandoah*, each carrying two officers and seven men, armed with pistols and cutlasses. For Marine Corps Private William Kenyon and his fellow Australian Confederates, this is first blood, but they can soon rest easy. The Confederate flag is hoisted, a shot is fired, and, even before the boats reach them, the whalers haul down their flags.

Waddell: 'Some officer, directing the pilot's attention to our flag, asked him if he knew it. He replied he had never before seen it, but as the boats were gone after the Yankees, it might be Jeff Davis's flag, for he had heard of a big war in America, and that in all the big battles the South had whipped the Yankees.

'When I told him what we were, he said, "Well, well, I never thought I would live to see Jeff Davis's flag.".'[3]

Thomas Harrocke remarks to Waddell that the island's five tribes are governed in their dealings not by the high principles of civilisation but by fear of violent retribution.

'Is not that very much the case with white people?' Waddell asks. 'It strikes me that the white tribe has more educated scoundrels than the dark races. All the villainy the world is governed by originated with the white man, and he has perpetuated it by introducing it among the uncultivated and semi-barbarians all over the world.'[4]

He has no doubt as to where the blame lies for corrupting the Edens of the Pacific.

'The missionaries and their followers who have visited these islands in their trading vessels have been detected in crime, and the islanders in many instances took revenge, and in return their thatched roof coverings would be burned by the crews of the vessels.'[5]

The American ships *Edward Carey*, the *Hector* and the *Pearl*, and the Hawaiian ship *Harvest* are boarded and claimed as prizes of the Confederate States of America. Their officers, stores, log books, charts and navigation instruments are taken to the *Shenandoah*.

Waddell then invites the King of Pohnpei, the Nahnmwarki, to the *Shenandoah* to inform him of the Confederates' intentions and ensure their actions do not compromise the island's neutrality – a matter that didn't seem to bother him unduly in Melbourne.

The King arrives with a retinue of chiefs and escorted by a flotilla of canoes, and climbs the companion ladder to be greeted by the Captain and Lieutenant Whittle, in full dress uniform.

His body glistening with coconut oil, the king is wearing a wide belt and breechclout, beads around his neck and a clay pipe through one pierced ear. While plying him with Wolfe's Aromatic Shiedam Schnapps – to which he takes quite a liking – Waddell, through Harrocke as interpreter, tells the King his version of the American Civil War or, as many a Southerner prefers to call it, the War of Northern Aggression.

'I explained to him that the vessels in port belonged to our enemies who had been fighting us for years, killing our people, outraging our countrywomen, and destroying our homes, and that we were ordered to capture and destroy their vessels whenever and wherever found, and that if the laws of His Majesty would not be violated, the vessels in port would be confiscated, and as there was little in them which the *Shenandoah* required, their contents would be presented to His Majesty to make such use of as he considered proper, and when his tribe had taken all they desired from the ships, I would take them to sea and burn them.'

The king quickly consults his chiefs and replies, 'We find nothing conflicting with our laws in what you say.'[6]

And he's more than happy with a gift of 70 muskets and ammunition taken from the *Harvest*. The muskets, intended as trade goods, are old, rusty and, if fired, likely to do more harm to the shooter than to the target.

The royal tour of the *Shenandoah* having ended with satisfactory outcomes for all involved, the King, keen to repay the

Southern hospitality, invites the *Shenandoah* officers to visit his residence.

While the officers are courting royalty, the crew – all given shore leave – are making the most of the island's natural attractions: the beaches, bush and freshwater swimming holes, but mostly the women.

There is no record of men from the *Shenandoah* fraternising with the island women, but when sexual favours could be procured for a plug of tobacco, it would be naïve to assume they did not. And they could not help but notice, on entering port, large numbers of women on the decks of the whaling ships. Plainly, the women were not selling sea shells.

Some officers and men make their way four miles up the coast to the mysterious ruins of Nan Madol. An ancient city built on a coral reef by an unknown civilisation, its massive walls, of stones weighing up to 50 tons, were quarried on the other side of the island. Local legend has it that the city was built by twin sorcerers who levitated the huge stones with the help of a flying dragon.

The question of how the stones were transported and erected is unanswered in 1865, and will remain an archaeological conundrum into the 21st century, as well as prime fodder for fanciful theories about lost continents, giants and alien visitors.

We'll never know what Australian Confederate Little Sam Crook might make of this stranger-than-fiction place, but it will make a hell of a yarn if ever he gets back home to Williamstown.

It's a little after noon on Sunday 9 April 1865 when a tall, grey-haired man of aristocratic bearing, in an immaculate grey tunic and buckskin gauntlets, and riding a grey horse, crosses the creek on the road to Wilmer McLean's farmhouse in the village of Appomattox Court House, Virginia.

He pauses only to allow his horse, Traveller, to drink, then rides on to the McLean place, a neat if unremarkable red-brick house, with elm trees shading the lawn and roses by the front porch.

The tall man dismounts and enters the house, where he sits in the parlour and waits in silence.

About half an hour later, a short, dark-haired, plain-looking man in a mud-spattered blue jacket comes riding down the road. He dismounts, steps onto the porch and hurries inside to join the tall man in the parlour. They shake hands.

Robert E. Lee and Ulysses S. Grant have met once before, during the Mexican War, and Grant mentions this, perhaps to break the ice. 'I have always remembered your appearance and I think I would have recognised you anywhere,' he says.

Lee replies, 'Yes, I know I met you on that occasion, and I have often thought of it and tried to recollect how you looked. But I have never been able to recall a single feature.'[7]

With what pass for pleasantries thus despatched, Lee asks Grant under what terms he would receive the surrender of his army. Grant repeats the terms he proposed in an earlier exchange of notes between the two, that 'the officers and men surrender to be paroled and disqualified from taking up arms until properly exchanged, and all arms, ammunition and supplies to be delivered up as captured property'.[8]

Lee knows he has no choice but to accept. What is left of his Army of Northern Virginia is surrounded, and Richmond has fallen. 'Those are the conditions I expected would be proposed,' he says.[9]

Three hours later, after details have been discussed and small compromises reached, General Grant puts the terms in writing, and both men sign the document.

The two great adversaries shake hands and leave the house together. As Lee, his expression unreadable, mounts Traveller, the Union soldiers in McLean's yard snap to attention.

One of the soldiers in the yard, 23-year-old Corporal Almer Montague, of the 1st Vermont Cavalry, a veteran of Gettysburg and the Shenandoah Valley campaign, is moved by the moment, and will later gather mementos of the historic event. In a letter to a friend, he writes:

'I have a few things that I have picked up that I wish to send by Uncle Lewis this morning and have just time. In the first place, the book they are in I got Appomattox Court House. The blotter paper was in the County Register. The leaf from the locust tree grew in front of the court house. The other two that I pinned together I picked off the bushes hanging over the steps of the very house in which General Lee surrendered, and the piece of stick is from the railing in front of the same.'[10]

As Lee takes the reins, Grant steps forward and raises his hat; Lee returns the compliment and rides off down the road.

It is customary on such occasions that the commander of the defeated side surrenders his sword, but Robert E. Lee did not do so. Ulysses S. Grant could not bear to take it from him.

On Monday April 10, Australians are yet to learn of Lee's surrender, but are relieved to read in their daily newspapers that the notorious bushranger Mad Dan Morgan has been shot and killed, ending a three-year rampage of cold-blooded murder, torture and arson.

After crossing the Murray River into Victoria, Morgan was raiding Peechalba Station, near Wangaratta, when a nursemaid raised the alarm. The station hands armed themselves, and when Morgan came out of the homestead he was shot in the back by stockman Paddy Quinlan, who had been hiding behind a tree.

Morgan, who had never given quarter to any of his victims, complained as he lay dying that it wasn't a fair fight.

And in a letter to the editor in Monday's *Sydney Morning Herald*, a reader helpfully suggests that police should use blood-hounds to hunt bushrangers, rather than employing Aboriginal trackers. He writes, 'Any person who has looked over a newspaper published in the slave states of America will see advertisements of slave-hunters who will guarantee to find any runaway Negro with their dogs.'[11]

The *Herald*'s correspondent is not yet aware that American slave-hunters will no longer advertise their services; that those days are over; that they ended just yesterday.

On the *Shenandoah*, Captain Waddell calls a meeting with the skippers of the captured whalers. Three of the four can offer no legal reason why their ships might be spared, but the master of the *Harvest*, John Eldridge, protests that his ship should not be confiscated because it is not an American but a Hawaiian vessel. He tells Waddell his ship was originally American, out of New Bedford, but had since been sold to interests in Honolulu. However, Captain Eldridge cannot produce a bill of sale to prove his claim, and Waddell doesn't believe him. Convinced the *Harvest* is under false colours, he orders that Eldridge and his officers be taken prisoner, and for the *Harvest*, along with the three other ships, to be set afire. It's a mistake, and one that will come back to haunt him.

Their whalers' crews, 130 men in total and mostly Hawaiians, are put ashore and, it's noted, are treated kindly by the islanders.

The four whalers are reckoned to be worth a total of almost $118,000 in prize money, but for Waddell the far greater prizes are captured charts of whaling grounds.

'With such charts in my possession, I not only held a key to the navigation of all the Pacific islands, the Okhotsk and Bering seas, and the Arctic Ocean, but the most probable localities for finding the great Arctic whaling fleet of New England, without a tiresome search.'[12]

On 12 April, Waddell and his officers go ashore to keep their appointment with the King. The royal residence is nothing fancy, just a one-room dwelling built of interlaced cane and roofed with coconut leaves, but in a pleasant riverside location where the fishing is good.

Inside, the Confederates – with Harrocke in tow to interpret – find the King seated on a woven mat with his queen beside him. The King invites them to sit – the seats are two wooden chairs, a box and a trunk – and immediately asks when they expect to leave and if they intend to kill their prisoners, which he considers the right thing to do. It seems he's not much of a one for small talk.

Waddell tells him he intends to set sail the following day, and that the prisoners would not be harmed. 'In civilised warfare,' he explains, 'men destroyed those in armed resistance and paroled the unarmed.'

'But war cannot be considered civilised,' the King replies, 'and those who make war on an unoffending people are a bad people and do not deserve to live.'[13]

Waddell impresses upon the King that when he gets home he will be sure to tell President Davis of his kind hospitality and the respect shown to the Confederate flag.

The King says, 'Tell Jeff Davis he is my brother and a big warrior; that we are very poor, but that our tribes are friends. If he will send your steamer for me, I will visit him in his country.'[14]

With that, he presents Waddell with two dead chickens and some coconuts to deliver to the President of the Confederate States of America with his kind regards.

The next morning, with the crew all present and correct, and almost all of them sporting tender new tattoos, courtesy of islander artists, the *Shenandoah* weighs anchor and steams out to sea, bidding farewell to the tiny island kingdom of Pohnpei – the only country on Earth to officially recognise the Confederacy as a sovereign nation.

Fred McNulty notes, 'After staying at Ascension Island 11 days, we hove our anchor and started for the coast of Japan. As we neared the coast, thousands of robins came on deck, and, falling exhausted from the rigging, were picked up in buckets full, and proved a great change from salt horse.'

He adds, 'Great events were going on then at home, but we were oblivious of their occurrence.'[15]

Jefferson Davis will never receive the chickens and coconuts from his Pacific Island admirer. What he does receive, on the same day the *Shenandoah* departs Pohnpei, is a letter from General Lee that begins, 'It is with pain that I announce to Your Excellency the surrender of the Army of Northern Virginia.'[16]

Davis, in poor health and increasingly out of touch with

reality, refuses to accept that Lee's surrender means the cause is lost. In his addled mind, he is the embodiment of the cause, and as long as he is at the helm the Confederacy will prevail. He clings to this belief even knowing that rebel soldiers, many of them sick, starving and emaciated, are limping into Union lines in their thousands, throwing down their arms in exchange for tinned beef and hardtack.

Jeff Davis is on the run. The Yankees have overrun his capital, and he is reduced to holding Cabinet meetings in a boxcar in a railway siding in Greensboro, North Carolina. Still, on 15 April he proclaims, 'I believe we can whip the enemy yet, if the people will turn out.'[17]

Davis doesn't know it yet but Abraham Lincoln, shot by an assassin the night before, died in the early hours of that same day. The assassination will harden Northern hearts and make reconciliation all the more difficult. And while the Confederacy continues to be led by a deluded, fugitive president, presiding over chaos, the war will not formally be over.

Chapter 15

The curious case of Eugenio Gonzales

How had it come to this? There had been a large show of public sympathy for the plight of Eugenio Gonzales. Hearts went out to this young man of African-American and Hispanic heritage who had served on the Confederate raider *Alabama*, and was wounded during the ill-fated battle with USS *Kearsarge*, in 1864. Since coming to Australia he had worked hard as a farm labourer and lived a quiet and respectable life, only to be savagely attacked to cries of 'Kill the black nigger!', and left for dead.

Yet here he is, on 20 April 1865, in the dock of a Victorian court, sentenced to 12 months' jail, with hard labour, for perjury.

Gonzales, 18, has been found guilty of falsely accusing Duncan McIntyre and his niece and nephew, Grace and John Sinclair, aged 12 and 15, of attempted murder. On 6 February, Gonzales told Flemington Police Court, 'I am in the employ of Mr Robert McDougal, of Essendon. On Saturday, 21 January I found a bull belonging to Mrs Sinclair on Mr McDougal's land. I was taking it to the house [to impound the animal], when Mr McIntyre came to take the bull from me. We had a fight, he struck me and knocked me down. The boy, John Sinclair, was at the fence, and called out, "Kill the black nigger!" McIntyre then called to the girl, Grace Sinclair, to bring a stone. She did so, and struck me on the back with it. I fell down, as dead.'[1]

Gonzales told the court he had been wounded in both legs during the battle between the *Alabama* and the *Kearsarge*, and came to Australia about nine months afterwards, on the *El Dorado*. It was not uncommon for free African-Americans to serve in the Confederate States Navy. Confederate naval regulations allowed a ship's captain a ratio of one black seaman to five white seamen.

A doctor who examined Gonzales shortly after the assault testified that he found him unconscious, bleeding from the mouth, and his back swollen from a recent blow. He had no discernible pulse, his eyes did not react to light, his extremities were cold, his lungs were congested and his teeth were clenched. In the doctor's opinion, he was close to death.

Another doctor gave similar evidence, agreeing that Eugenio Gonzales was dying as the result of severe injuries. Yet by some miracle he had recovered.

It might have seemed an open and shut case until the defence provided alibis for each of the defendants. Witnesses testified that, at the time of the alleged assault, Duncan McIntyre was in Melbourne, Grace Sinclair was fishing in a distant creek with her mother, and John Sinclair was away delivering produce all that day.

The case was dismissed, and Gonzales was indicted for perjury. At his trial, the alibis were repeated, with additional and persuasive detail, and the judge refused to allow as evidence a deathbed declaration by Gonzales because he had not died. The defence protested that it was unlikely a man anticipating death would perjure himself by swearing to a declaration that could send three people to the gallows, but the bench remained unmoved.

So here stands Eugenio Gonzales, found guilty as charged. However, the jury has recommended a lenient sentence, and the judge, in handing down 12 months – the maximum is 15 years – has accepted the jury's recommendation as 'tantamount to an expression of belief that Gonzales had been assaulted as he described, but that he had been guilty of overstating his convictions as to the identity of the persons who made the attack upon him'.[2]

Gonzales is taken down to the cells, there to await the wagon to transport him to Pentridge jail to do his time. However, his story doesn't end there. Observing the case with a keen and clinical eye was an eminent pathologist, Dr James Neild. An expert in forensic medicine, Dr Neild sees evidence of something the court did not see. His curiosity piqued, he sets out to investigate, and in August presents his remarkable findings to the Medical Society of Victoria, in a paper entitled 'On a Case of Feigned Haemoptysis and Collapse'.

He tells the Society, 'My attention has been directed to the case solely on account of the peculiar interest it seemed to possess as an example in that long list of feigned diseases, which form not the least part of that division of the study of medicine which I have had the honour of being appointed to teach in the Melbourne University.

'I cannot but regard it as a very unusual example of feigned disease. Indeed, the apparent absence of motive on the part of the impostor somewhat complicates the case, and almost points to the possibility of its serving not only as an instance of disease-feigning but also a curious phase of monomania.'

After briefly describing the court case, the injuries observed by two physicians, and the reasons for the judgement, he tells the gentlemen of the Society – some of whom must be squirming in their seats by now, 'Very properly, therefore, the case was dismissed, notwithstanding the very positive medical evidence tendered on the occasion, and which was, I am quite sure, given in perfectly good faith, and in the full belief that the symptoms as described were genuine.'

In other words, Neild, as delicately as possible, is telling his colleagues they've been fooled. In his opinion, Eugenio Gonzales is a consummate faker who, by long practice, has learnt how to deceive those who witness his supposed attacks of haemorrhage. Not only can he simulate haemoptysis (coughing up blood) but also loss of consciousness and collapse, and, for no apparent reason, he was willing to send three innocent people to the gallows.

To support his conclusion, Neild tenders a letter from Albert Read, the solicitor for Gonzales's alleged attackers. And it's a bombshell.

Read, dissatisfied with the jury's reluctance to convict, and the light sentence imposed by a sympathetic judge, decided to dig deeper.

Aware that the *Shenandoah* was in port, he met with Confederate officers and crewmen who had served on the *Alabama* up to the time of its sinking. All of them declared no such man had ever been on board that ship. Read then pieced together Gonzales's real story.

As a sailor on the ship *Aurora*, he arrived in Melbourne from America in November 1863, and was immediately taken to Melbourne Hospital for treatment of a back injury received when, during the voyage, he fell from the topsail yard of the ship onto the deck. On discharge from hospital he found work with a waterman named Antonio Losenlo, plying boats between suburban Footscray and Melbourne wharf.

Losenlo told Read that in the mornings he would often find Gonzales in a fit, foaming at the mouth and spitting blood, yet by breakfast time he would be fine. Gonzales did this so often that Losenlo was convinced he could throw a fit and haemorrhage at will. On other occasions he would be found with blood in his mouth and appear to be stone dead, but would come to after about an hour. Eventually, Losenlo told Gonzales he had had enough of his shamming, and sacked him.

Gonzales loafed around Footscray for a while, telling fortunes at the Ship Inn, but soon wore out his welcome by too often performing his haemorrhagic party trick. He crewed on a schooner but deserted after stealing money, then took the job as a farm hand for Robert McDougal.

The medical officer at Pentridge jail told Albert Read that even behind bars Gonzales was up to his old tricks, although he was now claiming to have been hit in the chest with a rock.

Read's letter concluded, 'Having given you the history of Gonzales, I leave you to judge of the value of his dying declaration, also of the medical evidence, showing with what great caution such evidence should be received, as well as how cautious medical gentlemen should be before giving such positive evidence that they could not be mistaken.'

On that cautionary note, Dr Neild's presentation to the Medical Society of Victoria concludes. Whether it's met by respectful applause or stony silence, we'll never know. Given that James Neild, who is not only a doctor but a poet and something of a bohemian, is not popular with the old guard, who regard him as a maverick, the latter is more likely. One medico, at least, registers his appreciation, only to taint it with a racist comment of sweeping proportions.

A certain Dr Black opines that the case confirms his own conclusions, gained while working in the West Indies, that 'coloured races were constitutionally disposed to habits of dissimulation, feigned diseases in that colony being among the most constantly observed phenomena of medical practice'.[3]

Chapter 16

The way north

'There were days not very long since when literary gentlemen wrote clever books about colonies, the right theory of colonisation, the sort of people that ought to colonise, and how they ought to be governed,' sniffs *The Times* of London on 24 April 1865:

> It was a great advance, so at least they thought, on the old material idea, of which, to say the truth, Robinson Crusoe was the leading type. But colonies, it is now very evident, will not be made by book, or by governments, or by societies, or by governors, or even by colonists themselves. Partly they take their own course; partly circumstances form them; those circumstances are sometimes so strong that you have little else to do but stand by at a respectful distance and see what comes of it.
>
> The colony, first the province of Victoria, was founded in quiet times; it is named after Her Majesty, and the capital after her Prime Minister. It was hoped that a few hardy fellows would go there, breed sheep, send us tallow and wool, and earn enough to

live comfortably and marry upon. That was only a few years ago, and Victoria has not had such a history as, we will say, Canada, but it has had some strange experiences. The fleece turned into a golden one, and, instead of a few shepherds and husbandman, Victoria has a population of near 700,000 pursuing every kind of trade, and, at the last date, carrying a protective tariff. But within those five and twenty years has come the demand for self-government, and Victoria is a virtually independent state. A little time since it was on the point of going to war with New South Wales, ostensibly on a question of duties, really for a 'correction' of the boundary line.

But now there has come a new question. All at once the *Shenandoah* makes its appearance in Port Phillip, carrying the papers, the chronometers, and some of the men of many Federal ships captured and sent to the bottom. The *Flying Dutchman* would not have been a more terrible visitor. There was no doubt about the ship or her history, for the crew let it all out, and were proud of their errand and their achievements, Melbourne of course was divided, but the Confederate cause is evidently tho more popular, and Captain Waddell became a 'lion' at the clubs and at parties.

We regret that the people of Melbourne should have displayed so much sympathy with a crew engaged in the destruction of ships coming upon errands of peace to their own distant ports.

Luckily for Victoria's governor, Sir Charles Darling, Her Majesty's Government does not share *The Times*'s air of despair of colonials behaving badly – not publicly, anyway.

If Governor Darling is anticipating a severe slap from Downing Street for his inept handing of the *Shenandoah* affair, he's relieved to receive a despatch from British Secretary of State, Earl Russell, thrashing him with a feather.

His Lordship writes:

I have much pleasure in informing you that Her Majesty's Government are of the opinion that, under the circumstances stated, you acted with propriety and discretion; and that there does not appear, at present, to be a necessity for any action on their part. With regard to your request that you may receive instructions as to the propriety of executing any warrant under the Foreign Enlistment Act on board a Confederate (public) ship of war, Her Majesty's Government are of the opinion that, in the case of strong suspicion you ought to request the permission of the commander of the ship to execute the warrant, and that if this request be refused you ought not attempt to enforce the execution; but in this case the commander should be desired to leave the port as speedily as possible, and should be informed that he would not be re-admitted.[1]

In other words, we'll forgive the cock-up, Charles, old chap, but do get it right next time.

In Irwin County, Georgia, on 10 May, Jefferson Davis is captured. With the President is his wife Varina, their four children, a small force of cavalry and a few others. Taken by surprise in the early morning by Union cavalry, the Confederates surrender without a shot being fired.

A popular story soon doing the rounds is that Davis almost

escaped when his wife persuaded the Union officer guarding their tent to let her mother fetch water from the creek. Permission was granted, and a person in a woman's coat and black head shawl left the tent and was headed for the creek when another officer noticed that Mrs Davis's 'mother' was wearing cavalry boots with spurs. He called on the 'old lady' to halt, and whipped off the shawl to reveal Jeff Davis. Another version of the tale has Davis making a break for it in a wig, bonnet and hoop skirt. The Northern press features cartoons depicting Davis fleeing in drag, and there is even a popular song titled 'Jeff in Petticoats'.

A verse of the songs runs:

Our Union boys were on his track for many nights and days,
His palpitating heart it beat enough to burst his stays.
Oh what a dash he must have cut with form so tall and lean.
Just fancy now the 'What is it? Dressed up in crinoline!'

The chorus goes:

Oh Jeffry D,
You flow'r of chivalree.
Oh royal Jeffry D,
Your empire's but a tin-clad skirt,
Oh charming Jeffry D.[2]

However, eye-witnesses on both sides refute the story. Among the most persuasive is an account by Davis's free-born African-American coachman and courier, James H. Jones, and another by one of the Union cavalrymen who arrested Davis. The soldier's account, as published in several newspapers and historical journals, tells us, 'Besides the suit of men's clothing worn by Mr Davis, he had on when captured Mrs Davis's large water-proof dress or robe thrown over his own fine grey suit, and a blanket shawl thrown over his head and shoulders.

'The story of the "hoop skirt, sun bonnet and calico wrapper" had no real existence and was started in the febrile brains of the reporters and illustrated papers of that day. That was a perilous moment for Mr Davis. He had the right to try to escape in any disguise he could use.'[3]

The way north finds fair winds and fine weather until the *Shenandoah* crosses the 43rd parallel. From then on, the weather grows increasingly cold and the winds turn fickle. Old hands feel it in their bones that something wicked this way comes, and, sure enough, from out of the north-east looms a vast black cloud, whipping the lazy rollers below into a boiling cauldron.

Waddell vividly describes the storm: 'So close did it rest upon the surface of the water that it seemed determined to over-whelm the ship, and there came in it so terrible and violent a wind that the *Shenandoah* was thrown on her side, and she bounced away as if in fight, like the stag from his lair, had started her.

'Squall after squall struck her, flash after flash surrounded her, and the thunder rolled in her wake. It was the typhoon. The ocean was as white as the snow as foamed with rage. A new close-reefed topsail was blown into shreds, and the voice of man was inaudible amid this awful convolution of nature.'[4]

Mercifully, the storm passes quickly and the ship, which had been forced westward by the gale, resumes its passage north. Two days on, though, another big blow pushes her off course for a while, but when she finally makes it across the 45th parallel the weather is colder but more settled. All hands breathe a sign of relief.

On 20 May, they sight the snow-covered Kuril Islands, and the next sail into the Sea of Okhotsk and run along the coast of the Kamchatka Peninsula, in the Russian far east, on the lookout for whalers.

There are no whalers in sight yet, but nature treats all on deck to spectacular displays of Arctic magic – beautiful mirages of such clarity that a snow-clad peak some 70 miles (113km) away appears much closer, and to have an identical but inverted image above it, peak touching peak, as if the sky were a mirror reflecting the earth below.

The magic spell is soon broken. On 27 May, as a thick fog clears, they find themselves in a field of ice stretching in every direction as far as the eye can see. The ice is at least five feet (1.5m) thick on the port side, and on the starboard side it rises to the height of the sails – lying stiff as boards across the masts, frozen from the drizzling rain of the previous night.

The ice floe is moving, slowly, with the ship caught in its grip. Fred McNulty recalls, 'It grated against the frail timbers that now only stood between us and death, as if envious that its realms had been invaded, and wanting to reach with its cold grasp the intruder.

'Lips unused to prayer now sent up a supplication. Added to all, as if to mock our miseries, a group of walruses climbed clumsily out of the sea and began disporting themselves so near that we could almost touch them.

'Gradually, as hope began to sink, the sun slowly came upon the scene. Though low in the north, it brought hope and warmth. The long, cold northern day that knows no sunset was upon us with its low, mocking noon. The sails began to lose their ridged bend, the ice loosened and we forged ahead. Then, lowering our propeller in the wake thus made, we pushed sternwise out of the terrible ice floe.'5

Two days on, while skirting an ice floe, they spot a ship heading straight for them. She's the *Abigail*, a whaler out of New Bedford, and she has mistaken the raider for a Russian supply ship en route to the port of Okhotsk.

When the Stainless Banner goes up and a shot splashes across her bows, the *Abigail* puts up no resistance and is duly boarded, looted and burnt. Her master, Ebenezer Nye, might well be the unluckiest skipper afloat, having previously lost a ship to the *Alabama*. When he and his mates are taken aboard the *Shenandoah* as prisoners, one of them turns to him in disgust and says, 'You are more fortunate in picking up Confederate cruisers than whales! I will never again go with you, for if there is a cruiser out there, you will find it.'6

Captain Nye tells the Confederates the war is over, but since he can offer no proof, they don't believe him. Twelve of the *Abigail*'s crew don't believe him either – or don't care – and enlist on the *Shenandoah*.

The booty from the *Abigail* includes 20 barrels of whisky, and the prize crew proceed to get roaring drunk. One sailor, Australian Confederate Thomas Swanton, gets so drunk he is ordered back to the *Shenandoah*, but when bundled into a boat jumps overboard. Lieutenant Chew reports, 'The water was below the freezing point and the cold bath did him much good. Had to lash him in the boat.'7

The rest of the revellers incur the wrath of Lieutenant Whittle, who notes in his journal, 'We brought off a great deal of liquor and many of our men and two officers got drunk. Put all in irons, gagged and triced up, right and left.

'I am determined that they shall not repeat it.'

One man did. The next day, Whittle writes, 'Put Mr Lynch [2nd carpenter] in irons for again being drunk. He being very insolent to me, I gagged him.'[8]

Chapter 17

The last shot

In 20 days, the *Shenandoah* has run from tropical heat to biting cold. As she labours through yet another gale, the mercury falls to several degrees below zero, and the pack ice is growing thicker.

The ship is in danger of being crushed when a lookout spots a passage through the ice, with open water beyond. She enters the passage under close and reefed sail, and in a short time is in water as calm as a mill pond while, on the weather side of the floe, massive chunks of ice are breaking off, throwing up sheets of water 20 feet (6m) high.

She's not out of danger yet. Now, she's sailing through rain and sleet which instantly freezes, encrusting the sails, braces, blocks, yards and all the running rigging in thick ice.

As the weather eases, the Captain knows what must be done, yet he pauses before giving the order, entranced by what he sees – more Arctic magic.

'The gale had passed over, and it was calm, the clouds were exhausted, the rosy tint of morn opened upon a scene of enchantment, and the sunlight burst upon us, the flash and sparkle from truck to deck, from bowsprit to topsail, awakened exclamations of enthusiastic delight over the fair ship.

'The disposition was evidently not to disturb, but leave to enjoyment the crystal mantle of the *Shenandoah*. Finally, the crew was sent aloft with billets of wood to dislodge the ice and free the running rigging. The large icicles falling from aloft rendered the deck dangerous to move upon, and it soon became covered with clear, beautiful ice, which was removed to the tanks, casks, and every vessel capable of receiving it.'[1]

Westward is a white world of ice; no fit place for hunter or quarry. The *Shenandoah* changes course for the North Pacific, and on the afternoon of 16 June enters the Bering Sea.

The hunt is on.

Amid the scramble to boost Melbourne's defences in the wake of the *Shenandoah*, the Victorian Government is considering an exciting new invention by Captain Horace H. Doty, late of the Confederate States Navy. As *The Argus* puts it, 'The Civil War in the United States, as might be expected from the inventive genius of the American people, has been prolific of improvements in the art of warfare.'[2]

Captain Doty's ingenious invention is an advanced design of 'submarine battery' – an explosive shell attached to the end of a long bar protruding from the prow of a semi-submerged vessel. During the Civil War, submarine batteries, or 'spar torpedoes', had been used with effect by the Confederate Navy. The term 'torpedo' in those days, applied to explosive shells. The self-propelled torpedo had not yet been invented.

In Captain Doty's improved device, when the shell strikes an enemy ship, wires in the bar, connected to a battery, make a circuit, which detonates the shell. It's said that a fast vessel armed with such a device could easily despatch several heavily armed frigates. Adding to its appeal, the device is simple, economical, safe, and can be used in the roughest seas and on the darkest night.

Victoria's defences would never include Doty's submarine battery, however. It seems the inventive Captain Doty was not all he appeared to be. Henry Harrison Doty, alias Horace H. Doty, was not a captain, and had never served in the Confederate Navy, nor in the Chilean Navy, as he also claimed.

And Doty did not invent the submarine battery. It had in fact been developed by Confederate naval officers Matthew Maury and Hunter Davidson. Maury, a naval scientist and Confederate agent in England, had served on the *Alabama* and escaped with Captain Raphael Semmes when the raider was sunk off Cherbourg in 1864. Captain Davidson founded the Confederate Submarine Battery Service, and in 1864, in Newport News, Virginia, skippered the semi-submersible torpedo boat *Squib*, which damaged USS *Minnesota*.

In 1865, Doty joined a band of mercenaries led by the two ex-Confederates – and which included the American artist James McNeil Whistler – on an expedition to supply torpedos and other arms to Chile, then at war with Spain. Whistler travelled separately to Chile, on the same vessel as Doty's wife, Astide.

Doty, paymaster on Davidson's ship the *Henrietta*, learned all he knew of military matters from listening to Maury and Davidson during the voyage to Valparaiso, then under Spanish bombardment.

The expedition was a failure. The mercenaries failed to sink the Spanish fleet, and the Chileans reneged on the £60,000 bounty promised to them. The entrepreneurs returned to England empty-handed, with Davidson accusing Doty of defrauding him of £100, and Doty accusing Whistler of seducing his wife during the voyage to Valparaiso.

Whistler, who had again travelled separately, arrived at Waterloo Station to find Doty waiting for him. Doty loudly accused him of being a cad and a scoundrel, whereupon Whistler lashed out and struck him. Doty, bigger and stronger than the feisty but slightly built Whistler, hit back with force, and the artist fled. Doty later challenged Whistler to a duel over the honour of his wife – who, as it turned out, was not his wife at all – but then withdrew the challenge.

The matter was far from settled, however. When Doty continued to make libellous accusations against Whistler, most offensively as a member of Whistler's gentlemen's club in London, the artist sought support from Captain Davidson, who didn't mince words:

'The character of the man H.H. Doty (alias Captain Doty) who was known to me only as a contractor with a Chilean agent in London in 1865 and afterwards as a shipped seaman on board my ship the *Henrietta*, in which I took a torpedo expedition to Chile, is too revolting for me to dwell upon in detail. Surely, no Society in England can be long deceived by this villain (and the woman with whom he travels as his wife).

'I have never known a more snake-like abject coward, and yet you say he belongs to a club in London! What kind of club can it be?'[3]

At 'Redmoor', his son's plantation in Amelia County, Virginia, a household name throughout the South puts a gun to his head and blows his brains out.

A wealthy slaveholder and leading advocate for secession in the years leading up to the war, 'Fire-Eater' Edmund Ruffin had a passionate hatred for abolitionists, Yankees and federal government, not necessarily in that order. One of the colourful characters of the Old South, with flowing white locks and aristocratic bearing, Ruffin claimed to have fired the first shot of the war, at the attack on Fort Sumter in 1861. He was 67 years old at the time.

On learning of Lee's surrender at Appomattox, Ruffin decides life is no longer worth living. He goes upstairs to his study, taking with him a rifle and a forked stick, and pens the last entry in his diary:

'I here declare my unmitigated hatred to Yankee rule – to all political, social and business connection with the Yankees and to the Yankee race. Would that I could impress these sentiments, in their full force, on every living Southerner and bequeath them to every one yet to be born. May such sentiments be held universally in the outraged and downtrodden South, though in silence and stillness, until the now far-distant day shall arrive for just retribution for Yankee usurpation, oppression and atrocious outrages, and for deliverance and vengeance for the now ruined, subjugated and enslaved Southern States.'

At this point, Ruffin is interrupted by news that there are visitors at the door. He entertains his guests, then, after they have left, returns to his study and writes, 'And now with my latest writing and utterance, and with what will be near to my last breath, I here repeat, and would willingly proclaim, my unmitigated hatred to Yankee rule – to all political, social and business connections with Yankees, and the perfidious, malignant and vile Yankee race.'[4]

That done, Edmund Ruffin wraps himself in a Confederate flag, puts the rifle muzzle in his mouth and uses the forked stick to pull the trigger. The percussion cap is detonated but fails to fire the rifle.

Hearing the noise, his daughter-in-law Jane alerts her husband, Edmund Junior, and they rush upstairs. But by the time they get to Ruffin's room, he has reloaded and, using his toe to squeeze the trigger this time, fired the fatal shot.

In Galveston, Texas, two days after Edmund Ruffin decided life was not worth the candle, Union General Gordon Granger, whose forces have just occupied the city, is standing on the balcony of Ashton Villa, the stately Italianate villa of wealthy Texas businessman James Moreau Brown. The ornate mansion balcony is a fitting site for the historic announcement the general is about to make to the townsfolk gathered below.

It has been more than two years since the Emancipation Proclamation, yet slavery has endured in Texas, where there are at least a quarter of a million people still in bondage.

In a strong, clear voice, Granger, a fearless, outspoken New Yorker with an impressive tally of battle honours, proclaims General Orders Number Three:

'The people of Texas are informed that, in accordance with a proclamation from the Executive of the United States, all slaves are free. This involves an absolute equality of personal rights and rights of property between former masters and slaves, and the connection heretofore existing between them becomes that between employer and hired labour. The freedmen are advised to remain quietly at their present homes and work for wages. They are informed that they will not be allowed to collect at military posts, and that they will not be supported in idleness either there or elsewhere.'[4]

Freed slaves in the restive crowd below the balcony stand silent in shock at first, then erupt in pure joy. This is more than emancipation – this is salvation, and the celebration of freedom on 19 June will become the black American Fourth of July. Henceforth, the anniversary of General Granger's proclamation will be known as June teenth, marked throughout America with picnics, parades and prayers of thanksgiving.

The mansion from whence the good news was spread has a macabre legacy, however. Ashton Villa, which was used as a hospital for Confederate wounded during the war, is said to be haunted by the ghosts of rebel soldiers – lost souls for the lost cause.

That same day, 19 June, Confederate agent James Bulloch pens a letter to Captain Waddell, telling him of Lee's surrender on 9 April and informing him that, since the surrender, the European powers have withdrawn belligerent rights to the Confederacy. Bulloch's orders to Waddell are to immediately cease offensive operations. His first duty now is to take care of the men under his command and to discharge and pay off the crew as soon as it is safe to do so, enabling them to return to their homes.

Bulloch advises him that if he does not have enough money to pay the crew in full he should pay them as much as he can and give each man a promissory note to pay the balance from his own account in Liverpool.

The letter also relays the disturbing news that, under a recent proclamation by the President of the United States, Waddell and his fellow Southerners dare not return to America.

The Australians on the *Shenandoah* knew from the outset that going home to resume their lives would risk arrest and imprisonment. Now, for the Americans on board, a homecoming could mean the noose.

Back in May, Lincoln's successor, Andrew Johnston, offered 'all persons who have, directly or indirectly, participated in the existing rebellion, except as hereinafter excepted, amnesty and pardon, with the restoration of all rights of property, except as to slaves, and except in cases where legal proceedings, under the laws of the United States providing for the confiscation of property of persons engaged in rebellion, have been instituted; but upon this condition, nevertheless, that every such person shall take and subscribe the following oath.'

People seeking a pardon must swear to 'henceforth faithfully support, protect, and defend the Constitution of the United States, and the union of the States thereunder' and to 'faithfully support all laws and proclamations which have been made during the existing rebellion with reference to the emancipation of slaves'.

And as if that isn't enough for old Johnny Reb to swallow, those to whom no amnesty will be granted included 'foreign agents of the pretended Confederate government' – such as James Bulloch; 'all who shall have been military or naval officers of said pretended Confederate government above the rank of colonel in the army or lieutenant in the navy' – such as James Waddell; 'all military and naval officers in the rebel service, who were educated by the government in the Military Academy at West Point or the United States Naval Academy' – such as the Captain and most of the officers of the *Shenandoah*; and 'all persons who have been engaged in the destruction of the commerce of the United

States upon the high seas' – such as the entire ship's complement of the *Shenandoah*, from captain to cabin boy.[5]

Bulloch's advice is to come to Europe and await further developments, but getting this vital news to the master of the *Shenandoah* is problematic. Bulloch sends copies of the letter to Britain's Foreign Minister Earl Russell, who agrees to forward copies to all British colonial authorities and to consuls in Japan, China and Hawaii. The hope is that the news will reach Waddell at some port or from some ship, somewhere soon. It does not.

In Sydney, the assassination of Lincoln has sparked widespread demonstrations of grief, with memorial services, public meetings to share outrage and sympathy, an official letter of condolence from the city's mayor to Mrs Lincoln, and even an undertaking by sorrowing citizens to wear mourning clothes for a month.

In Melbourne, US Consul William Blanchard lowers the consulate flag to half mast, and Yankee residents do likewise, but there is nothing like the public outpouring of grief seen in Sydney.

'Mr Abraham Lincoln was far above the average of Federal statesmen in his earnestness against slavery,' says *The Geelong Advertiser* in a backhanded compliment to the slain President, and continues:

> . . . and for his diverse faults, they were more those of ignorance and vacillation in a man so suddenly invested with so tremendous an authority, than of inherent defect of character.
>
> But while we regard the American Civil War as over, it would be idle to indulge in the belief that the Union is restored, or that the two parties who have been engaged in this death-struggle of four years, are now reconciled. The feelings which have been

generated by this war are not likely to die with the surrender of General Lee or the flight of President Davis. The nation which has endured so much, and fought so heroically in the endeavour to free itself from Northern domination, will hardly consent to forget the past, even though it gives up its arms.

The rebellion has been crushed out, but something else has been destroyed besides the Confederacy – the old unity; the old bonds have been dissolved; the silver chord is loosened; the golden bowl is broken forever. It is impossible that Northerners and Southerners can ever be again fellow-citizens as once they were. Under the immediate pressure of their present calamities, the South maybe quiescent for a time, but to believe that the spirit of a nation is entirely annihilated, which has the fame of Robert Lee and Stonewall Jackson, the memory of Richmond, of Charleston, of Gettysburg and Bull Run among its traditions, is to libel our kinsmen of the great Anglo-Saxon race.'[6]

More to the point, with the *Shenandoah* long gone, Melburnians are in need of new diversion; another novelty. And on 19 June they get one. A large male gorilla is now on display at the Museum of Natural and Applied Sciences, and curious citizens are queuing in their hundreds to visit the exhibit.

The museum's director, Professor Frederick McCoy, has described the old silverback, captured in central Africa, as 'the largest example of the monster ape recorded', with an expression 'more one of contented jovial jollity than malignity'.[7]

McCoy, a renowned palaeontologist, is active in the environmentally disastrous Acclimatisation Society, which favours importing English songbirds and rabbits to bring a touch of the Mother Country to the Australian bush (see Chapter 27).

He is also a rabid opponent of Darwinism, and is promoting the gorilla exhibit as proof positive that there is no distant link between humans and apes. He invites the public to see for themselves 'how infinitely remote the creature is from humanity, and how monstrous writers have exaggerated the points of resemblance when endeavouring to show that man is only one phase of the gradual transmutation of animals, which they assume may be brought about by external influences.'[8]

The professor's views are mainstream at the moment, but time and the weight of scientific opinion will eventually make a monkey out of him.

'Sail ho!' Overnight, thick fog made the lookout's job all but impossible, but a couple of hours ago he spotted whale blubber in the water – an encouraging sign. So far in these frigid climes, the Confederates' only contact has been with Inuit hunters.

'The *Shenandoah* was now north of the island of St Lawrence, under sail, with fires banked,' Waddell recalls. 'Several Esquimaux canoes with natives from the island visited us, and our crew struck up a brisk trade with them for furs and walrus tusks. It was interesting and curious, as we had no means of communication with them except through signs.'[9]

Fred McNulty's recollection differs markedly from that of his captain. 'They brought out walrus tusks and fur, which we declined to barter for. The cook, however, brought from the galley a slush bucket of odds and ends of grease and food, and our little stunted friends squatted upon the deck in silence, and dug deeply with their hands into the mixed viands. A pound of tallow candles to serve each as dessert, and when the king's meal to an Esquimaux was at an end they departed with full hearts and stomachs.'[10]

Now, at last, on the morning of Wednesday 21 June, from the masthead has come the cry the Confederates have been waiting for. Two sails are in sight. The *Shenandoah*, flying a Russian flag, gives chase, lobs a warning shot, and both ships heave to. They are the whalers *William Thompson* and *Euphrates*, both out of New Bedford.

By mid-afternoon, the *Euphrates* has been plundered and set afire, and the boarding parties have begun to transfer stores from the *William Thompson*, when a third sail is spotted. Again, the *Shenandoah* gives chase, only to discover on coming close enough to hail the ship that she's from a neutral country. She's the whaler *Robert L. Towns*, out of Sydney. The whaler's captain, Fred Barker, asks Waddell the name of his vessel, and Waddell, maintaining the Russian ruse, tells him she's the 'Petropauluski', which means nothing in Russian and is probably the first thing that popped into his head.

Barker, a Yankee, is not taken in by the charade. He's guessed the true identity of the vessel, not only because there is a burning ship in the distance, and another being raided, but because it so happens he was in Sydney when the *Shenandoah* was in Melbourne, and had read all about it in the papers. Giving nothing away, he sails north towards the Bering Strait to warn any Yankee ships he encounters that a Confederate raider is heading their way.

The master of the *William Thompson*, Captain Smith, is the bearer of bad news. Lieutenant Whittle records in his journal his reaction to learning of the assassination of President Lincoln and the attempt on the life of Secretary of State Seward: 'I only fear that these attempts will be put to the credit of some Confederates, but I am certain that it was not done by anyone from our side.'[11]

He's devastated by news that Charleston and Savannah have fallen, and, as a Virginian, is especially saddened to learn of the fall of Richmond. As for the report of Lee's surrender at Appomattox, he flatly refuses to believe it. 'Lee may have left a portion of his force to protect the retreat of his army, and even he might have been taken with this position, but as to his surrender of his whole army, and of his treating with General Grant for peace I do not believe a single word. There is no doubting the Confederacy has received in prestige a heavy blow, but further I do not believe.'[12]

The next day, five vessels are sighted near a large body of ice. The *Shenandoah*, flying the Stars and Stripes, makes for them and, passing close under the stern of the nearest ship, the New Bedford whaler *Milo*, invites her master, Captain Hawes, to come aboard with his papers.

'He complained,' Waddell recalls, 'and was surprised to learn the nationality of the steamer, and said he had heard of her being in Australia, but did not expect to see her in the Arctic Ocean.

'I asked for news. He said the war was over. I then asked for documentary evidence. He had none, but believed the war was over. I replied that was not satisfactory, but that if he could produce any reliable evidence, I would receive it.'[13]

When Captain Hawes can offer no such evidence, Waddell tells him he is willing to ransom the *Milo* if he will sign a bond for $40,000, payable to the Confederate government after the war, and take on board all of the *Shenandoah*'s prisoners. The skipper agrees, and returns to his ship with instructions to send all his boats and his entire crew to the *Shenandoah*. This is a stratagem on Waddell's part to prevent the *Milo* escaping while he pursues two other vessels that have realised something is amiss and are making a run for it.

As the escaping whalers enter the ice field, the *Shenandoah* runs close and parallel to the ice to separate the ships, then, when about a mile away from the furthest ship, fires at her twice, forcing her to heave to. The other vessel, the *Jirah Swift*, with a strong wind behind her, makes good her escape and heads for the Siberian coast.

The captured whaler is the *Sophia Thornton*, out of New Bedford. Her master, Captain Moses Tucker, and her mates are taken aboard the *Shenandoah*, which then resumes the chase of the *Jirah Swift*, with the *Milo* sailing behind.

The New Bedford barque *Jirah Swift* is a fast ship with a skilful master, Thomas Williams, and in a good breeze it takes three hours to get within firing range of her.

Lieutenant Grimball barks the order for the gun crew to man one of the ship's two Whitworths. There are five marines in the gun crew – Sergeant Canning, Corporal Alexander, and privates Kenyon, Reily and Brown – all Australian Confederates. They are preparing to fire a Whitworth 32-pounder. The first generation of modern artillery, this British-designed gun is state of the art – made of high-tensile steel rather than brittle iron, and loaded from the breech, not from the muzzle. Its 70mm-calibre barrel is rifled in a hexagonal design and it fires solid, hexagonal shot called 'bolts' that make a distinctive and eerie whistling sound when fired. Exceptionally accurate up to 9,000 metres, it's ideal for firing across water. Unlike an explosive shell, a bolt from a Whitworth has a battering effect on a target, capable of shattering a ship's hull and mowing down her crew with showers of splinters.

At Grimball's command, the gun is 'run out' with tackles until the front of the gun carriage is hard up against the bulwark and the barrel is protruding from the gun port. With five full turns of the handles, one of the gun crew opens the screw-threaded breech, and another loads a bolt and a waxed cartridge of black powder, pieced to align with the touch-hole at the back of the gun. The breech is closed, and the 'gun captain' – who in this instance would be Sergeant Canning – takes aim at the target, using the sights, turning the elevating mechanism, and by removing a locking pin in the carriage to move the gun from side to side.

When sure he has the target in his sights, allowing for the roll and pitch of the ship, the gun captain raises his arm to signal all is ready.

Grimball yells, 'Fire!'

Sergeant Canning ignites the powder with a fuse to the touch-hole; all jump aside to avoid the recoil and the flash from the touch-hole; the cannon booms, a shot whistles past the stern of the *Jirah Swift* and immediately brings her to heel.

The *Shenandoah*'s gun crew have the satisfaction of a shot well placed, and with the desired effect. They have done this many times before, though, so it's a matter of no particular moment to them.

It will be many months yet before they learn that off the coast of Alaska on this day, Thursday, 22 June 1865, at 5.45pm, they fired the last shot of the American Civil War.

Chapter 18

'An old grey-headed devil'

There have never before been such pirates. That is, pirates who don't know they are pirates.

On the capture of the *Jirah Swift*, Captain Waddell notes, with frank admiration, 'Captain Williams, who made every effort to save his barque, saw the folly of exposing the crew to a destructive fire and yielded to his misfortune with a manly and becoming dignity.'[1]

When Lieutenant Smith Lee, leading the boarding party, reaches the *Jirah Swift*, he finds Captain Williams and his crew already packed and ready to leave for the *Shenandoah*. Twenty minutes later, the *Jirah Swift* is on fire.

Williams tell Smith Lee he does not believe the war is over, although he feels certain the South will eventually surrender.

With all the prisoners now aboard, the *Milo* sets sail for San Francisco, and the *Shenandoah* heads off in search of more victims. Unbeknown to the Confederates, smoke from the burning *Sophia Thornton* and *Jirah Swift* is spotted by four ships a few miles away – an American whaler, a French vessel and two Hawaiian ships – all of which sail off to warn any American ships they encounter.

Meanwhile, when the *Milo* is out of sight of the *Shenandoah*, several of the prisoners on board, led by the captain of the *Abigail*, Ebenezer Nye, lower two whaleboats and set off through ice-bound seas, hoping to reach Cape Bering to warn the whalers there, a distance of about 200 miles (320km). Captain Nye, who has lost two ships to Confederate raiders, hopes to be third-time lucky, and this time Lady Luck is on his side. Two days later, the escapees are picked up by a Yankee whaler, the *Mercury*, make it safely to a friendly port and raise the alarm.

On the morning of Friday 23 June, the brigantine *Susan Abigail*, a trader out of San Francisco, falls prey to the black raider. The Confederates help themselves to the weapons, calico, twine and other goods intended to be traded with the Inuit for furs.

San Francisco newspapers on board tell of the removal of the Confederate Government to Danville after the fall of Richmond, and President Jefferson Davis's proclamation that the South would not give up the fight.

Waddell claims the news includes a report that the better part of Lee's Army of Northern Virginia have joined with General Joe Johnston's forces in North Carolina, 'where an indecisive battle had been fought with General Sherman'.[2] If such a report exists, it is entirely without foundation.

Waddell further claims the *Susan Abigail*'s master, Captain Redfield, tells him, 'Opinion is divided as to the ultimate result of the war. For the present, the North has the advantage, but how it will all end no-one can know, and as to the newspapers, they are not reliable.'[3]

The *Susan Abigail* is set ablaze, and two of her crew join the *Shenandoah*, which Waddell interprets as proof they do not believe the war is over. 'They were not pressed to ship, but sought service under our flag,' he writes.[4]

Lieutenant Whittle's take on the news from America is not quite in accord with his captain's version. He notes in his journal: 'The vessel which we captured today is one of the latest arrivals from San Francisco and brings the confirmation of the assassination of Lincoln, fall of Charleston, Savannah, Wilmington, Richmond and the surrender of General Lee with 16,000 men. The news, if true, is very bad, but there's life in the old land yet. Let us live with a hope. The God of Jacob is our refuge. Oh let us trust in him.'[5]

That same day, in the Choctaw Indian Territory, Oklahoma, the last active rebel army unit, the Cherokee Mounted Rifles, commanded by Cherokee chief and Confederate general Stand Watie, rides into Fort Towson to surrender.

Watie's battalion of Cherokee, Seminole, Creek and Osage warriors has won a reputation as a brave and formidable force in the west, but after fighting on for 75 days after Lee's surrender in the east, Watie has accepted that continued resistance is futile, and is the last rebel general to lay down his arms.

There is now only one Confederate combat unit still active – the *Shenandoah*.

The tally is rising fast. On 22 June the *General Williams*, out of New London, is captured and burned, and on the following day six New England whalers are captured – the *William C. Nye*, the *Nimrod*, the *Catherine*, the *Isabella*, the *Gypsy*, and the *General Pike*. All are burned except the *General Pike*.

Waddell: 'The *General Pike* lost her master, and the mate was in charge of her, who asked as a special favour to be allowed to ransom her. He said, "If you ransom the *Pike*, her owner will think me so fortunate in saving her that it will give me a claim on them for the command."

'All the prisoners were sent to the *General Pike*, and she was given a certificate for San Francisco.'[6]

Next morning finds the *Shenandoah* under sail with a head wind, and the sails of escaping ships in sight. Keeping her distance so as not to raise suspicion, she follows them.

Fred McNulty describes what happens next as 'our greatest day's work – perhaps the greatest destruction ever served upon an enemy in a single day by one ship'.[7]

In a thick fog, on the morning of 28 June, something suddenly sweeps across the *Shenandoah*'s bows, and the men on deck can just make out the outline of a ship. In the fog, she almost collided with the raider.

The fog lifts to reveal not one but 11 ships lying at anchor in a wide bay. The bay is East Cape Bay – now Cape Dezhnev – on the Russian coast, and the ships are all Yankee whalers – the *Favorite*, the *James Murray*, the *Brunswick*, the *Congress*, the *Nile*, the *Congress*, the *Hillman*, the *Isaac Howland*, the *Nassau*, the *Martha 2nd*, and the *Covington*. And all of them are sitting ducks.

The *Shenandoah* steams into the bay, flying an American flag, whereupon all 11 ships do likewise. Fred McNulty tells us, 'Soon the work of demand, surrender, debarkation and conflagration began. Two were saved and bonded to take home the other crews.

Then followed the torch and auger. Never before had these latitudes beheld such a dread scene of devastation as this, as ship after ship went up in flames.

'We had been ordered to wipe out the whaling marine of the enemy; and now, after the government that had so ordered had been itself destroyed, we, unwittingly, were dealing the enemy our hardest blows – not our enemy, if we knew the facts, and we were making of ourselves the enemy of mankind.'[8]

Waddell writes:

We had heard of the whale ship *James Murray* off the island of Ascension, and after reaching the Bering Sea had heard again of her and also of the death of her master, whose widow and two little children were on board.

While our boats were being armed preparatory to taking possession of the prizes, a boat from the whale ship *Brunswick* came to the steamer, and the mate in charge of the boat, ignorant of our true nationality, represented that the *Brunswick* had struck a piece of ice a few hours before which left a hole in her starboard bow 20 inches below the water line, and asked for assistance.

To their application we replied, "We are very busy now, but in a little while we will attend to you."

The mate thanked us, and he was asked which of the vessels was the *James Murray*. He pointed her out. The *Brunswick* laid on her side, her casks of oil floating her well up, and her master, seeing his vessel a hopeless wreck, had offered his oil to any one purchaser among the masters of the other vessels at 20 cents per gallon.[9]

The *Shenandoah*, now in position to threaten the whaling fleet with her guns, hoists the Stainless Banner, and armed boats are launched to board the ships and bring their masters and papers to the *Shenandoah*.

'The American flags were hauled down instantly,' says Waddell.'[10]

All but one, that is. On the whaler *Favorite*, Old Glory still flaps in defiance.

Thomas Young, an old salt in his mid-sixties, is master of the *Favorite*, out of Fairhaven, Massachusetts, with a cargo of 500 barrels of whale oil and 3,300 pounds of ivory. He watches with rising anger as the rest of the fleet – chased and boarded by the *Shenandoah*, give up without a fight.

Seeing a boat shove off from the *Shenandoah* and make for his ship, he arms himself with a pistol and an old blunderbuss – a short, muzzle-loading firearm used for shooting whales – and climbs onto the cabin roof. When the raider's boat comes close, he aims the blunderbuss at the head of the officer in charge of the boarding party and yells, 'Stand off!'

The rebel officer at first laughs off the threat as a joke; an empty gesture. Then, noting the determined look on the old skipper's face and the unwavering aim of his blunderbuss, he orders his men to turn and row back to the *Shenandoah* with all speed.

On the *Favorite*, Captain Young's officers and crew are quaking with fear, expecting the next few minutes will bring the flash and thunder of a broadside from the *Shenandoah*'s guns. Desperate to prevent a bloodbath, they beg him to surrender, but Young is resolute. He'd be happy to die, he tells them, if he could take the commander of the privateer with him. Realising further argument is useless, Young's officers somehow remove his ammunition and the percussion caps for his pistol without him noticing, then they and the entire crew lower boats and abandon ship, leaving their captain to face the wrath of the raider alone.

Young knows only too well what shot and shell can do, having run a Union supply ship up the Potomac early in the war, dodging Confederate shore batteries all the way – a very risky business. Still, he stands his ground.

'Besides,' he tells himself, 'I have only four or five years to live anyway, and I might as well die now as any time, especially as all I have got is invested in my vessel, and if I lose that I will have to go home penniless and die a pauper.'

From the *Shenandoah*, Young hears the cry, 'Fire, but fire low!' Nothing happens. Waddell gave the order to fire but had immediately countermanded it on noticing that one of his boats was in range.

Soon, the boarding party comes alongside for a second time, and the rebel officer calls on Captain Young to strike his colours.

'I'll see you damned first!' Young snaps.

'If you don't do it, I'll shoot you!' says the Confederate, aiming his pistol at the captain.

'Shoot and be damned!' shouts the captain, raising his weapon. He squeezes the trigger. Click.

'Goddammit!' Realising his gun is unloaded, he has no option but to surrender, and is taken to the *Shenandoah*, clapped in irons and imprisoned in the topgallant forecastle.[11]

No accounts of this incident identify the Confederate officer involved in the standoff with Captain Young. However, given that this officer threatens to gag the captain unless he cooperates, it's likely to have been William Whittle.

Four hours after being taken prisoner, Young is bundled on board the *Nile*, to be sent to San Francisco. There, he will claim Waddell called him an 'old grey-headed devil' and refused to send him to Honolulu with the other bonded vessel, the *James Murray*, because 'he wasn't fit company for ladies'.

As his ship burns to the waterline and disappears beneath the waves, Captain Young watches his entire life savings go down with it. To rub salt into the wound, the Confederates also relieve him of a library of some 200 books, $120 in cash, a gold watch and even his shirt studs.[12]

Captain Waddell's only comment on the incident is that 'seeing someone on her deck with a gun, an officer was sent to capture her and send her master to the *Shenandoah*. That vessel was the bark *Favorite*, of New Haven, and her master was drunk from too free a use of intoxicating liquor.'[13]

Waddell was wrong about the ship's home port – the *Favorite* was out of Fairhaven, Massachusetts, not New Haven, Connecticut – but he might well have been right about her skipper's level of sobriety.

All the ships are set alight except for the *Milo* and the *James Murray*, which are ransomed. And Waddell sends a message to the widow of the late captain of the *James Murray*, whose body has been pickled in whisky, informing her that she and her children are under the protection of the *Shenandoah*, assuring her no harm will come to her or to the vessel because Southerners do not make war on women and children. Nor, it seems, on pickled skippers.

To support his contention that he is as yet unaware the war is over, Captain Waddell argues that of the 336 crewmen of the captured ships, the nine who enlisted – 'all intelligent soldiers, men who had been taught to respect military authority and who knew how to uses the Enfield rifle' – were not the sort of men who would join a lost cause.

'The enlistment of those men in the Confederate service is evidence that if they had heard any report of the military failure of the South, they considered it so unreliable as not to hinder their seeking service in the *Shenandoah*.'[14]

As the ships burn, he paints a vivid picture: 'An occasional explosion on board some of the burning vessels betrayed the presence of gunpowder or other combustible matter. A liquid flame now and then pursued an inflammable substance which had escaped from the sides to the water, and the horizon was illuminated with a fiery glare presenting a picture of indescribable grandeur, while the water was covered in black smoke mingled with flakes of fire.'[15]

Most of the ships destroyed hail from New Bedford, Massachusetts, known as the whaling capital of the world. New Bedford is also a haven for fugitive slaves, and has been since well before the war. The town has a thriving African-American community, raised the first black regiment of the war, and counts among its favourite sons the abolition movement leader Frederick Douglass, who in 1838, as a runaway slave, found freedom and tolerance there.

For all that, though, whaling is New Bedford's life blood, and when news arrives of the rebel raider's decimation of its fleet, the citizens are aghast.

Not everyone is caught unawares. One prominent New Bedford firm has been tipped off by a New York merchant that the raider is on the prowl, on the proviso that the firm does not warn the fleet. The merchants are hoping the damage done by the *Shenandoah* will inflate the price of whale oil. It does, but not for long.

The whalers of New Bedford have been wary of the *Shenandoah* since January when *The Standard* newspaper reported the raider's arrival in Melbourne. From now on, *The Standard* and other publications will cover the ship's movements – or possible move-ment – almost daily, as the toll of captures and burnings mounts.

On 31 July, *The Standard* reports:

This is a more severe blow than New Bedford has experienced since the British invasion and destruction of the shipping and business part of the town in 1778. It took many years for the place to recover from the effects of that wanton raid, and now, our city being on the decline, this second act of British vandalism is doubly severe.

We may reasonably expect, however, that the present season will see the last of such piratical disasters to the whaling business, and our merchants, by exhibiting a renewed spirit of enterprise, may do much to retrieve the past. Let the full number of vessels be immediately fitted for the fishery, and we may confidently trust that before they arrive on the cruising grounds the pirate will be among the things that were. In consequence of the news, whale oil is going up, and this should be an additional incentive to embark in the business.

Some month ago, a communication was addressed by Messrs. Williams & Haven, of New London, in behalf of the Pacific whaling interests, to the Navy Department, setting forth the danger of the fleet being attacked by the *Shenandoah*, and answer was received that several naval vessels were then in the Pacific Ocean, and others on their way to join the squadron, and no danger need be apprehended. Many war risks have been can-celled by the owners of vessels on this assurance of safety. Still, there is no available force now at hand to cope with the pirate. The present wholesale destruction of vessels will doubtless incite the Government to do as much as to lock the door now that the horse has been stolen, and we have confidence that the Pacific will in a few months swarm with our cruisers and the pirates will either be driven from the seas or run up at the yard-arm.

The total value of the vessels belonging to this port was $237,000, and the total insurance amounts to but $116,425. War policies had been cancelled and ceased by limitation, amounting to about $80,000. The Mutual Marine and Pacific Mutual offices had no war risks on any of the captured vessels.

There is much excitement among our merchants and at the insurance offices, and no more war risks will be taken on vessels cruising in the Pacific and Arctic Oceans until further advices are received.

A dispatch received by Messrs Swift & Allen from Captain Williams, of the barque *Jireh Swift*, dated San Francisco, 20th inst., states that his vessel was burned by the pirate off Cape Thaddens, 22nd June. She had taken four hundred barrels whale oil thus early in the season.

As panic spreads, headlines get bigger and bolder.

'The pirate *Shenandoah*! She steers in the tracks of whalers, terrible havoc expected!' screams New Bedford's *Whalemen's Shipping List and Merchants' Transcript* on 25 July, followed on 1 August by 'Destruction of whaleships by the pirate *Shenandoah*!' then, on 22 August, by 'The late destruction of whalers,' and on 29 August by 'Further destruction of whaleships.'

The New York Times takes up the cry with 'The Pirate *Shenandoah*', on 27 August.

And *The Republican Standard*, of Bridgeport, Connecticut, splashes with 'The pirate *Shenandoah* still at work' and 'Wholesale piracy' in its 31 August edition.

All fanning the flames, it could be said, yet there is genuine cause for alarm. The *Shenandoah* will destroy almost $900,000 worth of whaling ships and cargoes from New Bedford alone, a blow made all the more painful by the fact that most of the damage is done after the war is over.

In the end, of the 46 whalers captured and torched by the *Shenandoah*, the *Alabama* and other Confederate raiders, 25 are out of New Bedford. The damage to the whaling fleet will soar to $2 million, and the world's whaling capital will never recover.

Back in 1861, when the Civil War seemed far away, New Bedford boasted a fleet of some 60 whaling ships, plying their lucrative trade in the Atlantic, the North and South Pacific, the Indian Ocean and Hudson Bay. Typically, a whaler returning with, say, 500 barrels of whale oil and 200 barrels of sperm oil could average more than $100,000 a season.

Then the raiders came. Within a year, several New England whaling ports had closed completely. Boston's whaling fleet was reduced to only five ships, and Salem's to just one. The danger was simply too great, and insurance premiums had skyrocketed. By 1863, the number of barrels of whale oil had dropped by half.

Still, New Bedford whalers continued the hunt. By 1864 they comprised almost two-thirds of the Yankee fleet and were keeping the industry alive – barely.

Not any more. Now that the wolf is on the fold, residents fear their city might soon be yet another abandoned port, like Nantucket. One resident, Leonard Ellis, writes, 'Our idle wharves were fringed with dismantled ships. Cargoes of oil covered with seaweed were stowed in the sheds and along the river front, waiting for a satisfactory market that never came.'[16]

Small wonder, then, that in the port of New Bedford, Massachusetts, the name Waddell would henceforth be a dirty word.

Then again, it cuts both ways. Captain Waddell has a low opinion of whaling skippers. In his experience, 'All the captains and masters were more or less under the influence of liquor, and some of them swore their sympathy for the South, while others spoke incoherently of cruiser fire and insurance. A drunken and brutal class of men, I found the whaling captains and masters of New England.'[17]

As the burning New Bedford fleet lights the sky, a scene of destruction Captain Waddell found so exhilarating, the *Shenandoah* heads northward, into dangerous waters once again, closing up fast with floes and icebergs, until the risk of being trapped in the Arctic Ocean, possibly for months, forces her to turn south. She reaches East Cape and open water just as a vast ice field is closing the strait.

It is perpetual daylight at these latitudes, but as the ship reaches St Lawrence Island, she is sailing blind in a black fog, and runs shuddering and shrieking into a massive ice floe. Blocked in the ice, the *Shenandoah* is in danger.

Sailors scramble to take in all the sail, then use grapnel anchors and lines to swing her away from the ice. After several hours of heaving and hauling, helped along by gentle steaming, the ship inches her way towards open water.

At entry on the ship's log for 1 July reads, 'At 1.30am, entered a field of heavy ice; honed everything back, furled all sail and got up steam; lowered a boat and ran out lines ahead; made fast to large cakes of ice, and commenced hauling through, turning engine over slowly, breasting off with spars; struck large masses of ice several times, but sustained no material injury. At 4.30 got out of ice.'[18]

The raider might be safely out of the ice at last, but it is not out of danger. Waddell is concerned that if enemy squadrons in the Pacific have learnt of the *Shenandoah*'s movements from the ransomed ships, they could easily blockade her and force her into battle. He is determined to avoid a fight, reasoning that even if the *Shenandoah* wins a battle, she would most likely sustain some damage and be forced to put into a port for repairs. He's been there and done that, in Melbourne, and he has no wish to do it again.

'We knew but too well the character of the neutrality of the first naval power of the earth to suppose that any government bordering on the Pacific coast would endanger its existence by receiving a Confederate cruiser for repairs and thus incur the displeasure of the worst government under the sun.'[19]

High-minded sentiments, some might say, from a man who played the British neutrality laws like a fiddle.

Chapter 19

All pirates now

In the scramble to be – or be seen to be – on the winning side, British public opinion turns against the *Shenandoah*. The former Confederate raider is now perceived as a pirate ship and her captain and crew as buccaneers. The press calls on British warships that cross her path to treat her as they would any pirate, and blow her out of the water.

Unbeknown to the men of the *Shenandoah*, their actions having been authorised by a country that no longer exists, the Stainless Banner offers them no more protection than the Jolly Roger.

It has been more than a century since the end of the so-called Golden Age of Piracy, in the Caribbean; the age of Blackbeard and Captain Kidd. And it's a decade since the British Navy all but eradicated piracy from the Atlantic and along the Barbary Coast of North Africa. Nevertheless, fear and loathing of marauding buccaneers are ingrained in the psyche of a maritime nation. For Britons, the pirate remains a bogey – still out there somewhere on the high seas, priming his pistol, honing his cutlass, ready to strike.

The United States Navy, too, has had considerable success in stamping out piracy, particularly on the Barbary Coast, as well as river piracy. In the 1860s, and for many years after the Civil War, Americans in the Northern states will equate piracy with the Confederate raiders. Such is the depth of this enmity that in 1872, when the Captain Kidd of his day – the notorious American pirate and blackbirder Bully Hayes – returns to the United States, he is condemned by *The San Francisco Bulletin* as 'a vile and brutal miscreant who should be hanged on the same gallows with *Alabama* Semmes and *Shenandoah* Waddell'.[1]

In Australia, where Bully Hayes is equally as infamous, and the names Waddell and Semmes as familiar, piracy, in earlier days, mostly meant 'piratical seizure' of ships by escaping convicts. Since the establishment of the first European settlement, in Sydney in 1788, at least one ship a year had been stolen by desperate men and women.

Piratical escapes were most common in Hobart, Tasmania, and Newcastle, north of Sydney. In Newcastle, despite strict regulations on arrivals and departures, and sentries guarding the wharves, convicts successfully made off with vessels ranging from pilot boats to schooners, none of which was ever heard of again.[2]

The last person hanged for piracy in Australia – and possibly in the British Empire – was James Camm, executed in Hobart in 1832 for his part in the seizure of the brig *Cyprus* in Recherche Bay. The previous year, at London's Execution Dock, two of Camm's fellow escapees became the last people in Britain to be sent to the gallows for piracy.

In America, the last person hanged for piracy was Albert Hicks, in 1860. Hicks, a sailor, murdered the skipper and two crew members of the sloop *A.E. Johnston*, while at sea out of

New York, took all the money on board and escaped in a yawl. Convicted of piracy and triple murder, he was hanged on Bedloe's Island – now Liberty Island – in New York Bay, as an estimated 10,000 people watched from boats. It was a gala occasion.

On the morning of 1 July 1865, a motley force of some 300 Confederate soldiers, deserters, misfits and adventurers splash across the Rio Grande into Mexico. Known as the Iron Brigade – a Missouri cavalry division with a reputation for brutality – the exiles are led by General Jo Shelby, who refused to surrender after Appomattox and has fled south of the border rather than live under the Yankee yoke.

The Iron Brigade is leaving one civil war for another. Mexico is occupied by French troops of Napoleon III, with an Austrian puppet emperor, Maximilian, on the throne, at war with the republican forces of Benito Juarez, the unseated president. It is Shelby's intention to offer the services of his brigade to both sides, and accept the best offer.

Privately, he has a grander plan – to take command of the winning army and then the government, and establish a new Confederacy on the ruins of the Mexican Empire.

After planting the Stars and Bars in Mexican soil, the Iron Brigade rides south towards Monterey. A hot reception awaits them.

Ploughing through the North Pacific in fine weather again, and no longer dreading the call of 'Ice ahead!' Captain Waddell hatches his most daring plan. 'It was the 5th of July when the Aleutian Islands were lost to view and the craft made for the parallel where west winds would hasten her over to the coast of California, for I had matured plans for entering the harbour of San Francisco and laying that city under contribution.

'The newspapers which were captured gave intelligence of the disposition of the American naval vessels and I was not unfamiliar with their commanding officers or their sagacity.'[3]

Waddell's plan to capture an entire city seems outrageous yet is achievable. There is only one Yankee warship in the port of San Francisco – an ironclad under the command of Captain Charles McDougal, an old shipmate of Waddell's. They served together on the *Saginaw*, which Waddell dismisses as barely seaworthy, and he remembers McDougal as being 'fond of his ease', and no match for any officer of the *Shenandoah*.

He plans to enter the port at night to ram and board the ironclad, make Captain McDougal and his crew his prisoners, then, come daylight, train all guns on the city. San Francisco would be his without firing a shot or taking a life. It is bold but beautifully simple, and Waddell is sure it could work.

But as the *Shenandoah* nears the California coast, he has second thoughts, reasoning that perhaps it would be wise to check with a ship recently out of San Francisco before steaming into port at full speed ahead with a rebel yell.

At a public meeting in Brisbane, Queensland cotton growers and merchants attempt to drum up support for a petition calling on the colonial government to avert what they insist is an impending disaster. Queensland's fledgling cotton industry, they claim, is at risk of total annihilation as a result of the end of the American war.

Peace, say the cotton producers, is bad for business. The likelihood of renewed competition from America, compounded by the withdrawal of the government subsidy, threatens to decimate the profits of Queensland producers accustomed to being able to charge extravagant prices for their product.

The colony's cotton barons are concerned that even allowing for cotton destroyed during the war, there may well be a considerable stockpile in the South – enough to flood the market and send the price of a bale plummeting. In a twist of logic that suggests the Thirteenth Amendment has no more force in law than, say, a draft business plan, the cotton producers warn that although the North professed to abhor slavery during the war, it will now find that slave-grown cotton makes good commercial sense – too good to resist. Unable to compete, even with a cheap labour force of Kanaka field hands kidnapped by blackbirders, they predict that Queensland's flourishing cotton fields will soon lie abandoned, choked with weeds. The cotton barons call on the colonial government to increase the bounty and postpone its withdrawal for three years. Otherwise, like Hanrahan in John O'Brien's famous poem, they'll 'all be rooned'. They win few hearts and minds, however, by clamouring for protection at the first sign of free competition after years of shamelessly exploiting the cotton famine. They don't get their wish, and, within a few years, a return to the lower, pre-US Civil War prices, helped along by floods and the boll weevil, will send Queensland's King Cotton to his grave.

And in the fields where he reigned supreme for those few short years, the Kanakas who picked the cotton will be slashing sugar cane.

Chapter 20

The darkest day

In America, with the guns of the North and South now silent, the war-weary, reunified nation is looking westward. It's a cultural shift born of Manifest Destiny and nurtured by gold fever. America has discovered the Wild West – an enduring fascination that arguably begins at 6pm on Friday 21 July 1865, in the town square of Springfield, Missouri, scene of the first recorded Western showdown.

On the street, two men face each other. One is former Union soldier, lawman and luckless gambler James Butler Hickok, better known as 'Wild Bill'. The other is Hickok's erstwhile best friend, Davis Tutt. A falling-out over a woman has poisoned their friendship, and so it has come to this – a new kind of gunfight; the first quick-draw duel.

When the opponents are 75 yards (68.5m) apart, Tutt draws first but Hickok draws faster. Tutt misses but Hickok does not. Shot through the heart, Tutt cries out, 'Boys, I'm killed!' then falls to the ground dead. With blood in the dust of a Missouri street, the Civil War is yesterday's news.

A legend in his own lifetime, Wild Bill Hickok will go on to kill 36 men before being shot in the back by Jack McCall, a drunken, down-on-his-luck gold miner, while playing poker in a saloon in Deadwood, Dakota Territory, in 1876.

'A sail!' For the men of the *Shenandoah*, the moment the *Barracouta* hove into view is the stuff of nightmares. An entry in the ship's log for Wednesday 2 August, by Lieutenant Dabney Scales, officer of the watch, reports, 'Having received by the British barque *Barracouta* the sad intelligence of the overthrow of the Confederate Government, all attempts to destroy the shipping or property of the United States will cease from this date, in accordance with which the First Lieutenant Wm. C. Whittle Jnr. received an order from the commander to strike below the battery and disarm the ship and crew.'[1]

It had been shaping up to be a perfect day. The ship was gliding gently along in a light breeze, moving parallel to but a safe distance from the California coast, when at 12.30pm she sighted and gave chase to a barque that turned out to be a British ship, 13 days out of San Francisco, bound for Liverpool. The Confederates boarded the *Barracouta*, and, this time, what they learnt was undeniable.

After checking the ship's papers and satisfying himself that she was British, the boarding office, Sailing Master Irvine Bulloch, asked the captain for news of the war.

'What war?' the captain asked.

'The war between the United States and Confederate States,' Bulloch replied.'

'Why, the war has been over since April,' said the captain.[2]

Recent San Francisco newspapers on board confirm Bulloch's worst fears. All Confederate forces have surrendered, Davis has been captured and the entire government has collapsed. The cause is lost.

He returns to his shipmates with this melancholy news, and with a warning from the *Barracouta*'s captain that Federal cruisers are hunting for them everywhere, intent on hanging them all from the yardarm.

'We knew the intensity of feelings engendered by the war, and particularly in the hearts of our foes towards us,' says Whittle. 'We knew that every effort would be made for our capture, and we felt that if we fell into the enemy's hands we could not hope, fired as their hearts were, for a fair trial or judgement, and the testimony of the whalers, whose property we had destroyed, would all be against us.

'Even during the war we had been opprobriously called pirates, and we felt that if captured we would be summarily dealt with as such.'[3]

Captain Waddell is desolate. 'My life has been checkered from the dawn of my naval career and I had believed myself schooled to every sort of disappointment, but the dreadful issue of that sanguinary struggle was the bitterest blow, because unexpected, I had yet encountered. It cast a gloom over the whole ship and did occupy my thoughts.'[4]

He will later state that had the *Barracouta* been a Yankee vessel, he would have sunk her regardless of the news she carried. His justification is his belief that the Washington Government was disseminating false reports, making it impossible to believe the newspapers. Where and how he learnt this, he doesn't say. Nor does he explain why a San Francisco newspaper on a British ship is believable, while a San Francisco newspaper on an American ship, namely the *Susan Abigail*, was not.

The *Shenandoah*'s First Officer, charged with the task of disarming the ship, declares this day 'the darkest day of my life'. Brooding in his cabin, pouring his despair into his journal, William Whittle writes that the *Barracouta* 'brought us our death knell, a knell worse than death'. He continues:

Our dear country has been overrun; our President captured; our armies and navy surrendered; our people subjugated. Oh, God, aid us to stand up under this, thy visitation.

There is no doubting the truth of this news. We now have no country, no flag, no home. We have lost all but our honour and self-respect, and I hope our trust in God Almighty.

Were men ever so situated? The Captain gave me an order to dismount and strike our battery, turn in all arms except the private arms, and disarm the vessel, as no more depredations, of course, upon the United States shipping will be done. We went sorrowfully to work making preparations but night coming on, we will await tomorrow to finish our work. Hoisted propeller and made all plain sail.

I feel that were it not for my dear ones at home I would rather die than live. Nearly all our work in the Arctic must have been done after this terrible visitation, but God knows we were ignorant.

When I think of my darlings at home, and all my dear ones, my heart bleeds in anguish.[5]

A meeting of officers is called to discuss the best course to pursue, and each man offers an opinion. Some favour sailing to Melbourne; some to Valparaiso; others to New Zealand.

The Captain reminds them it is his responsibility to preserve the honour of his men and of the flag. The right thing to do, he says, is to run for a European port. 'A long gauntlet to run, to be sure, but why not succeed in baffling observation or pursuit? The enemy had gloated over his success and would, like a gorged serpent, lie down to rest.'[6]

Denied the greater glory, Waddell now reaches for a lesser one. He will never surrender to a Yankee; he will outwit and outrun his pursuers, even if it means sailing around the world; he will have his page in history, come hell or high water.

'I felt sure a search would be made for her in the North Pacific and that to run the ship south was important for all concerned,' Waddell writes. 'Some of the people expressed a desire that I should take the *Shenandoah* to Australia or New Zealand or any port rather than attempt to reach Europe.'[7]

The notion of returning to Melbourne is attractive to some, but there is cause to wonder whether Australians would welcome losers as warmly as they had welcomed underdogs. Could the romance be rekindled? They will never know. The Captain's mind is made up. The *Shenandoah* will run for England and surrender at a neutral port. He will pursue no other course; consider no alternative.

The crew are now called to assemble aft. In a brief speech, the Captain gives them the bad news and tells them of his decision to sail to Liverpool. The men give three cheers, all return to their duties, and the ship's prow is pointed to Cape Horn.

According to some sources, the crew petition Waddell to sail for Sydney, which is the nearest British port. He agrees to do so, but after 24 hours heading for Australia changes course for Cape Horn, thence to England. Among his officers, opinion is divided on whether Cape Town or Liverpool is the safest choice, but by most accounts the consensus is to head for Liverpool.

With her guns swung below decks and her ports sealed, the *Shenandoah* is once again a peacetime vessel, not that that would prevent any American man-of-war from cheerfully blowing her out of the water.

At Glasgow Infirmary, in Scotland, English surgeon Joseph Lister, disturbed by the high death rate following surgery, tries a simple but radical new approach. A maverick among his contemporaries, he does not consider unwashed, blood-stained hands a badge of professional pride, and does not accept the prevailing theory that infection is caused by airborne germs and cannot be prevented.

In August, after testing the antiseptic effects of carbolic acid – a derivative of coal tar – on surgical instruments, incisions and dressings, Lister applies a solution of carbolic acid to the leg wound of an 11-year-old boy run over by a cart. The wound does not become infected, and within six weeks the boy's broken bones have mended.

Sadly, the birth of sterile surgery has come too late for the American Civil War wounded. The more than 12,000 surgeons who served in the Union army treated some 400,000 wounded men – more than half of them for gunshot and artillery wounds – and performed more that 40,000 operations. On the Confederate side, far fewer surgeons treated about the same number of men. Injuries to limbs were common, and the only known way to prevent infection was amputation. Still, even for minor injuries, the most common cause of death of wounded soldiers was infection.

An estimated three out of five wounded Union soldiers, and two out of three Confederate casualties, died of infectious diseases. It can only be guessed how many of those deaths might have been prevented by clean hands and a dash of carbolic.

It's not long before the antipathy towards the *Shenandoah* is given a dollar value. On 7 August 1865, owners of the San Francisco whaler *William C. Nye*, captured and destroyed by the Confederates on 26 June, send the British Government a bill for US$280,212.50 – about $4 million in today's money. The itemised account includes $35,000 for the vessel, $20,000 for the boats, whaling guns and other materials, $7,087.50 for the 150 barrels of whale oil aboard, $118,125 for the season's catch that went down with the ship, and $100,000 worth of whalebone.

The first of many such accounts to be presented, its authors see it as a legitimate claim against Britain and, by association, its Victorian colony for flouting international neutrality laws, but it is also motivated by a seething resentment of the British Empire's unofficial yet transparently obvious support for the Confederacy. That support, whether real or imaginary, has reopened old wounds from the War of Independence; the ill feeling is apparent in repeated descriptions of the *Shenandoah* in the American press as the 'English pirate'.

In Dayton, Ohio, on 7 August – the same day Britain is slapped with the first *Shenandoah* bill – former slave Jourdan Anderson dictates a letter to his old master, Colonel Patrick Henry Anderson.

The colonel – with his cotton plantation now struggling to

survive in the post-war South – has written to Jourdan begging him to return to the plantation at Big Spring, Tennessee, to work for him as a free man. Jourdan had escaped with his wife Mandy and their three children in 1864, when Union soldiers raided the plantation.

This is part of Jourdan's reply:

Sir, I got your letter and was glad to find that you had not forgotten Jourdon, and that you wanted me to come back and live with you again, promising to do better for me than anybody else can.

I have often felt uneasy about you. I thought the Yankees would have hung you long before this, for harboring Rebs they found at your house. I suppose they never heard about your going to Colonel Martin's to kill the Union soldier that was left by his company in their stable.

Although you shot at me twice before I left you, I did not want to hear of your being hurt, and am glad you are still living . . .

I want to know particularly what the good chance is you propose to give me. I am doing tolerably well here. I get $25 a month, with victuals and clothing; have a comfortable home for Mandy – the folks call her Mrs. Anderson – and the children – Milly, Jane, and Grundy – go to school and are learning well. The teacher says Grundy has a head for a preacher. They go to Sunday school, and Mandy and me attend church regularly.

We are kindly treated. Sometimes we overhear others saying, 'Them colored people were slaves' down in Tennessee. The children feel hurt when they hear such remarks, but I tell them it was no disgrace in Tennessee to belong to Colonel Anderson. Many darkeys would have been proud, as I used to be, to call you master. Now if you will write and say what wages you will give me, I will be better able to decide whether it would be to my advantage to move back again . . .

Mandy says she would be afraid to go back without some proof that you were disposed to treat us justly and kindly; and we have concluded to test your sincerity by asking you to send us our wages for the time we served you. This will make us forget and forgive old scores, and rely on your justice and friendship in the future. I served you faithfully for 32 years, and Mandy 20 years. At $25 a month for me, and $2 a week for Mandy, our earnings would amount to $11,680 . . .

If you fail to pay us for faithful labors in the past, we can have little faith in your promises in the future. We trust the good Maker has opened your eyes to the wrongs which you and your fathers have done to me and my fathers, in making us toil for you for generations without recompense . . .

In answering this letter, please state if there would be any safety for my Milly and Jane, who are now grown up, and both good-looking girls. You know how it was with poor Matilda and Catherine. I would rather stay here and starve – and die, if it come to that – than have my girls brought to shame by the violence and wickedness of their young masters. You will also please state if there has been any schools opened for the colored children in your neighborhood. The great desire of my life now is to give my children an education, and have them form virtuous habits.

Say howdy to George Carter, and thank him for taking the pistol from you when you were shooting at me.
From your old servant,
Jourdon Anderson[8]

It's not known if the colonel ever wrote back, but it's safe to assume he did not, and that Jourdan and Mandy Anderson never got the wages owed them for their years in bondage. They never returned to Big Spring plantation; they lived long and useful lives in Ohio, and raised 11 children.

That same week, in Australia, Melbourne's *Argus* publishes an editorial Colonel Anderson would surely have endorsed, but would have left Jourdan Anderson sadly shaking his head:

It is evident that emancipating the slave is not so simple a measure as Mr Lincoln expected. The sudden gift of freedom to four millions of half-civilised men, who understand nothing of the principle involved in it, entails responsibilities that are not readily discharged.

What is to become of them? Socially, the Negro will never be amalgamated with the white population. To all intents and purposes he is an inferior being, whose very conditions of existence imply the absence and the impossibility of an equal human status. In the face of all this, he is not only made socially free, but he clamours to be made politically enfranchised.

Virtually, it means nothing less than the subjection of the whites to the dominion of the blacks, a contrast so violent that it would be comic if its consequences were not so terrible. Of course, it is not apprehended that the whites will become the hewers of wood and drawers of water for their former bonds-men, but it is pretty certain the black will not readily work for the white. Liberty, to him, is personal liberty, the liberty to do nothing, to indulge in his natural propensities of sloth, to get his salt pork and rum at other people's expense, and practise polyg-amy and Obeah without interruption from his more fastidious fellow men – this is what emancipation conveys to his mind, and he will not be long in discovering that, whatever else may be the advantages of the franchise, it has this special attraction for him – that it spares him the necessity of working.[9]

In Montevideo harbour to take on supplies, Captain Christopher Rogers of USS *Iroquois* learns that the *Shenandoah* is within strik-ing distance. Without waiting to finish loading, Rogers weighs anchor and steams off in pursuit. The *Shenandoah*, although faster than the *Iroquois*, would be no match for its 50-pounder gun and four 32-pounders. Rogers hunts the *Shenandoah* through the Mediterranean, around South America and across the Pacific to Singapore, but always misses her by a few weeks.

When the *Iroquois* gives up the chase and returns to America, the pursuit is taken up by the US Navy's Pacific Squadron, under Rear Admiral George Pearson. The squadron, formed to protect the Arctic whaling fleet from Confederate raiders, is under orders to track down and destroy the *Shenandoah* at any cost, but none of Pearson's six sloops-of-war ever catch a glimpse of her.

Chapter 21

Oh, Pattie!

William Whittle is wallowing in sorrow. 'When I think that all our privations, trials, loss of life and blood since the war have such an end, I scarce know what to think or do. We are certainly a pitiable people. To think of our poor country being overrun, and of our people subjugated, conquered and reduced to a state of slavery, which is worse than death.'[1] Slavery is only a fate worse than death for white people, presumably.

With his misery matched by rain and squalls, Whittle has taken to continuously rereading his letters from his beloved Pattie, and pleading with the Almighty.

'To know how I feel would give anyone the blues. How my position is altered: no country; no home; no profession, and alas, to think the fondest wish of my heart, i.e., to marry, must be abandoned. Oh my darling Pattie, how can I give thee up? God grant me support!'[2]

The Confederates have no way of knowing for sure, although they might easily have guessed, that one of the ships they bonded rather than burned had by now alerted Washington of their movements. The realisation is dawning that, to avoid capture, the *Shenandoah* will have to sail around the world without touching land, while being hunted all the way.

From the outset, they frequently sight ships, and will continue to do so. Some ships that spot them send up signals, but the *Shenandoah* does not reply. She is a ghost ship now, or desires to be. All on board are counting the closing miles and are fixed on the same objective – getting to the other side of the world as soon as possible; and arriving there safe and sound.

Setting course for her final destination, the ship is continually under sail because she has only seven days' supply of coal, which is kept in reserve for when steam will be most needed, such as when rounding the Horn.

Once Confederates, they are wanderers now, cast upon the seas of a world that changed without them noticing, and has turned against them.

McNulty laments that they can't even expect to make money from the venture, 'which usually follows successful privateering'. Still, unlike the inconsolable first officer, he's philosophical about the way things have turned out:

We had sailed against the flag of the United States, not to plunder its citizens but to destroy its commerce. We were imbued with no grasping thoughts of wealth. The success of our cause was what we had sailed for, and now that we had no cause we were poor indeed.

What we had done was all under the open mandate of honourable warfare, recognised as such by the oldest and most powerful of the maritime and naval nations, when she declared we were belligerents, thus recognising that the flag we bore was a national flag.

But, on the other hand, we knew the United States had never recognised the Southern States to be in secession, and, inasmuch as we were unsuccessful, we could hardly know what to expect. But the vastness of the movement, greater in extent and completion than anything in history, embodying within itself millions of men who had sprung full armed and as in one step to war, was beyond the pale of international or of national precedent.[3]

After passing east of Cape Horn on 16 September, the mood on the *Shenandoah* is made gloomier still by howling gales, looming icebergs and cold, moonless nights. Waddell recalls, 'The struggles of our ship were but typical of the struggles that filled our breasts upon learning that we were alone on that friendless deep without a home or country, our little crew all that were left of the thousands who had sworn to defend that country or die with her, and there were moments when we would have deemed that a friendly gale which would have buried our sorrowful hearts and the beautiful *Shenandoah* in those dark waters.'[4]

He fancies that the ship shares their despair, and no longer moves as swiftly as she used to.

Again, he is requested to put in to Cape Town, and again he refuses, keeping well to the east and keeping a polite distance from any sail to avoid being recognised.

'Bloody Bill' Anderson will once again live up to his nickname today. It is nine o'clock on the morning of Wednesday 27 September, as he and his band of Missouri guerrillas, disguised in Yankee uniforms, ride into Centralia, Missouri, to cut the railroad.

William T. Anderson, a sadist, killer and rapist, leads about 80 irregulars who target Union soldiers and loyalists in Missouri and neighbouring states, and are notorious for their brutality. While Bloody Bill claims to fight for the Confederacy, he once told Charles Strieby, a neighbour he was trying to recruit, 'I don't care any more than you for the South, Strieby, but there is a lot of money in this [bushwacking] business.'[5]

On 21 August 1863, guerrilla bands led by Anderson, George Todd and William Quantrill descended on the town of Lawrence, Kansas, where they murdered more than 150 unarmed men and boys. It was the bloodiest civilian massacre of the war.

The New York Times declared, 'Missouri is today more dangerously disturbed, if not more dangerously disloyal, than Mississippi. More contempt for the army and for the government is daily poured forth there – more turbulence in talk and in action is indulged in – and human life is less safe than anywhere else within all the military lines of the United States. In this latter respect, the condition of Missouri is fearful. Not a day passes that does not chronicle house-burnings and murders.'[6]

In Centralia, Bloody Bill and his band terrorise the townsfolk and loot the town before blocking the rail line.

An approaching train, spotting the blocked line, slams on the brakes, but by the time the engineer realises the men in blue uniforms are not Union troops it's too late, and the guerrillas have boarded. The train's 125 passengers include 23 Union soldiers headed home on leave. At gunpoint, Anderson orders the soldiers to strip off their uniforms, after which, he and his men casually gun down the unarmed soldiers, then mutilate the bodies. They set fire to the train and the rail depot, then ride away.

That afternoon, a troop of Union mounted infantry led by Major Andrew Verne Emen Johnston – known to his men as 'Ave' Johnston – rides into Centralia. Told of the murders, Johnston sets off in pursuit of Bloody Bill. He soon catches up with the guerrilla band, and orders his men to dismount and form a battle line. The 155 Union troops outnumber Anderson's men, but their muzzle-loading rifles are no match for pistols when the mounted guerrillas charge their line. The bluecoats' first volley kills several of the guerrillas but they are quickly overrun and, in the end, 123 Union soldiers lie dead, Ave Johnston among them.

History will call this atrocity the Centralia Massacre. History will also take note of the young guerrilla who shot and killed Ave Johnston. His name is Jesse James.

It's October now, and although the *Shenandoah* is clipping along nicely in fine weather and feeling the first welcome lifts of the south-east trade winds, the first officer's cabin still contains a broken-hearted rebel and a shrine to the girl he left behind.

'I spent most of the day in my rooms, reading the Services for the day and reading the letters of my darling Pattie,' Whittle writes. 'Oh, how awful it is that there seems to be no prospect of my ever being able to ask her to be mine. When I asked before I had a profession to support us, but how changed! I have lost all and have to commence again, with a dark future. Oh, how I love that girl! Oh, how sad and heartbreaking to give up hope of her being mine.'[7]

Whittle is also haunted by fears that the damned Yankees have murdered his silver-haired father, a commodore in the Confederate Navy, as well as his sisters and brothers. Why he might imagine such a thing, he doesn't say, and in time he'll find his fears were unfounded.

Whittle's diary entry for Sunday 8 October, reveals the depth of his self-pity: 'One year ago today, I sailed in this ship from London. It has been a year of constant anxiety and Labour from then till now. And to have such a sad, inglorious, pitiable and miserable end is truly heartbreaking.'[8]

Whittle's low spirits appear to have become widespread. Even though, with the trade winds now in her favour, the ship is making more than 200 miles (320km) a day, below decks dissent is festering. The mildest slight, the smallest grievance, becomes a cause for open hostility. Stripped of their identity and purpose, the officers have lost their old camaraderie, which has given way to petty spite, malicious rumour and suspicion. Relations are so toxic that when the Captain sends champagne to the wardroom when the ship recrosses her outbound route, three of the officers walk out.

Master's Mate Cornelius Hunt is accused – behind his back – of having a secret stash of several hundred dollars taken from a Yankee whaler, and fingers are pointed in all directions when sailmaker Henry Alcott reports that someone has forced open his sea chest and stolen his opera glasses.

Lieutenant Whittle, whose dismay at such ructions distracts him from pining for Pattie, tells us, 'I determined to have a search as this is one of very many instances of theft. I had the berth deck cleaned and overhauled each bag, but did not find the thief.'[9]

It has to be supposed that the ugliness that's infected the wardroom has found its way to the topgallant forecastle. The crew could hardly fail to notice the conflicts among their officers, and it doesn't help that the ship hasn't been resupplied for more than five months, and food and water are running low.

While it's likely there have been lapses in discipline among the crew as a result of the officers' distractions, there's no record of Lieutenant Whittle tricing anyone up during the remainder of the voyage. Perhaps, amid mutinous rumblings, he didn't dare, or maybe he simply couldn't be bothered any more.

The collapse of morale even shows in the *Shenandoah* herself. Above and below decks she's looking increasingly dirty, disordered, unloved. Just when it seems the melancholy ship can't get any more miserable, as she crosses the equator, scurvy breaks out among the crew. Unfortunately, Assistant Surgeon Fred McNulty, whose affection for the bottle has grown more and more fervent in recent weeks, can no longer perform his medical duties. When he's not abusing someone or trying to pick a fight, he's stumbling about like a drunken sailor (because that's what he is) or sitting slumped in a stupor.

On Tuesday 10 October, Lieutenant Whittle is informed that McNulty is on a wild binge. He finds him in a drunken rage, abusing Captain's Clerk (and Melbourne recruit) John Blacker. Whittle offers to help McNulty to his cabin, whereupon McNulty pulls a gun on him and threatens to shoot him. Whittle snatches the gun away and reports the incident to the Captain, who orders McNulty confined to his quarters.

The next day, as the ship enters the North Atlantic, Waddell tells Whittle to cancel McNulty's confinement if he is sober. Whittle does so.

The matter doesn't end there. Lieutenant Whittle is summoned by the Captain, who has just had a conversation with Fred McNulty. It seems the Assistant Surgeon told the Captain he had not been drunk; that his harsh language to John Blacker was a response to Blacker using insulting language about the Captain;

and that he had not threatened Whittle with a pistol but had merely intended to show it to him.

'I at once sent for two officers who sustained me in saying that he was drunk,' Whittle writes. 'I learned from two sources that the quarrel between himself and Mr Blacker originated in his own abusive language and that Mr Blacker said nothing of the Captain, and taking everything in connection I conclude that he tried to make it appear to the Captain: first, that he was a partisan of his; and second, that my report about his being drunk and drawing the pistol was an act of cruelty on my part. I made up my mind that my report should not be so treated or considered, for his every ground was false.'[10]

With Lieutenant Scales as a witness, Whittle confronts McNulty, who denies he was drunk, but in the next breath admits that he was. Whittle then asks him why he didn't tell Captain Waddell the truth, to which he replies, 'Well, didn't I?'

'No!'

McNulty repeats the claim he made to the Captain that he was not brandishing the pistol in a threatening manner. When Whittle refutes this, he says, 'Well Sir, when we get onshore there is a way to settle things.'[11]

The next day, McNulty sends Whittle a note formally challenging him to a duel: 'Sir, I demand an explanation and withdrawal of the language you applied to me in the presence of Lieutenant Scales last evening. Should the demand appear extravagant, such other satisfaction as is looked for between gentlemen is expected at your earliest convenience.'[12]

The formal challenge is delivered by McNulty's second, Sidney Smith Lee, who Whittle considers 'the only man in the mess with whom I am not on good terms'.[13]

Whittle's note in reply declares, 'Under the circumstances I have to accede to your demand for such satisfaction as you desire. As the ship is not a place where such a thing can be settled, as soon as we get on shore, full satisfaction will be given you.'[14]

In the United States Navy, the rules of duelling were included in the midshipman's handbook until duelling by officers was banned in 1862. Southerners, however, still hold to *The Code of Honour: Rules for the Government of Principals and Seconds in Duelling*, set down in 1838 by John Lyde Wilson, a former governor of South Carolina.

The Code of Honour is similar to the 1777 Irish *Code Duello*, accepted world-wide as the official rule book, but also allows a challenger to post a public notice to disgrace a man who refuses to fight.

The Code Duello prescribes what is an acceptable form of apology on the part of the person challenged in order to avoid a duel without dishonour; the correct etiquette for delivering a challenge – never at night, rather with a cooler head next morning; the proper procedure for duelling with pistols and with swords; and the types of wounds acceptable for honour to be satisfied. Although the object is not to kill but to satisfy honour, deaths are not uncommon.

If Whittle and McNulty ever met on the field of honour, we'll never know. Whittle's journal and his later writings make no mention of it, so either the duel never happened or William Whittle won.

On Monday morning, the general seemed to have rallied a little. Doctor Madison tried to cheer him, saying he should hurry up and get well because Traveller had been in the stable a long time now and needed exercise. That afternoon, though, he took a turn for the worse. He didn't seem to notice his family gathered around his bed, and called out, 'Tell Hill he must come up!'

Last night, while he slept, a fire was lit in the hearth and Colonel Johnston sat by him in the dark.

This morning, those with him clearly heard him say, 'Strike the tent!'

Those were the last words he would ever speak. At 9.30am on Wednesday 12 October 1870, Robert E. Lee died.[15]

The Royal Navy announces that it will soon be equipped with a weapon of mass destruction – the self-propelled torpedo. Invented by a Royal Navy engineering officer, the torpedo contains a charge of up to 10,000 pounds (4535kg) of gunpowder, and travels 20 feet (6m) below the surface at a speed of 600 feet (180m) a second, with a range of up to 1800 yards (1645m). The weapon's means of propulsion and other details are being kept secret as yet.

'The greatest advantage of this invention,' says Sydney's *Empire*, 'is that it can be as effectively used by the slowest or by the fastest vessels, and even by fixed forts and batteries facing the sea.

'The great objection to this invention is that it is absolutely and irresistibly destructive, so that the combined fleets of the whole world could be destroyed in an hour.'[16]

On the 'birthday of the *Shenandoah*' – the anniversary of when, on 14 October 1864, the *Sea King* met the *Laurel* at Madeira and the last Confederate raider was born, William Whittle writes:

Since this day 12 months ago, how many changes have we gone through. Then we were all rejoiced at and proud of having an opportunity of serving our country; alas, how changed; now, we are plunged into the most heart-breaking despair of having no country to serve.

Oh, God! Give us strength and faith to resign ourselves to thy will. To me, the day is more dead in as much as it is the birthday of the dearest being on earth to me. This day 22 years ago my darling Pattie was born.

Most solemnly do I invoke God's blessing upon her. Oh God, guard, rule and lead her I humbly pray, and grant that I may yet be able to call her mine own. It is the fondest wish of my heart, next to seeing my country free. Are not both hoping without hope? It would appear so, but the same hand which afflicts can bless and aid. At dinner today, I filled my glass with port wine and silently drank her health.[17]

Getting good or bad news from A to B in 1866 is a matter of patience, hope and luck. Mail delivered by steamship across the Atlantic between, say, Liverpool and San Francisco takes about 10 days. Mail between San Francisco and Sydney takes about the same, while mail between Britain and Australia can take from 60 to 70 days, depending on the weather and the route taken. The telegraph has brought instant communication wherever a wire can be strung between two places, but there will be no trans-atlantic telegraph cable until 1866, no cable connecting Australia to the rest of the world until 1872, and no ship-to-shore radio until 1907.

And yet, in the Blue Ridge Mountains of Virginia, a man is flying a kite on a copper wire, Benjamin Franklin-style, from a mountain top. It is October 1865, and the man is Mahlon Loomis, a Washington DC dentist who, like Ben Franklin before him, is fascinated by the natural wonder of electricity.

Loomis has come to the Blue Ridge for a bold experiment. He believes the earth is surrounded by an electromagnetic field he calls the 'electric sea', and that the power of that force can be used to send a signal from one place to another without the need for wires. Loomis called his discovery the 'aerial telegraph'. Later, others will call it wireless telegraphy or radio. No-one has tried this before. It is 30 years before the invention of radio will be credited to the Italian inventor Guglielmo Marconi.

To test his theory, Loomis has an associate fly a second kite from a mountain top 14 miles (22.5km) away. The wire from one kite is attached to the ground through a telegraph key. The other kite's wire is grounded through a galvanometer to measure electrical current. With the kites acting as antennae, Loomis taps the telegraph key. The galvanometer registers a response. It works!

Loomis is convinced that his invention could revolutionise communications by 'causing electric vibrations or waves to pass around the world, as upon the surface of some quiet lake one wave circlet follows another from the point of the disturbance to the remotest shores, so that from any mountain top upon the globe another conductor, which shall pierce this plane and receive the impressed vibration, may be connected to an indicator which will mark the length and duration of the vibration; and indicate by any agreed system of notation, convertible into human language, the message of the operator at the point of the first disturbance.'[18]

Mahlon Loomis's discovery could have changed the world as early as 1865, including the ways the world waged war or attempted to avoid it. But, like many people ahead of their time, he was ignored, dismissed as a crank, decried as a fraud. Later duplications of his experiments would prove that he did indeed transmit radio signals as he had claimed, but it was all too late for this pioneer. He died in 1886, a broken man, poor, unsung and all but forgotten.

Consider how different this story might have been if the world had listened to the inventive dentist. James Bulloch could have let Captain Waddell know the war was over, and Pattie could have told William Whittle that, pirate or not, she'd still marry him.

Chapter 22

'All hands to bury the dead'

'I give our noble old vessel about 15 more days to land us safely in some English port,' writes William Whittle on Sunday 22 October, 'after having borne us over upwards of 50,000 miles of water on the most wonderful and eventful cruises ever made. What will become of us after we get there, God alone can tell. For myself, I have little or no faith in the existence of honour among nations when that honourable course may clash with interest.

'Oh God, never were any men in such a terrible situation of suspense and misery![1]

The *Shenandoah*'s executive officer is still in the doldrums, but at least he makes no mention of Pattie.

During the day, they pass several ships heading south, and, as is now the standard practice, avoid contact with them. That night, they cross the Tropic of Cancer into the North Temperate Zone, and the sun obliges by dropping the temperature to a bracing 59 degrees Fahrenheit (15°C).

It has now been 112 days since the men of the *Shenandoah* last sighted land, and 195 days since last they stepped ashore.

On 25 October, 500 miles (805km) south-east of the Azores, comes a cry from the masthead that had once brought a rush of joy but now brings a feeling of dread. 'Sail ho!'

On the horizon, from the look of her masts and sails, she's most likely a steamer. That means she could be a Federal cruiser, and, what's worse, she has clearly spotted the *Shenandoah*.

Changing course would be a dead giveaway, so the crew try to slow the *Shenandoah* down by lowering the propeller and throwing out a drag, hoping to put more distance between her and the mystery ship. It doesn't work.

This could be the end for the last Confederate raider, yet, as the sun sets, her master is moved to quote Byron:

> *Slow sinks, more lovely ere his race be run,*
> *Along Morea's hills the setting sun;*
> *Not, as in northern climes, obscurely bright,*
> *But one unclouded blaze of living light,*
> *O'er the hush'd deep the yellow beam he throws.*[2]

After nightfall, Waddell sends a lookout to the masthead. The news is not good. The ship is a man-of-war for sure, and she's no more than three miles (4.8km) away. There's nothing for it now but to put up steam and turn south under cover of darkness.

It's a risky manoeuvre but it works. By 9pm, when the moon rises, their nemesis is nowhere to be seen. She was the US warship *Saranac*, and she had just missed the last chance to capture the notorious pirate ship *Shenandoah*.

Two of the *Shenandoah*'s crew are desperately ill. Seaman William Bill, a Hawaiian also known as Bill Sailor, is dying of syphilis, his body covered in ulcers. Marine Sergeant George Canning, who joined in Melbourne, is bedridden, suffering from what he claims to be a festering gunshot wound to the lung, received at the Battle of Shiloh while aide-de-camp to Confederate General Leonidas Polk.

Several weeks earlier, Canning told Midshipman John Mason that he had a wife in Paris, somewhere in the Saint-Germain district. He asked Mason if he would be kind enough send her his belongings if he died. Mason agreed, and Canning told him he would write down the address. He never did.

William Bill passes away peacefully in his hammock on Thursday 26 October, and his body is prepared for burial at sea first thing next morning. This is not indecent haste. Superstitious sea dogs fear that if a dead sailor is left on board too long, his ghost can conjure a storm.

On Friday morning, the entire ship's company, apart from the moribund Sergeant Canning, assemble on the poop deck at the call, 'All hands to bury the dead!' William Bill's body, sewn into a canvas shroud made from his own hammock – with the last stitch through the nose, to make sure he's dead – and draped in a Confederate flag, is placed on a plank.

The Captain reads from the Bible, 'I am the resurrection and the life. He that believeth in me, though he were dead, yet shall he live.'[3] Then, 'We commit the body of our brother William to the deep.' At that, the marines fire a volley, the plank is lifted and the corpse slides over the rail and into the sea.

Four days later, Canning dies and is dropped over the side with all due ceremony. The cause of death is listed as 'phthisis', a now archaic term for tuberculosis of the lung, which is probably closer to the truth than Canning's claimed war wound.

Whittle describes Canning's burial as 'an affecting sight',[4] a charitable comment given Whittle's apparent disgust at Canning's abusive treatment of Edward Weeks, his black servant. To his last breath, Canning did nothing but curse and deride Weeks, who nonetheless continued to care for the dying man. Surgeon Lining, too, found the late unlamented sergeant a contemptible character who thought only of himself.

It might seem ironic that these Southerners – committed as they are to the preservation of slavery – should be repulsed by the ill-treatment of a man they consider a racial inferior. It is a hallmark of their code, however, that in dealings with persons of any class, creed or colour, propriety overrides all other considerations. In other words, they simply can't abide bad manners.

If there is irony here, it is that Melbourne recruit George Botriune Canning, a man who mythologised himself, has unwitting made history by firing the last shot of the war, and as the last man to die in the service of the Confederacy.

There is an intriguing postscript to Canning's story. Descendants have claimed that family research reveals he did not die aboard the *Shenandoah* but was allowed to secretly leave the ship, shortly before she arrived in Liverpool, so that could spend his last days with his family in France. It's believed that despite his terminal illness he somehow found his way to a nephew's home in Nanterre, where he lingered for several months, died and was buried there, or perhaps in Paris.

It's assumed that the several accounts of his death and burial at sea were part of an organised cover-up. It is difficult to accept, though, that on humanitarian grounds, officers of the *Shenandoah* would conspire to fake the death of a man they despised.

Chapter 23

Liverpool and limbo

Under sail, 500 miles (805km) south-east of the Azores, the *Shenandoah* turned her head north, and, pushed along by a strong south-westerly, is now within 700 miles (1,125km) of Liverpool.

As the wind drops and the seas calm, 11 sails are sighted, and the Confederates count themselves lucky they're not under steam.

Captain Waddell explains why. 'The ship continued under sail during the daylight, because if we had gotten up steam it would have been observed, and as each sail was ignorant of the character of the other, it would have directed attention to the steamer, and one of them might have been a Federal cruiser.

'As soon as night received us in her friendly folds, steam was applied and we were off for St. George's Channel.'[1]

The closer they get to their destination, the stronger grows Lieutenant Whittle's feeling of dread. 'Somehow or other I look forward to our safe arrival in an English port with very little hope,' he writes. 'I feel some way or other as though some great calamity was hanging over me. Why, I can't divine – or what

I can't imagine, as it really seems to me that our cup of grief is already full. I trust that I am only gloomy without cause, God grant it.'[2]

About 300 miles (480km) from Cape Clear Island, off the southernmost tip of Ireland, Paymaster Breedlove Smith begins the unenviable task of paying the officers and crew. The total amount required to pay each man his due is $30,000, but there is only a measly $4,000 in the kitty. Per man, that's only about $1 for each $7 owed.

Later, Captain Waddell who, with Lieutenant Whittle, oversees the procedure, will offer one version of the settling of accounts. Master's Mate Cornelius Hunt will offer a radically different version.

On the evening of Friday 3 November, the Confederates sight the Irish coast, their first landfall since the Aleutian Islands, 122 days and 23,000 miles (37,000km) ago.

Late at night on Guy Fawkes Day, Sunday 5 November 1865, the *Shenandoah* steams by the beacon in St George's Channel, bound for the Mersey and the Liverpool docks. The beacon is a welcome light but a lonely one on this Guy Fawkes Day – there are no celebratory fireworks for the raider's return.

Here is Fred McNulty's melodramatic account of the raider's return:

> Up from the water rose the Welsh hills. Distance lending her charm to her purpling heather, smoothed down their rough exterior as they rose from the water, bright in the autumn sunlight. Now the clear headlands of the Anglesey, rising high out of St George's Channel, stood more near, and a pilot swept alongside.

He asked us to show our flag. We say we have no flag. Then answers the servant of the nations, 'I cannot go on board your ship.' A hurried consultation – an anxious exchange of inquiring looks – what shall we do now – we have but one flag – shall we raise it? It was the flag to which we had sworn allegiance. Shall we lift it once more to the breeze, in defiance of the world – if needs be – and, defying all, be constant to that cause which we had sworn to maintain until we knew there was no Confederacy, and that ours, in truth, was a lost cause?

'We will!' say all hearts with one acclaim. 'And let this pilot, or any other, refuse to recognise us if they will.'

Then, for the last time, was brought up from its treasured place below, the sacred banner of the fair South, to wave its last defiant wave, and flap its last ensanguined flap against the winds of fate, before going forever upon the page of history. Out upon the free day it flashed, and the far shores of England seemed to answer its brave appeal – that the banner that had led a million men to many victorious battles should now have one more and final recognition, should once more be recognised a flag among the flags of nations.

The grim old sea dog, tossing his boat at stern, beholds go up the outlawed banner! He sees it floating in the wild, free air, and anticipates his England's decision that it shall be recognised for this one last time. He calls for a line, swings himself over the old war-ship's side, and up the noble Mersey, 13 months after the departure from the Thames, and just six months, lacking four day, after the war ended, sailed the Confederate ship-of-war *Shenandoah*.[3]

In stark contrast, Waddell's typically unembellished recollection of the event is that the pilot comes aboard at around midnight, and when told the vessel is the *Shenandoah*, exclaims, 'I was reading a few days ago of your being in the Arctic Ocean!'[4]

Waddell asks the pilot for news from America, and the answer confirms what he was told on the *Barracouta*.

Come morning, the *Shenandoah* steams up the River Mersey in a heavy fog. The pilot's orders are to anchor her beside the British warship *Donegal*, and, as soon as she drops anchor, a lieutenant from the *Donegal* comes aboard and officially informs the Captain and his officers that the war is over.

Shortly afterwards, Captain James Paynter of the *Donegal* comes aboard and tells Waddell he will telegraph the Foreign Secretary, Earl Russell, for instructions. Under Paynter's orders, the gunboat *Goshawk* is lashed alongside, and her master, Lieutenant Alfred Cheek, along with customs officers and an escort of marines, take possession of the ship.

Lieutenant Cheek has been given orders that all on board are to remain on the vessel. When told that some men have already gone ashore, the commander is unfazed. He turns to Captain Waddell and says with a smile, 'Oh, you won't leave the vessel, I know, so it doesn't matter about the lads going on a bit of a lark.'[5]

A waiting game begins. The crew, some of them again showing signs of scurvy, are anxious to get ashore after nine months at sea, and within a few days several have deserted and there are dark mutterings among the rest.

Should they sit around waiting to be arrested and hanged as pirates? Should they jump ship and take their chances? Or should they seize the ship, sail off and hoist the Jolly Roger? If pirates they're called, then pirates they'll be!

For 13 months after leaving England as the *Sea King*, the *Shenandoah* had evaded pursuit, captured 38 vessels valued at

$4,172,233, destroyed 32 and bonded six, fired the last gun in the name of the Confederacy, and circumnavigated the globe, a distance of some 60,000 miles (96,500km), crossing every ocean except the Antarctic.

Captain Waddell would later boast, 'I claim for her officers and men a triumph over their enemies and over every obstacle, and for myself I claim having done my duty.'[6]

To the men of the *Shenandoah*, those are achievements to be proud of, and yet, here, rocking gently at anchor in the Mersey, about to surrender their ship to the British, it's as if it had all been for nothing.

At 10am, 6 November 1865, the last Confederate flag is hauled down. Cornelius Hunt turns away. He cannot bear to watch. William Whittle, tears streaming down his face, does the same.

They would get no sympathy from Sydney's *Empire* newspaper. Unaware that the Confederate cruiser's raiding days are over, the edition of 7 November fulminates:

From California we learn what the *Shenandoah* steamer has been about since Captain Waddell was lionised in Melbourne, and a display of indignation was got up by sympathisers with the Slave Confederacy and admirers of flash ruffianism against the Executive of Victoria for venturing to hint to the pirates that British law and international rights must be respected in Port Phillip.

With the instinct of a cowardly robber, albeit to the dazzled eyes of his Australian admirers he presented the aspect of a hero, the commander of this steamer made for the whaling grounds of the Bering Straits where he might be sure he would meet plenty of valuable property and no armed vessel.

The infamy attached to the crimes of the *Shenandoah* is

reflected on those in Britain and Australia who gave their coun-
tenance to the evil designs of her commander. And, as it is said,
the harbourers of some of the bushrangers were greatly relieved
when the fatal and just bullets laid the robbers low in death,
those whom false sentiment or thoughtlessness has betrayed into
sympathy with the criminal career of Captain Waddell and his
associates, may well desire the tidings that will assure them of the
destruction of the *Shenandoah*.[7]

Where once flew the Stainless Banner, up goes Old Glory. It is
Saturday 11 November 1865, and Captain Thomas Freeman
of the US Navy has come aboard to take possession of the
Shenandoah. She is now proclaimed a United States man-of-war,
and Freeman's orders are to take her to New York.

Noting her neglected condition – a sure sign of low morale –
Captain Freeman orders the vessel scrubbed throughout with
chloride of lime before sailing.

An inspection of the ship provides a detailed inventory of the
spoils of war. Besides the armaments, the list includes 51 chronometers, 23 sextants, three compasses, seven marine clocks, two
barometers, about 70 books, a sabre, a double-barrelled shotgun,
a rifle, a blunderbuss, navigational charts, a stuffed sofa, a divan,
tables and chairs, three tons of powder, 1,500 pounds of tobacco,
250 pounds of tea, containers of sperm oil, six casts of spirits, stores
of salt beef and pork, a large number of flags of different nations,
and, in the safe, a bag containing $828.38 in gold and silver coins.

Across the Atlantic, on the evening of 15 November, the *Nile*
docks in the port of San Francisco. Aboard are the officers and

crew of 11 other ships that had fallen prey to the *Shenandoah* in the Arctic on 28 June.

The master of the *Nile*, Captain Fish, tells the waiting press that all the vessels were looted and burnt except for his ship and the *James Murray*, both of which were bonded and despatched to San Francisco and Honolulu. He reports seeing ships burning as the *Nile* left the scene, and that he last caught sight of the *Shenandoah* heading south-west towards St Lawrence Bay.

Under the headline, 'The *Shenandoah* again', *The San Francisco Evening Bulletin* captures the mood of the moment:

We have now had three arrivals of 'bonded' vessels from the *Shenandoah*, bringing us the news of her operations down to the 29th of June. She commenced her ravages among our whalers by capturing and burning the *Edward Casey*, the *Harvest*, the *Pearl*, and the *Hester*, at Ascension Island, on the 1st April. Since that time she has done a good stroke of business on behalf of her English backers, and has run up a nice little bill for them to settle at some future day.

The barques *Milan* and *Vernon*, lumber vessels belonging to Pope and Talbot, of this city, arrived here last evening from Puget Sound. The *Milan* left Puget Sound on the 23rd of July. She reports that at the mouth of the Straits of Fuca [Strait of Juan de Fuca, Canada] she saw a three-masted steamer, with her royal yards up. The *Vernon* left Puget Sound the day after the *Milan*, and she reports having seen, near the mouth of the Straits of Fuca, a three-masted steamer, with her royal yards all up, and that the steamer ran round her in a circle three times. The captains of the *Milan* and I both say the steamer was nothing like any of the British war steamers around Victoria [Canada]; and the description they gave of this strange vessel corresponds with that given of the British pirate *Shenandoah*, by the men of the whaling fleet.

We do not consider it probable, however, that the pirate has ventured to approach this coast, after sending three vessels to report her operations. After destroying the whale fleet in the Arctic, she has doubtless gone in the opposite direction from that to which her 'bonded' vessels were sent; and the next heard of her will probably be in Australia, hobnobbing with her English friends.[8]

Among the prisoners disembarking from the *Nile* are Captain Green and 21 men from the *Nassau*, Captain Wood and 24 men from the *Congress*, Captain Ludlow and 15 men from the *Isaac Howard*, Captain Macomber and seven men from the *Hillman*, Captain Holly and 12 men from the *Waverly*, 10 men from the *Martha 2nd*, six from the *Brunswick*, 11 from the *Covington*, and Captain Young of the *Favorite*, who has quite a tale to tell.

In England, reporting the latest on the raider's return, *The Illustrated London News*, unlike Sydney's *Empire*, does not editorialise:

The arrival of the late Confederate cruiser *Shenandoah* in the port of Liverpool, and her surrender by Captain Waddell to the commander of HMS *Donegal*, Captain Paynter, by whom, in obedience to the orders of our Government, she has since been given up to the consular agents of the United States Government, have been already made known to our readers.

Long after Lee's surrender and Davis' capture, Captain Waddell sunk, burned, and otherwise destroyed whole fleets of whalers in the Ochotak Sea and Behring's Strait. Nothing more was heard of the *Shenandoah* until her arrival a fortnight since in the Mersey. She had no guns on deck, all her armament being stowed away below in boxes. The crew of the *Shenandoah* numbered 133 men; and as soon as she was surrendered, Captain Waddell and some of the officers separated.

Since setting out on her work of destruction, the *Shenandoah* had destroyed thirty-seven vessels, the majority of which were whalers, and these were destroyed after the cessation of hostilities. To show how the operations of the *Shenandoah* affected the sperm oil market, we may state that her depredations amongst the whaling fleets has caused sperm oil to run up from £70 to £120 per ton, and it is likely to advance still further, as, until the news of the surrender of the *Shenandoah* reaches the port whence whalers depart, the Arctic seas will certainly be bare of the customary amount of whaling vessels.[9]

Swooping in for the kill, US Ambassador to Britain Francis Adams writes to Britain's Secretary of State Earl Clarendon, requesting that the *Shenandoah* and all the property on board be seized at once, and then handed over to the United States. Adams' letter, along with a letter from Captain Waddell detailing the ship's movements since leaving England, and other related documents, are referred to three eminent jurists for a legal opinion.

The jurists are Attorney-General Sir Roundel Palmer, Sir Robert Phillimore, the Advocate-General in Admiralty, and Solicitor General Sir Robert Collier, who in 1862 had advised the government to seize the Confederate ships being built at Liverpool. His advice, which would have prevented the *Alabama* going to sea, was ignored.

On the matter of the *Shenandoah*, their advice is as follows:

We think it will be proper for Her Majesty's Government, in compliance with Mr Adams' request, to deliver up to him, on behalf of the US, the ship in question, with her tackle, apparel etc, and all captured chronometers of other property capable of being identified as prize of war, which may be found on board of her.

With respect to the officers and crew, if the facts stated by Captain Waddell are true, there is clearly no case for any prosecution on the grounds of piracy in the courts of this country, and we presume that Her Majesty's Government are not in possession of any evidence which could be produced before any court or magistrate for the purpose of contravening the statement or showing that the crime of piracy had in fact, been committed.

With respect to any of the persons on the *Shenandoah* who cannot be immediately proceeded against and detained under legal warrant upon any criminal charge, we are not aware of any ground upon which they can properly be prevented from going on shore and disposing of themselves as they think fit, and we cannot advise Her Majesty's Government to assume or exercise the power of keeping them under any kind of restraint.[10]

Instructions are sent to Captain Paynter to release all officers and men who are not British subjects. So, in the early evening of Friday 19 November 1865, the steamer *Bee* pulls alongside the *Shenandoah*, and Captain Paynter steps aboard with good and bad news.

The good news is that he has been ordered to release the raider's officers and crew without charge. The bad news is that only those who are not British subjects are to be released. In other words, the Australian recruits, other colonials and British nationals, will be prosecuted for breaching the foreign enlistment laws.

Captain Waddell summons his officers and crew to the quarterdeck, and calls for the roll books. As each name is called by First Lieutenant Whittle, the man answering to that name is asked by Captain Paynter, 'What countryman are you?'

The men have anticipated a check of nationality, and have rehearsed the response. To a man, all claim to be true-born sons of Dixie. And even though some of those replies are spoken in accents closer to Richmond, Victoria, than to Richmond, Virginia, Captain Waddell duly affirms each claim as true and correct.

Captain Paynter declares himself satisfied there are no British subjects aboard, and tells the ship's company that all 110 of them are free to go ashore.

This announcement is met with loud cheers and, no doubt, sighs of relief, as the men rush off to gather their possessions and prepare to board the waiting *Bee*.

We will never know what passed between the two captains at this time. Perhaps it was the ghost of a smirk from the Englishman, an appreciative nod from the Confederate. It's highly unlikely that Paynter – a bluff old salt in the same mould as James Waddell – was fooled by the amateurish performance. For reasons of his own – perhaps a quiet admiration for the master and men of the one that got away – he chose to turn a deaf ear.

Certainly, Waddell's memoirs reveal a mutual respect between the skippers, and Waddell writes, 'Captain Paynter visited me several times and gratified me by expressing his approval of the good conduct exhibited by those who had so recently been under my command under circumstances so painful. "It is," said he, "the result of a good discipline and confidence in your rectitude."'[11]

Then again, it may be that Paynter, accustomed as he was to the mandatory well-scrubbed and clean-shaven appearance of Royal Navy sailors, simply could not conceive of the scruffy, full-bearded, motley crew of the *Shenandoah* as Britons.

A *Liverpool Mercury* correspondent at the scene reported, 'Before leaving the vessel, they gave three lusty cheers for Captain Waddell, their late commander. Captain Waddell, in feeling terms, acknowledged the compliment, and said that he hoped the men would always behave themselves, as brave sailors ought to do.'[12]

With that, the crew bid farewell to the *Shenandoah* and board the ship taking them to the landing stage and freedom, but also to an uncertain future. And after all they've been through together, most of them will never meet again.

A few days after leaving the ship, James Waddell suffers bouts of haemorrhaging from the lungs, and for a while is close to death. At around this time, he learns that his wife, Anne, who had sailed for America the day after he left England on the *Sea King*, 13 months earlier, had been arrested upon her arrival in the United States.

On the orders of Lincoln's Secretary of War, Edwin Stanton, Anne was imprisoned on the dubious charge of being the wife of a pirate, and later released after signing a declaration that she would neither see nor communicate with her husband for the duration of the war. Circumstance dictated that Anne would honour that agreement, whether she wanted to or not.

She and her husband are reunited in England, and make their home at Waterloo, near Liverpool. In time, and with Anne's care, James Waddell regains his health.

Waddell would never forgive Edwin Stanton for the harsh treatment of his wife. In his memoir, he writes, 'If it be true that Mr Stanton committed suicide, no wonder he cut his unhaltered throat, his horrible crimes could in no way be expiated so well as in his violation of the sixth commandment. Is murder suicide?'[13]

The rumoured suicide is one of several canards concerning Edwin Stanton. A chronic asthmatic, he died of respiratory failure in Washington DC, on Christmas Eve 1869. A favourite of conspiracy theorists to this day, Stanton was also rumoured to have suffered bouts of insanity, to have dug up the body of his mistress to make sure she was dead, to have slept with his wife's corpse, and to have masterminded the assassination of Abraham Lincoln. There is no credible evidence to support any of these claims.

A scalp is required – for appearance's sake, at least. After all the sound and fury, Her Majesty's Government must place someone, anyone, in the dock for violating the Foreign Enlistment Act. Since James Waddell, his officers and crew have avoided prosecution, the finger is pointed at Peter Corbett, master of the *Shenandoah*'s previous incarnation, the *Sea King*.

On 27 November, in the Court of Queen's Bench, London, Captain Corbett, a British subject, is indicted on 55 counts of breaching the act. The most serious of these charges are that he incited men to serve on a foreign warship, that he did likewise upon the high seas, and that the offence was committed on board a British vessel.

The case for the prosecution does not run smoothly. While some witnesses swear that crewmen from the *Sea King* and the *Laurel* were induced by Corbett to join the Confederate service, with offers of high pay and prize money, other witnesses testify that nothing of the sort occurred.

The judge tells the jury that given such conflicting evidence, their verdict will simply depend on which side of the story they believe. The jury retires, only to return five minutes later with a verdict of not guilty.

Across the Atlantic, the case fuels further resentment. The way America sees it, the ostensibly neutral British have colluded in the arming and manning of enemy vessels, turned a blind eye to the illegal recruitment of seamen in the colony of Victoria, and have allowed all those involved in the affair to walk free. Demands for the extradition to the United States of Waddell and his officers have been ignored.

In London, US Ambassador Francis Adams is convinced that because Britain accepted responsibility for the returning *Shenandoah*, the United States can sue the British Government for compensation for the damage done by the raider. In Washington, Secretary of State William Seward is of a like mind, and the wheels are set in motion for a massive claims action.

Meanwhile, in an affidavit to the US Consul in Liverpool Thomas Dudley, a young sailor who served on the *Sea King* and then on the *Shenandoah*, William Temple, claims that while in Melbourne, the Governor of Victoria, Sir Charles Darling, met in private with Captain Waddell on board the *Shenandoah*. Temple also claims that the ship's officers were well aware recruits had come aboard, that all the recruits were British subjects, and that they were enlisted in the Confederate service within sight of land. Temple's affidavit includes a list of all the men recruited in Melbourne.

To US Ambassador Adams, these revelations are dynamite; vital new evidence to support criminal charges and a claim for damages. The trouble is, Governor Darling and Captain Waddell never met. In a despatch to London, Darling insists that during a church service he saw an officer later identified to him as Waddell, but that they never spoke, nor met, on that or any other occasion.

In Temple's defence, it's suggested that perhaps he mistook the Mayor of Melbourne for the Governor, but the sailor's credibility is severely compromised.

As for his claims regarding the Australian recruits, when put to Captain Waddell he issues the usual emphatic denial, standing, as usual, on his honour as an officer and a Southern gentleman.

Even though William Temple's claim that Darling met Waddell might well be an innocent mistake, and although he is correct concerning the recruits, he is labelled a liar with a grudge against his former captain. To the continuing frustration of the United States Government, the so-called Temple Affair comes to nothing.

Chapter 24

Bad blood

On Christmas Eve 1865, in Pulaski, Tennessee, six former Confederate soldiers – enraged at the Reconstruction laws imposed on the defeated South – meet at the law offices of Judge Thomas M. Jones. The six men – lawyers John Lester, Richard Reed and James Crowe, with Frank McCord, whose family owns the town's newspaper, *The Pulaski Citizen*, along with John Kennedy and Judge Thomas's son Calvin Jones – vow to oppose the influx of Northern 'carpetbaggers' exploiting commercial opportunities and filling official positions in the South, and in particular to actively oppose the granting of voting and other (limited) civil rights to freed slaves. To that end, they form a secret society they call the Ku Klux Klan (Ku Klux after the Greek word kyklos, meaning 'circle', and Klan for 'clan', representing their Scottish-Irish heritage).

Later apologists for the original Klan will describe it as a social club for disenfranchised Confederate veterans, but from the very beginning it is dedicated to intimidation and terror.

Hundreds of thousands of freed slaves in the South have found themselves not only struggling to survive, with no money, no prospects and little or no education, but also surrounded by a vast majority of hostile whites.

Houston Hartsfield Holloway, a former slave in Georgia, writes, 'For we colored people did not know how to be free and the white people did not know how to have a free colored person about them.'[1]

The Klansmen, determined that no free black person should be 'about them', take to terrorising freed slaves in their homes on night rides, dressed in robes made of bed sheets and wearing hoods, as if they are ghosts of dead rebel soldiers.

They give themselves grand titles – Grand Magi, Grand Cyclops, Grand Turk, Knight Hawk, and Lictor – and elect as their first Grand Wizard the ex-Confederate general Nathan Bedford Forrest.

General Forrest, who will later deny any association with the Klan, had already earned a chapter in the annals of infamy. At the Battle of Fort Pillow, Tennessee, on 12 April 1864, his troops massacred the Union garrison of 500 mostly African-American soldiers after they had surrendered. Sources on both sides confirmed that the Union troops were shot and bayoneted after throwing down their arms.

In his report of the battle to his superior officer, General Leonidas Polk, Forrest writes, 'The river was dyed with the blood of the slaughtered for two hundred yards. The approximate loss was upward of five hundred killed, but few of the officers escaping. My loss was about twenty killed. It is hoped these facts will demonstrate to the Northern people that negro soldiers cannot cope with Southerners.'[2]

The American military historian David Eicher would call Fort Pillow 'one of the bleakest, saddest events of American military history'.[3]

'Before reaching Liverpool, there was money on board of the ship which was captured prior to the surrender of the Southern armies, and other money which had been captured after the surrender of the Southern armies. The former I directed to be divided among the officers and crew according to the law on the subject of prize money, of which I declined to receive the portion which I would be entitled to, and it was divided among the officers and crew with the rest of the money.'[4]

That's Captain Waddell's recollection, but it's not how Cornelius Hunt remembers it.

'For the many and valuable services he rendered to his native country during the hour of her trial, [Confederate agent James Bulloch] steadfastly refused to receive any compensation,' Hunt writes. 'A short time prior to the final collapse, several thousand pounds of the Public Fund came into his hands, which he laid aside, not knowing how else to dispose of it, to provide for the immediate necessities of such naval officers of the Confederacy as the close of the war should leave homeless and proscribed in England.'[5]

Hunt says each officer is allocated £200 from the fund 'as recompense for the long service they had rendered, and for which they could never hope to receive any other compensation'.[6]

Hunt claims Bulloch appointed Waddell to distribute the money; that his former captain had 'shamefully abused that trust',[7] and that this is the real reason he was so stubbornly determined to take the *Shenandoah* to Liverpool rather than to Sydney or Cape Town.

According to Hunt, after disembarking in Liverpool, and before the ship's officers have been made aware of Bulloch's provision for them, Waddell summons them all to his rooms at George's Hotel, where he interviews them one at a time, and doles out £50 to £100 each, except for a few favourites, who receive the full £200. The rest of money, Waddell keeps for himself.

Hunt also claims Waddell pays the crew only one-third to one-half of what is owed them, with a vague promise to pay the rest at some time in the future. Hunt says that for weeks afterwards, Waddell's residence is 'besieged by these poor men clamouring for the hard-earned pittance out of which he mercilessly defrauded them'.[8]

Hunt's accusations don't stop there. He claims Waddell threatens to withhold the pay of a sailor who has souvenired the ship's flag, unless he hands it over. When the sailor, who values the Stainless Banner more than money, refuses to give it up, Waddell nevertheless relents and pays him.

It is noteworthy that James Bulloch, who, according to Hunt, supplied the funds Waddell misappropriated, makes no mention of what would have been a scandalous affair, and continues to hold Waddell in high regard. Nor do the journals and memoirs of any other officers support Hunt's claim, which suggests it is, at worst, a callous libel, motivated by some grudge against the Captain or, at best, a wildly overdramatised version of a minor incident or misunderstanding.

Waddell gave the money captured after Lee's surrender to the paymaster of the *Donegal*, for which he received the following receipt, dated 8 November, signed by a clerk and witnessed by the paymaster, 'Received of Captain James I. Waddell a bag said to contain $820.28, consisting of mixed gold and silver, as per papers annexed to bag.'[9]

Concluding what he insists is a 'truthful narrative', Cornelius Hunt records, 'It is exceedingly painful for a sailor to write such things concerning a commander under whom he has served. Had Captain Waddell been contented with simply enriching himself at the expense of those who shared the toils and perils of that cruise, which has made his name famous, I should have been silent, for the credit of the service to which I had the honour to belong, but when, after all his officers had left England, and he therefore felt secure from personal chastisement, he ventured to publish that atrocious libel concerning their honour and their courage, I could not in justice to myself and my associates do less than exhibit the man to the world in his true colours.'[10]

The 'atrocious libel' Hunter refers to is in a letter from Waddell, in Liverpool, to a friend in Mobile, Alabama, dated 27 December 1865. In it, Waddell repeats his denial of the allegation that the *Shenandoah* continued her depredations despite being aware the war had ended. He states that on 2 August, upon being convinced by the master of the British barque *Barracouta* that the Confederate cause was indeed lost, he immediately set a course for Cape Horn.

That statement is followed by the assertions that so outraged Cornelius Hunt:

The Barracouta news surprised me, and among some of the officers I witnessed a terror which mortified me. I was implored to take the vessel to Australia; that to try to reach a European port would be fatal to all concerned. Petitions were signed by three-fourths of the officers, asking to be taken to Cape Town, arguing and picturing the horrors of capture, and all that sort of stuff.

I called the officers and crew to the quarter-deck, and said calmly to them. 'I intend taking this ship to Liverpool. I know there is risk to be run, but that has been our associate all the time. We shall be sought after in the Pacific and not in the Atlantic.'

They supported my views, and then followed a letter from the crew, signed by 71 out of 110 men, saying they had confidence in me, and were willing, nay, desired to go with me wherever I thought best to take the vessel.

I had of course a very anxious time – painfully anxious – because the officers set a bad example to the crew. Their conduct was nothing less that mutiny.

I was very decided with some of them. I had to tell one officer I would be Captain or die on the deck, and the vessel should go to no other port than Liverpool."

Waddell's letter concludes:

So ends my naval career, and I am called a pirate. I made New England suffer, and I do not regret it. I cannot be condemned by any honest-thinking man. I surrendered to the British Government, and all were unconditionally released. My obstinacy made enemies among some of the officers, but they now inwardly regret their action in the Cape Town affair.[12]

Chapter 25

The long way home

On bidding farewell to the ship, Lieutenant Frank Chew vowed that, with the death of the Confederacy, he would never go to sea under another flag.

Knowing they risked the noose for piracy if they returned to the United States, Frank Chew, Dab Scales and Jack Grimball sought advice from Commodore Matthew Maury, the former Confederate envoy in England, then in exile in France. Through Maury's influence, they gained work as surveyors for Emperor Maximilian in Mexico, and settled in the town of Carlota, an ex-Confederate enclave near Vera Cruz.

Carlota was the largest enclave of the New Virginia Colony – conceived by Maury, who was an old friend of Maximilian – and numbered among its first settlers Jo Shelby, the Confederate cavalry general who led his Iron Brigade across the Rio Grange into Mexico rather than surrender (see Chapter 19).

Shelby's cavalry rode from the American Civil War into the civil war being waged between the Juarista rebels and the forces of France's puppet Emperor Maximilian. Shelby had hoped to provide his brigade's services as a foreign legion to whichever side made the better offer, but fate decided for him when, south of Monterey, the brigade blundered into the middle of a battle. The French garrison at Matehuala was under siege by rebel troops. The 500 French troops were outnumbered four to one, when, just as all seemed lost, the Confederate cavalry charged the rebel lines and saved the day.

Maximilian was grateful, although not grateful enough – or foolish enough – to risk the Southerners taking control of his army, which was, as previously stated, Shelby's ultimate aim. The Emperor declined Shelby's offer, but as consolation offered him and his comrades free land in the Córdoba Valley.

The Iron Brigade – now a fighting force without a fight – was disbanded, and, while many of its men scattered, others stayed. As word spread, hundreds of ex-Confederates headed south of the border to take up land grants in the colony.

In early 1867, when Maximilian's government fell to Republican forces, the New Virginia Confederates were suddenly no longer welcome in Mexico, and soon the colony was abandoned.

Frank Chew had already left Mexico by then, however. In 1866 – two years before all former Confederates were granted a full pardon – the rules had moderated enough for him to quietly return to Missouri. There, he married Mary Willie Windsor, in 1872, and by 1880 was working as a railroad freight agent in St Louis. Frank Chew died on 11 January 1894, aged 52, survived by his wife, Mary, and their five children.

Dab Scales also made it home to Memphis in 1866, and by 1869 he had established a thriving law practice in the city. In

1885, he married Susan Winchester, and they had three children. He was elected a State Senator in 1895, served in the US Navy during the Spanish–American War, and was a vestryman at his local Episcopalian church. Dabney Minor Scales died on 26 May 1920, aged 79. His obituary describes him as 'singularly sincere and just and conscientious; his manner was gentle, but in principle he was firm as a rock.'[1]

Jack Grimball arrived back in his native Charleston in January 1867, after struggling to make a success of raising cattle. He had written to his parents the previous year of difficulties hiring labour and of crime in the New Virginia colony. On his return, he studied law, and practised in Charleston and then New York City from 1868 to 1883, before retiring to become a rice planter in South Carolina.

John 'Jack' Grimball died in Charleston on Christmas Day 1922, at the age of 82.

After departing Liverpool, William Whittle, Sidney Smith Lee, Orris Browne and John Mason had sailed for Argentina, which – like Mexico – welcomed former Confederates. After trying their hand at prospecting for a while, they bought 50 acres at Rosario, on the Rio Parana, where they raised cattle and poultry, and grew vegetables.

Before leaving for Argentina, John Mason travelled to Paris, hoping to somehow honour the promise he made to Sergeant Canning to deliver his possessions to his family. Since Canning had died without telling him an address, Mason placed ads in newspapers and waited for a reply. Two men responded – one who claimed Canning owed him money, and another who said he was Canning's brother. Both could have been telling the truth but Mason was unconvinced, and turned them away.

In 1867, after Orris Browne's father managed through influential friends to obtain pardons for his son, Browne and Mason immediately returned to Virginia. There Browne spent the rest of his days as a successful farmer. 'Hollywood Place', his market garden and orchard in Cape Charles, was said to be the largest in the state. Whittle and Lee left a few months later, having stayed on to sell the Rosario farm. It proved difficult to dispose of the property, and Whittle, who was all but flat broke, worked on a river boat to help raise the money to get home.

Later in life, Browne, who was a great admirer of William Whittle, wrote to him, 'You were during the cruise of the ship the real commander of her in many tight places and at times you were the only man who could have directed Waddell.'[2] Orris Applethwaite Browne died in Baltimore on 28 September 1898. He was 56.

Lee returned to work his farm in Stafford County, Virginia, and for a while was also skipper of the steamer *Ironsides*, plying between Acquia Creek and Washington DC. Sidney Smith Lee Jnr passed away on 14 April 1888. He was 51 years old.

On his return, John Mason studied law at the University of Virginia, then settled in Baltimore, where he became a highly respected lawyer, and married Helen Jackson of New York, the daughter of a US Navy officer. They had five children. John Thompson Mason died in Baltimore, aged 57, on 9 March 1901.

Home again, William Whittle served until 1890 as the captain of an Old Bay Line steamer on the Baltimore, Norfolk and Portsmouth run. He then worked as a superintendent for the Norfolk and Western Railway, and in 1902 became a director and vice-president of the Virginia Bank and Trust Company.

Whittle's path crossed that of his former captain only once. When returning by rail to Baltimore, while waiting to change trains at Annapolis Junction, he ran into James Waddell, who greeted him warmly. Soon afterwards, however, Whittle read in the press the letter by Waddell that had so offended Cornelius Hunt. Finding himself accused too of 'nothing less than mutiny', from then on, Whittle wanted nothing more to with his old skipper.

And yes, William did marry his beloved Pattie. They had six children. William Conway Whittle died on 5 January 1920. He was 79.

Whittle's journal, a 300-page daily record of his adventures on the *Shenandoah*, was lost until 1980, when a descendant, Mary Whittle Chapman, discovered it while cleaning out her late grandmother's attic. The Whittle family donated the journal to the Museum of the Confederacy in Richmond, Virginia.

Curiously, the entries covering the *Shenandoah*'s visit to Melbourne are missing. Those pages were torn from the journal at the end of the cruise or sometime later.

Surgeon Charles Lining, too, went to Argentina, where he worked as a government surgeon at Santiago del Estero until 1874. He then returned to the United States and practised medicine in Paducah, Kentucky, until his death at age 63, on 23 February 1897.

The *Shenandoah*'s assistant surgeon, Fred McNulty, made his way to Chile after the surrender, and enlisted as a surgeon in the Chilean Navy. In 1869, during Cuba's battle for independence from Spain – the Ten Years' War – he attempted to join the Cuban Patriot Army but was prevented from travelling to Cuba by American authorities.

That same year, after being pardoned, he returned to the United States and settled in Boston, where he took up a position as superintendent of the Boston Lunatic Hospital, and later opened his own private 'home for the treatment of mental and nervous diseases', called Pine Grove Retreat, at Roslindale.[3]

Frederick J. McNulty died at his home in Boston on 14 June 1897, aged 62.

Cornelius Hunt had the distinction of being the first of the *Shenandoah*'s officers to publish a memoir of his experiences – however doubtful its veracity in parts – and in 1869 joined a group of Civil War veterans, both blue and grey, recruited as mercenaries to fight for Ismail Pasha, the Khedive of Egypt. The Khedive, known as Ismail the Magnificent, wanted to expand his country's interests at the expense of Turkey, but since Egypt was nominally part of the Ottoman Empire, this spelt trouble. Undaunted, Ismail ordered his American troops, led by ex-Union and ex-Confederate generals, to invade the Sudan and Ethiopia.

It didn't go well. By 1879, after a series of crushing defeats for Egypt, the war was over and Ismail was forced to abdicate.

We'll never know how much action Cornelius Hunt saw. Sometime in 1873 he was thrown from his horse and died – the only American to die in the service of Egypt.

James Bulloch remained in Liverpool, where he prospered in the merchant trade. Through James's connections, his brother Irvine Bulloch made a career as a cotton broker there, and both lived out the rest of their days in England.

For these brothers in exile, in the years to follow, the only strong connection with their relatives on the other side of the Atlantic would be regular visits from their nephew Theodore 'Teddy' Roosevelt, a future president of the United States, although they returned at least once – secretly and under assumed names – to visit family in America, including Teddy Roosevelt.

Irvine Bulloch died on 14 July 1898, aged 56, while on a visit to Wales. His Confederate Navy officer's sword is on display at the Merseyside Maritime Museum, in Liverpool.

When James Bulloch died, in Liverpool, on 7 January 1901, a dark whisper followed him beyond the grave. To this day, he is suspected of having been involved in a plot to kidnap Abraham Lincoln; that as the controller of covert naval operations in Britain, acting on the orders of the Confederacy's Secretary of the Navy, Stephen Mallory, he provided secret funds to the blockade runner and Confederate spy Patrick Christopher Martin; that the funds were intended for John Wilkes Booth, who planned to kidnap Lincoln, and who, when the attempt failed, murdered the President.

There is no evidence that Bulloch ever met or communicated with Martin or any other of Booth's co-conspirators. And the only document believed by some to support the claim that he provided covert funds to Martin is a request from Mallory to Bulloch, on 24 August 1864, to pay a Captain P.C. Martin $31,507 for a cargo of provisions, clothing and ordnance.

Clouding the issue is a claim that Booth's co-conspirator was not Patrick Christopher Martin but Colonel Robert M. Martin, a Confederate agent who had tried and failed to kidnap Lincoln's Vice-President, Andrew Johnston, in Louisville, Kentucky. Colonel Martin also tried and failed to burn down New York City. He planned to start the conflagration by lighting a fire in his hotel room, but when he closed the door on leaving the room, the fire went out.

In 1905, on a whistle-stop tour of the South, President Theodore Roosevelt told the citizens of Roswell, Georgia – birthplace of the Bulloch brothers:

It has been my very great good fortune to have the right to claim my blood is half Southern and half Northern, and I would deny the right of any man here to feel a greater pride in the deeds of every Southerner than I feel. Of all the children, the brothers and sisters of my mother who were born and brought up in that house on the hill there, my two uncles afterwards entered the Confederate Service and served with the Confederate Navy.

Men and women, don't you think I have the ancestral right to claim a proud kinship with those who showed their devotion to duty as they saw the duty, whether they wore the grey or whether they wore the blue? All Americans who are worthy of the name feel an equal pride in the valour of those who fought on one side or the other, provided only that each did with all his strength and soul and mind his duty as it was given to him to see his duty.[4]

Of the 42 Australian Confederates, one, George Canning, was dead, and 12 are known to have made it home to Victoria. The remaining 29 men either resettled elsewhere in Australia or, once ashore in Liverpool, melted into the crowd or joined a ship bound for parts unknown.

For the 12 returning Melbourne recruits, there was no prospect of a pardon, as there was for the Southerners. Having dodged the hangman in England, surely the wise thing to do would be to assume another identity and start a new life or at least to lie low until the heat died down. But they didn't do either. They resumed their lives as if nothing had happened. And there is no record of the hamlike fist of the law rapping on anyone's door – perhaps because the authorities' handling of the *Shenandoah* Affair had been so inept that the returning Australian Confederates were left unmolested out of sheer embarrassment.

Little Sam Crooks, when he wasn't out fishing, could be found back at his old waterfront haunts in Williamstown, no doubt holding court with tall tales and true of his adventures on the famous rebel raider.

When Sam, who never married, died at age 52, on 30 June 1876, the passing of such a colourful local character warranted an obituary in the *Williamstown Chronicle*:

Samuel Crook, an old identity in Williamstown, died on Thursday night. He was a little clean-shaved, nautical-looking man, who might be seen almost any day down the 'front' in the neighbour-hood of the steamboat jetty or Pier Hotel.

He came to Williamstown very many years ago, when it was only a village, and with a few short intervals when he went to sea, he remained here till Thursday night.

He was one of the few men who joined the Confederate priva-teer *Shenandoah* when she called into this port. He got away in her, and followed her fortunes in her destructive career amongst the United States whalers and merchantmen, and was with her up to the time that Captain Waddell discharged his heterogeneous crew in Liverpool. 'Little Sam', as he was known, had a fund of interesting reminiscences of the *Shenandoah*, than whose crew none was better fed or better paid, as it subsequently proved at the expense of the British Government.

An industrious, peaceable, very un-privateer-looking man was Samuel Crooks, who handed in his checks on Thursday night. In the evening, he was down the front as usual, but during the recent foggy weather his old complaint, asthma, had been more than usually troublesome. He went to his home in Waterman's Row, or Stanford Place, as it is now called, and at twelve o'clock was taken very ill with the asthma. Dr Figg was sent for, but a quarter of an hour after midnight it was all over – he was dead. His remains will be interred in the cemetery tomorrow afternoon.[5]

Of the other sailors, Thomas Strong returned to Melbourne but didn't stay long. Bold as brass, he asked for his old job back, well aware his former employer, George Washington Robbins, had been a paid informer for US Consul William Blanchard when the *Shenandoah* was in port. When Robbins refused to hire him, 'on patriotic grounds', he shipped on a foreign vessel and left Australia, never to return.[6]

John James returned to his home in Williamstown, as did John Kilgower, later listed in local directories as a shipwright. John Spring and John Moss went home to Emerald Hill (now South Melbourne), Thomas McLean to Carlton, Henry Sutherland to Yarraville, James McLaren to Richmond, and John Collins and William Green to Sandridge, where Green was later listed as a bootmaker.

Of the marines – David Alexander, Henry Reily and William Kenyon – it's understood that Alexander eventually returned to Australia, but his fate is otherwise unknown, as is that of Reily, and of Canning's long-suffering servant, Edward Weeks.

After the surrender, William Kenyon remained in England until 15 June 1867, when he shipped as an ordinary seaman on the *Martha Birnie*, bound for Sydney. On arriving in Sydney, he travelled home to Melbourne, where he found work as a coal and wood merchant.

By 1872, Kenyon was the licencee of the Happy Home Hotel, in Sandridge, and had married Sarah Stenniken. He and Sarah would have five children.

But if contentment had set in for the former Confederate marine, it was about to be disturbed in March of that year, when the past came knocking, albeit politely.

As repeated demands by the United States for compensation for damages inflicted by Confederate raiders elicited the rote response that Her Majesty's Government did nothing wrong, American diplomatic correspondence grew more and more fevered. When the total amount claimed reached a staggering $2 billion, the Americans suggest Britain could give them Canada as a down-payment, to which the British response was the diplomatic equivalent of 'Seriously?'

At last, in February 1871, both sides agreed to sit down together and thrash out an agreement on the *Alabama* Claims – so-called because, of the three main Confederate raiders, the *Alabama* did the most damage. She took 69 prizes and a tonnage of 45,217. The *Shenandoah* took 38 prizes and a tonnage of 14,958. The *Florida* took 36 prizes and a tonnage of 19,870. The total of prizes taken was 284, and the total tonnage was 142,899.

Three months later, Britain and the United States signed the Treaty of Washington. Under the terms of the treaty, Britain officially expressed regret for the damage done by the Confederate raiders, without admitting guilt, and both sides agreed to submit the *Alabama* Claims to an international tribunal.

In Switzerland, later that year, a tribunal of five arbitrators – British, American, Swiss, Italian and Brazilian – met at the Hotel de Ville in Geneva. Their brief was to exorcise any devils in the detail, and put a dollar value on the claims.

Britain was represented by the eminent Scottish judge and notorious rake Sir Alexander Cockburn; the United States by the sepulchral former ambassador to Britain, Francis Adams; Brazil by Viscount d'Itajuba, whose diplomatic credentials were essentially a handsome face and a nodding acquaintance with the Emperor of Brazil; for Italy, and president of the tribunal, Count Sclopis, Italy's respected Minister for State; and for the Swiss, the no-nonsense senior bureaucrat Jacques Staempfli.

For over a month, this B-list of the great and the good squabbled over statements, reports and affidavits from assorted players in the *Florida*, *Alabama* and *Shenandoah* sagas. A major point of contention was the liability of the colonial authorities in Melbourne. Sir Alex Cockburn, supported by Viscount d'Itajuba, disagreed with the majority view that the Melburnians were negligent. In the dissenters' opinion, the colonials were not at fault. Rather, the blame lay with the dishonourable behaviour of Captain Waddell, whose lies the authorities had accepted.

The majority view prevailed, however, and the cost to Britain of the *Shenandoah*'s sojourn in Melbourne was estimated at almost $5 million.

The official tasked with gathering evidence in Australia for the *Alabama* Claims is the US Consul in Melbourne, Thomas Adamson Jnr.

William Blanchard had resigned as US Consul in Melbourne in 1866, citing ill health. However, his resignation came just as American merchants in Melbourne were demanding he be sacked for certain improprieties. The traders accused Blanchard of being involved in dodgy deals, an accusation he indignantly denied.

Thomas Adamson had previously been the American consul in Honolulu, but had been reprimanded and removed to Melbourne after refusing to lower the consulate flag to half-mast on the death of Hawaii's Queen Dowager, Queen Kalama Hakaleleponi

Kapakuhaili. Adamson had grudgingly lowered the flag only after Commander William Truxton, of the US warship *Jamestown*, sent his marines to lower it by force if necessary.

In Melbourne, Adamson took testimony from Michael Cashmore, who on 2 February 1865, when aboard the *Shenandoah* on business, swore that in the mess room, one of the sailors slurping soup called his name. He was surprised to see that the man – who, like the others, was in Confederate uniform – was a gold miner he knew.

Asked what he was doing there, the miner replied, 'I joined them this morning.'

Cashmore then asked the man if he thought joining the *Shenandoah* would be more profitable than digging for gold.

'The pay is nothing to boast of,' he replied, 'but there is a chance of making a good deal in the shape of prize money.'

The unnamed recruit assured Cashmore the experience would be 'nothing new' to him because he had previously served aboard a British man-of-war.[7]

Another witness, George Washington Robbins, a Melbourne stevedoring contractor born in Louisiana – and the man who had refused to re-employ Australian Confederate Thomas Strong – swore that back in New Orleans he was acquainted with *Shenandoah* paymaster Breedlove Smith and one of the ship's engineers. Robbins, the consul's former stooge, reported that while spying on the ship he had seen six boatloads of men go aboard. He also claimed to have told the police but they had ignored him.

Robbins had reason to believe that a man named Ross, who had since died, was actively engaged in recruiting sailors for the Confederate cruiser.

Could Ross have been the mysterious Mr Powell? Consul Adamson would never know. Frustrated at every turn by hostile witnesses, sealed lips and conveniently faulty memories, he reported having little luck in 'obtaining legal evidence to establish what by common report I believe to be true'.

'The dirty work was no doubt done by a low class of people, such as boarding house runners, ship chandlers, etc, etc, and between deaths and removals they have disappeared from the scene.

'The repairs were made by people still living who refuse to testify. The active sympathy of high government officials was undoubtedly shown and exerted on behalf of the *Shenandoah*, but we cannot place an ex-governor, Chief Secretary or Crown Solicitor on the witness stand.'[8]

Then, just when it all seemed a monumental waste of time and effort, George Washington Robbins turned up with news that his foreman at the port knew the whereabouts of *Shenandoah* men who returned to Melbourne.

Adamson hurried to Sandridge, where he was told these men could be produced for 'a consideration'. He promised to be generous, and, the following day, the foreman brought a former *Shenandoah* man to be interrogated, and said he would bring three more the next day.

The man sitting calmly across from the Consul was William Kenyon, formerly Private Kenyon, Confederate States Marine Corps. Speaking freely, Kenyon told Adamson that after hearing that the *Shenandoah* needed men, he and some others decided to enlist. He had heard, too, that the ship's commander did not want to see them come on board, and that at 11pm on the night before the *Shenandoah* left port, he and six others rowed themselves out to the vessel. There was only one man on deck to meet them, and they immediately went below and hid in various parts of the ship. The next day, when the ship was six or seven miles outside Port Phillip Heads, he and 41 other men went on deck and enlisted in the Confederate service – a procedure that took several hours.

Kenyon told the Consul he served as a marine on the *Shenandoah*, and was involved in the capture of American vessels in the Pacific and Arctic oceans, and in the Okhotsk Sea.

Tantalisingly, Adamson noted that Kenyon had 'a most startling recollection of the capture of a vessel called the *Jireh Swift*'. Just what that 'startling recollection' was, Adamson didn't say, but it could well be that Kenyon mentioned being on the gun crew that fired the last shot of the war.

From Kenyon, the Consul learnt details of the surrender at Liverpool, and how the Australians and other British subjects among the ship's company had escaped prosecution by passing themselves off as Southerners.

So far, so good, until: 'After Kenyon had made his above statement in answer to my questions, I asked him to make the same in presence of a Notary Public. He agreed to do so and I hastened to call on my solicitor who agreed to verify the declaration.

'I was not absent three minutes, but on my return Kenyon said he must first see another person before he would subscribe the deposition. All arguments were fruitless and he went away. Later on he returned and vacillated but would not come to positive terms. I then sent for the other men, but before they could be reached Kenyon had seen them, and, as it appears, persuaded them to place themselves in his hands in order to get a large sum from me for their evidence.'[9]

For whatever reason, the former Confederates did not come back to bargain and consequently didn't get a penny, and the

Consul didn't get the evidence he needed. For the second time in his diplomatic career, Thomas Adamson Jnr was forced to lower the flag – albeit metaphorically this time.

At last, on 15 September 1872, exhausted by circuitous argument, the arbitrators of the *Alabama* Claims sharpened their pencils and figured out the bill. The total cost to Britain was $15.5 million, payable in gold, within one year. Thus, the Geneva Tribunal gave the Treaty of Washington its blessing.

A cartoon of the day, titled, 'The apple of discord at the Geneva Tribunal', shows the personification of England, John Bull, aiming a crossbow à la William Tell at Uncle Sam, who is standing in front of a tree, with an apple on his head. The apple is labelled 'Alabama Claims' and the arrow aimed at it is labelled 'peaceful arbitration'. Looking on, seated on a platform are the top-hatted, sombre-faced tribunal members, and, safely behind a fence, the crowned heads of Europe. An insert in a corner of the cartoon shows the apple skewered by the arrow, and John Bull and Uncle Sam embracing – friends again.[10]

For Britain, however, friendship would not come cheap. The tribunal had put the blue pencil through the unreasonable – such as the claim that Britain's aid to the rebel raiders prolonged the war by two years – and ticked the acceptable – namely, the damage done – thereby paring down the compensation claim from $2 billion to $15.5 million.

While that was a significant reduction, to put it into a modern perspective, $15.5 million in 1872 is the equivalent of about $300 million in 2015, which is hardly small change. And it's surely no coincidence that 1872 was the year the United States overtook Britain as the global economic leader.

The Confederate raiders could never have guessed that laying a shot across a Yankee whaler's bow would change the world. Yet, in some ways, that's what happened. The Treaty of Washington, when ratified by the United States Senate, ended the risk of hostilities between America and the British Empire. Henceforth, the two powers would remain firm allies. The treaty also opened the door to the official recognition of Canada by the United States, and revised the laws of neutrality so that the *Shenandoah* saga might never be repeated.

There was but one matter that the British declared non-negotiable. Her Britannic Majesty's commissioners, on the instruction of the Home Office, made it abundantly clear to the Americans that the use of the split infinitive would simply not be tolerated. They demanded that in the wording of the treaty, words must not be inserted between the preposition 'to' and a verb. On that seemingly small yet semantically seminal matter, the British were victorious.[11]

All the men of the *Shenandoah* had surrendered, but apparently no-one had told the ship. When Captain Freeman headed her down the Mersey, bound for New York, it seems the old rebel raider was determined never to enter a Yankee port, and that the Atlantic conspired with her.

On reaching the open sea, the *Shenandoah*'s propeller began vibrating so violently that it shook the entire vessel. Then, savage gales and huge seas mercilessly battered the ship until, low on fuel and after losing all her sails and at risk of foundering, Freeman had no choice but to limp back to Liverpool for repairs.

There she sat, unloved and unwanted, an embarrassment to Britain and a headache for America, until 22 March 1866, when she was put up for auction by the US Government.

The winning bid, of £15,750, was from an agent on behalf of the Sultan of Zanzibar. The famously hedonistic Sultan, Majid bin Said Al-Busaid, had amassed a vast fortune from the East African slave trade. He renamed the ship the *Majidi*, after himself, and had her refitted as his luxury private yacht. No expense was spared. It can only be assumed that what went on below decks of the *Majidi* was beyond the wildest dreams of the most sex-starved crewman on the *Shenandoah*.

In 1879, Sultan Majid died, and in April of that year, during the reign of his son Barghash bin Said – a reformer who outlawed the slave trade and modernised his country – the *Majidi* was wrecked by a hurricane. Salvaged by a British firm, she was taken to Bombay for repairs, and in July steamed out of Bombay headed for Zanzibar, never to be seen again.

Off Mozambique, a British warship, the *Briton*, picked up a boat with sailors who claimed to be the only survivors of the *Majidi*. Some said she foundered; some said she was scuttled.

The fate of the last Confederate raider would remain a mystery. What's sure, though, is that the lucky ship's luck finally ran out.

Chapter 26

The horse has bolted

Signs of changing times were appearing: some for better; some for worse.

In March of 1868, taking action belatedly after years of tacitly supporting slave labour, the Queensland parliament voted to tighten the laws on blackbirding. Under the Polynesian Labourers Act, importers of Pacific Island labourers now had to be licensed, and pay a £500 bond, to be forfeited should there be proof that any islanders had been kidnapped. Employers were obliged to provide workers with a daily ration of bread or flour, beef or mutton, vegetables or rice, salt, soap and tobacco, and a yearly allocation of two shirts, two pairs of trousers, two blankets and a hat.

While the new laws marked the beginning of the end of slavery in Australia, they would be too often observed in the breach.

In a Sydney court, in March 1868, the famed and flamboyant Victorian advocate Butler Cole Aspinall, defender of the Eureka rebels and the *Shenandoah*'s Charley, was embroiled in the most difficult case of his career. His client was Henry James O'Farrell, 35, an Irish-born Australian from Ballarat, on trial for his life for the attempted assassination of Prince Alfred, Duke of Edinburgh and second in line to the British throne.

On 12 March, the 23-year-old Prince, the first member of British royalty to tour Australia, was on his second trip to Sydney after visiting Adelaide, Brisbane and Melbourne, where he was the biggest sensation since the *Shenandoah*. At a picnic in the harbour-side suburb of Clontarf, to raise money for Sydney Sailors' Home, Albert was presenting a donation to the charity when O'Farrell walked up behind him and shot him in the back.

William Vial, a coachbuilder, wrestled with O'Farrell and tried to turn the gun on him but shot a bystander instead. The crowd, assuming Vial was the assassin, began savagely beating him, then, realising they had the wrong man, took to bashing O'Farrell and screaming for him to be lynched. Someone found a rope and the angry mob was about to string O'Farrell up from a tree when the police waded in and managed to get him safely aboard a steamer, bruised and bleeding but alive.

He told one of the police, 'I don't care for death. I'm sorry I missed my aim. I made a bloody mess of it.' He then claimed to be a Fenian and called out, 'God save Ireland!'[1] O'Farrell, a chronic alcoholic with a history of mental illness, and recently released from an asylum, later denied being an Irish rebel from the Fenian Brotherhood.

The Prince's wound, just to the right of the spine, was serious but not fatal, and within a few weeks he had made an almost complete recovery.

In court, Aspinall sought to have his client found not guilty on the grounds of mental illness. But with the public, politicians and press baying for blood, he didn't have a prayer. O'Farrell was sentenced to death, and, despite a plea for clemency by the Prince himself, went to the gallows at Darlinghurst Jail on 21 April.

Outside the jail, where a large crowd waited to celebrate the moment, at 9pm, when the would-be assassin was launched into oblivion, police and soldiers were posted in expectation of a Fenian attack that didn't come. Inside the jail, politicians and invited guests from the city's elite were seated comfortably to observe the execution. The condemned man, calm but silent, mounted the scaffold and shook hands with a priest. The hangman pulled a lever, and, at nine minutes past nine, a doctor declared that it was officially all over for Henry O'Farrell.

It wasn't all over for the public, however. It fact, reaction to the shooting was just the beginning. Sweeping across the land like a dust storm came a wave of mass hysteria. At public demonstrations, thousands wept and wailed for grief and guilt, loudly reaffirming blood-ties to the Motherland and bemoaning the awful shame that such an outrage should have happened in a land so loyal to the royal.

And with the shame came blame. Persecution of the Irish, particularly but not exclusively Catholic Irish, ran rampant. Whipped up by the press and politicians – and despite clear evidence that O'Farrell was no Fenian but was simply mad – sectarian division and mistrust became part of the social fabric, and would remain so for a century or more.

Amid this orgy of cringing and breast-beating, hospitals, public buildings, streets, ships, bridges, parks and countless baby boys throughout Australia were named after Prince Alfred. And in New South Wales, the scene of the crime, the penitent government proclaimed 28 April 'a day for general thanksgiving to Almighty God for His great mercy in preserving the life of His Royal Highness from the hand of the assassin, Henry James O'Farrell, at Clontarf, on the 12th ultimo, and in restoring to him his wanted health and strength'.[2]

On Christmas Day 1868, in the cause of securing 'permanent peace, order, and prosperity throughout the land, and fully restore confidence and fraternal feelings among the whole people', the President of the United States granted a complete amnesty to all former Confederates.

'Now, therefore, be it known that I, Andrew Johnston, President of the United States, do hereby proclaim and declare unconditionally and without reservation, to all and to every person who, directly or indirectly, participated in the late insurrection or rebellion a full pardon and amnesty for the offence of treason against the United States or of adhering to their enemies during the late civil war, with restoration of all rights, privileges, and immunities under the Constitution and the laws which have been made in pursuance thereof.'[3]

There were no exceptions, no catches, no oaths to swear, no fine print. At last, all the rebels could go home. Many had already done so, but now the way was clear for the return of America's pirate enemy number one – James Iredell Waddell.

Provoking comments regarding horses and stable doors, the British Parliament passed a new Foreign Enlistment Act, replacing the Act of 1819, with tighter provisions 'to prevent the enlisting or engagement of Her Majesty's subjects to serve in Foreign Service, and the building, fitting out, or equipping in Her Majesty's Dominions vessels for warlike purposes without Her Majesty's licence'.[4]

The new Act, said London's *Spectator*, 'greatly improves the old Act, but we doubt whether it is even yet stringent enough. It enables the Government to prohibit the building as well as the escape of *Alabama*s, but it compels the Admiralty to release them on receipt of a bond that they are not to be employed for any illegal work. In the case of any rich Power wanting ships, would that amount to anything more than an increase in the price?

'Again, the Government is not invested with power to seize contraband of war, but, at present, only warns dealers by proclamation that if caught it may be confiscated – an absurdity when it only has to be carried across the Channel.'[5]

Still, there was no cause for alarm. Any would-be enemy raider would now have to contend with the Royal Navy's new self-propelled torpedo.

The explorer William Gosse, while trekking westward from Alice Springs telegraph station, on a expedition through central Australia, in July 1873, headed towards what he first assumed to be a hill, only to find it was a huge rock, two miles (3.2km) long and 1,000 feet (305m) high, rising out of the desert. Gosse and Kamran – one of three Afghan cameleers in his party – climbed to the top, and Gosse declared the rock a natural wonder.

A rival explorer, Ernest Giles, had set out for the landmark at the same time as Gosse, vying with him to be the first to get there. But when Gosse reached it first, he had the honour of naming it. As naming discoveries after one's self was simply not the done thing, he didn't name it Gosse Rock, and Kamran Rock was quite out of the question. In the time-honoured British tradition of naming unforgettable places after forgettable people, he called it Ayers' Rock, after the South Australian Premier and mining magnate Henry Ayers.

Ayers' main claim to fame came in the nick of time. Three days later, he was voted out of office. Had Gosse reached the rock on 22 July instead, it might have been named Blyth Rock, after incoming Premier Arthur Blyth.

Of course, the rock already had a name. The local Anangu people called it Uluru, but William Gosse didn't bother to ask them. Perhaps he thought they hadn't noticed it.

From the beach at Drummond Island, on 24 October 1873, a fleet of canoes set out to welcome home survivors of the 1871 Carl massacre, in which 70 men kidnapped from the Pacific island, in the remote Gilbert group, were murdered by the infamous Australian blackbirder James Murray.

The 27 men, who sailed home on the *Alacrity* after working on Fiji plantations for two years without pay, were at last gazing at familiar sands, with the sounds of greeting from family and friends bouncing across the water. Their employers, claiming they had broken their three-year contract by leaving Fiji after two years, paid them out with just £12 in goods between all 27 of them. The traders who shipped them home had taken their cut, and each islander would step ashore with only a knife, a pipe and a plug of tobacco to his name.

A few weeks earlier, a blackbirding ship for Queensland plantations, the schooner *Jason*, sailed into Hervey Bay after 'recruiting'

96 Kanakas, 10 of whom died on the way, and another after the ship anchored.

The skipper of the *Jason*, James Taylor, insisted the men were treated well and that when they took ill he did all that could possibly have been done for them. A Queensland Government agent, John Stewart, who accompanied the blackbirders to ensure all their dealings complied with the Polynesian Labourers Act, agreed. A 30 per cent mortality rate was, well, just one of those things.

Chapter 27

The blame game

Although Captain Waddell was safe from prosecution under the general amnesty of 1868, due to his recurring poor health, he and Anne did not return to America until 1875, when he was hired by the Pacific Mail Line to take its new steamer, *City of San Francisco*, on its maiden voyage to Sydney.

Back home in America, to his dismay, Waddell made the papers again. When *The New York Times* reported on 2 December that his ship was set to sail without him, it seemed his piratical past had caught up with him.

'Captain Waddell, who arrived in command of the Pacific Mail steamer *City of San Francisco*, will not take her on her first trip to Sydney, via Honolulu, being threatened with arrest by the Hawaiian authorities on a charge of piracy, for the destruction of the Hawaiian barque *Harvest* during his operation against the Arctic sailing ship in the rebel steamer *Shenandoah*. Captain Lachlan will take his place temporarily pending arrangements to secure Waddell's freedom from molestation by the Hawaiian authorities.'[1]

Weeks later, Australians excitedly awaiting the arrival of the first steamer built especially for the Sydney mail run learnt the reason for the delay. One newspaper reported:

'In command of this magnificent vessel comes a gentleman who rendered himself somewhat notorious during the "late unpleasantness", and whose record is not particularly satisfactory to ship owners and other interested parties in San Francisco.'

The report outlined the Hawaiian charge of piracy that caused Waddell to be stood down, then commented, 'This must be a hard blow to Captain Waddell, as he naturally thought the consequences of the war had passed into history, and were likely to trouble him no more.

'Many persons in Melbourne will recollect the visit of the *Shenandoah* in 1865, and the favourable impression made upon those with whom he came in contact, by her intellectual and gentlemanly commander.'[2]

But if Waddell was still thought of fondly in Australia, it's hardly surprising that he had few friends in San Francisco, the city he had once planned to hold to ransom. His appointment as master of a new ship named for the city was met by fury and threats of violence. Old whalers howled for him to be lynched, and men burst into his hotel intent on shooting him.

A San Francisco correspondent, sparing no vitriol, reminded readers that Waddell, 'while in charge of the cruiser *Shenandoah*, [was] the author of more destruction to Northern commerce than any other naval officer belonging to the South.

'I believe, if my memory serves me, Waddell, while in command of the vessel named, was the hero of a little episode in the harbour of Melbourne.

'While he was carrying fire and sword upon the high seas he burnt a Hawaiian vessel, in company with three flying American colours, for which act, it is urged, he is amenable to law as a pirate.

'So the echoes of the old conflict, in one shape or another, are yet heard. It is said the Pacific Mail directors at New York make their selection of officers from ex-Confederates, for the purpose of conciliating the Democratic majority in the present Congress. They want a subsidy.'[3]

It was indeed true that Waddell had friends in Washington, among the Southern Democrats. Congress was soon to vote on the Reciprocity Treaty, a free-trade agreement between the United States and the Kingdom of Hawaii that would boost the islands' economy, in exchange for granting to the Americans land that would one day be Pearl Harbor naval base. Some 60 Congressmen threatened to vote against the treaty unless the Hawaiians dropped the charges against Waddell.

It worked. Waddell returned to the helm of the *City of San Francisco* and set out for Australia, arriving in Sydney on 4 May 1876.

Oh, how the mighty had fallen. In Sydney there were no welcoming crowds, no heaving bosoms, no nods and winks from the powers that be, as was the case in Melbourne not so long ago.

Some sources have claimed Waddell called into Melbourne on the mail run to Australia, where he was once again feted and fussed over, but that claim is incorrect. The Captain did not return to Melbourne, and had he done so he would have found it rather different from the vibrant city that had treated the Confederates to the time of their lives.

The roaring days were over, and the city's golden glow, just beginning to fade in 1865, was gone. The gilt was peeling. Drovers pushed cattle down streets where, not so long ago, toffs and diggers busily went about the business of hopes and dreams. Many of the theatres in Bourke Street had been replaced by opium dens and gambling joints, and the fancy women in opulent bordellos by bedraggled street-walkers. The pimps and petty thieves had lost their flash but the hard men were harder, the shutters were up and the copper's night-stick cracked with crazy rage.

Melbourne's condition wasn't terminal, merely a case of the post-goldrush blues. Australia's jewel in the south would recover from this funk, and soon, but for the moment the aurelian gods had abandoned it, and it was feeling a little sorry for itself.

Sydney didn't lay out the good silverware for the old rebel, nor would Waddell have expected it to. Nevertheless, the day after the ship's arrival, an open letter to Captain Waddell appeared in *The Sydney Morning Herald*, signed by 31 passengers on the *City of San Francisco*.

'We, the undersigned passengers beg you to accept our acknowledgements of the skill, vigilance and admirable discipline with which the ship was commanded by you during the voyage from San Francisco to the English colonies, and at the same time we desire to express our sense of obligation to your unvarying courtesy and attention, and that of your officers, which have added much to the pleasure of our passage.'[4]

Had the bluff old seadog discovered his softer side at last? Well, maybe. He could always turn on the Southern charm if the need arose.

Of the 30 days Waddell spent in Sydney on his second and last visit to Australia, nothing is known. There were no published notices of his attendance at dinners, soirees or such events. We can only assume he passed the time quietly – perhaps his health was troubling him again – and when he departed for San Francisco, the only record of his leaving was a few words in the 'Clearances' column of *The Sydney Morning Herald* shipping news for 2 June. It read, '*City of San Francisco*, steamer, 3,000 tons. Waddell, for San Francisco.'

There would be no glowing testimonial from Waddell's passengers on the *City of San Francisco*'s 1877 run from San Francisco to Panama. Off the coast of Mexico, on 18 May, at 9.18am, on calm seas and under a clear blue sky, she struck an uncharted rock and sank.

No lives were lost. All 101 passengers were evacuated from the sinking vessel onto a Mexican gunboat and taken to Acapulco, thence to Costa Rica for passage back to San Francisco. It was hardly the ideal holiday cruise itinerary, and although passengers were left damp and disappointed, and news of the disaster sparked a fall in stocks in Pacific Mail, most interested parties blamed the rogue rock rather than the ex-rebel skipper. Waddell was exonerated by an official inquiry, and remained with the company for a few more years, albeit in an on-shore role.

In 1878, tension between Britain and Russia over Russia's expanding influence in the Balkans and the Eastern Mediterranean reached breaking point. London, seeing Russia's actions as a threat to British interests, warned Moscow that further expansion would incur the wrath of the Empire.

In February, when the Czar thumbed his nose at the warning, and continued to move his troops westward towards Constantinople, the British fleet set sail for Mediterranean waters. War seemed inevitable.

In America, meanwhile, a fanciful tale was spreading. So the story went, a plot had been uncovered to fit out a privateer to prey on British merchantmen should hostilities break out between Britain and Russia. And the commander of the privateer was to be none other than the former master of the rebel raider *Shenandoah*, Captain James Waddell.[5]

As it turned out, no shots would be fired across the bows of British ships by Waddell or anyone else. In May, war was averted when Britain and Russia settled their differences.

By 1878, it was apparent that American shipping had not yet recovered from the ravages of Confederate raiders during the Civil War, and the consequent transfer of ownership from American to foreign owners.

However, long-term studies had concluded that although the raiders were widely held responsible by the public and in the press, they were not entirely to blame. *The Vernon Pioneer* explained: 'It will surprise many to learn that although these causes accelerated the decline in our ocean carrying trade, they did not produce it. The transfer of the trade from America to foreign bottoms had been going on for many years before 1861, and the process was so steady and uniform that even if there had been no war between the North and South the ultimate result would not have been very different from what it is now.'

Citing new research, the paper took to task Senator Blaine, of Maine, for claiming the decline in the maritime economy was entirely due to the rebel raiders.

Everything else has gained renewed growth since 1864, why has not the shipping? If the causes assigned by the Maine Senator are the true causes, why does the decline continue 13 years after the causes themselves have ceased to exist? It is 20 years since the panic and prostration of 1857, and it is 13 years since the Confederate cruisers swept the high seas – and in this time the trouble, instead of growing lighter, has grown heavier.

We have not even begun to regain our lost supremacy on the seas. The statistics to which we allude prove conclusively that the steady decline of our ocean-carrying trade from 1826 to the present time must be due to other causes than our Civil War, and that even the lighter tariff of the years that preceded the war had no perceptible effect in checking the downward progress. As the skill of our American shipwrights has never been called in question, or their ability to build as stout and as fleet ships and at as little cost as the ship builder of any other nation, it is obvious that the loss of our carrying trade cannot be attributed to heavier cost of vessels or to defective workmanship. The causes of the decay of the American mercantile marine must therefore be looked for elsewhere.[6]

The fault, according to *The Vernon Pioneer*, lay principally with the English, who, to achieve faster passages and justify higher charges, had abandoned sail for steam and iron for wood, and with America's own shipowners, who somehow failed to notice that times were changing. As a result, America's fleet of mostly wooden sailing ships simply could not compete.

After all the years of border disputes between New South Wales and Victoria, an unstoppable invasion force finally crossed the Murray River. In March 1879, a plague of rabbits, which had thus far been confined to the Victorian side of the border, hopped into New South Wales, on the way to becoming the worst environmental pest in Australian history, spreading faster than any introduced mammal ever, anywhere in the world.

And it was all the fault of one Victorian farmer. Thomas Austin, an English gentleman who had been fond of a spot of rabbit shooting back in the Old Country, was disappointed to discover on migrating to Victoria that, while there were plenty of native animals to massacre, there were no rabbits.

Austin was a member of the Acclimatisation Society of Victoria, a group of homesick Britons dedicated to populating the colony with familiar species to blow away. In 1859, he arranged for a nephew in England to send out 72 partridges, some sparrows, thrushes and blackbirds, five hares and 12 rabbits to his property, Barwon Park, near Winchelsea, in southern Victoria, as game for shooting parties.

Austin's dozen rabbits bred like the proverbial, and although he tried to contain them, they soon escaped into the wild. There would have been enough predators on his property to keep the rabbit numbers in check, but Austin and his friends had killed them all. Five years on, 14,000 rabbits had been shot on Austin's property alone, with millions more to come beyond its boundaries as they began nibbling and burrowing their way across the continent.

Still, it must have seemed like a good idea at the time. As far as Thomas Austin was concerned, 'The introduction of a few rabbits could do little harm and might provide a touch of home, in addition to a spot of hunting.'[7]

Chapter 28

Requiem for a lost cause

The world would last hear of James Iredell Waddell's exploits – with equal measures of irony and empathy – as the master of a sloop on Chesapeake Bay, chasing oyster pirates.

After the Civil War, Chesapeake Bay in the state of Virginia supplied half of the world's oyster harvest. New Englanders, whose oyster beds had been exhausted, took to poaching from Virginian oyster beds, incensing the watermen with legitimate claims on the crop. There had been violent clashes until the Virginia authorities, deciding there has been too much blood in the water, banned dredging for oysters.

When the poaching continued unabated, Virginia's governor, William Cameron, moved to take on the oyster pirates, whose vessels were now armed. His determination gave birth to the State Fisheries Force, popularly known as the Oyster Navy. The fleet consisted of a mere handful of vessels, but the man appointed its commander was the formidable old rebel James Iredell Waddell.

In 1884, two weeks after his appointment, at the mouth of

the Honga River, on the eastern side of the Chesapeake, Captain Waddell ran the sloop *Leila* into the midst of a pirate fleet and opened fire. In less than a quarter of an hour, one pirate ship was sunk, three had run ashore, three were captured and the rest had fled. It was the beginning of the end for the Chesapeake oyster pirates. Maryland's Natural Resources Police, the oldest conservation law enforcement agency in America, celebrates Waddell's 1884 victory as its foundation day.

It's no stretch of the imagination to picture the old commander of the famous *Shenandoah*, watching the fleeing pirates from the humble quarterdeck of the *Leila*, smiling with nostalgic pride and thinking out loud, 'Well, sir, it takes one to know one.'

That was the Captain's last hurrah. There would be no more battles, no more controversies, no more causes, just or unjust, won or lost, for this son of North Carolina.

At his home in Annapolis, Maryland, on 16 March 1886, with his wife Anne by his side, James Iredell Waddell died. He was 62 years old.

On the day of his funeral, the Maryland legislature suspended proceedings as a mark of respect, and the pallbearers included former shipmates from the *Shenandoah*. Each year since, on the anniversary of Waddell's death, the Maryland division of the United Daughters of the Confederacy assemble at his grave-side in Old St Anne's Cemetery, Annapolis, to commemorate Confederate Navy Day.

In 2015, on the website findagrave.com, comments included this from an Australian: 'Whilst you did not know my relatives in Melbourne, my great-great-grandfather met you and your crew. May you rest in peace in the arms of the Lord.'

*

William Kenyon, Australian Confederate, died of heart failure at his home in Sandridge, on 14 November 1915. He was 71 years old.

On the day he died, across the world, on a ridge above a hitherto unremarkable Turkish beach, four of his fellow Victorians lay dead in the dust. Trooper William Hall of the 4th Light Horse, a 22-year-old Greenvale farmer, had been killed defending the precarious position called Ryrie's Post. Not far from him lay the bodies of 21-year-old Private Harry Hardy of the 24th Infantry Battalion, a farm hand from Abbotsford; Private George Rushton, 27, also of the 24th Battalion, a Melbourne electrician; and Private Charles Harris, 21, of the 21st Infantry Battalion, a labourer from Murchison.

These young men were four of the eight Australians killed on the heights at Gallipoli that day – the day after Lord Kitchener, Commander-in-Chief of the British Army, arrived on the beach below in a small boat to survey the Australian positions. He told the men gathered around him, 'The King has asked me to tell you how splendidly he thinks you have done. You have done splendidly, better, even, than I thought you would.'[1]

Two hours later, Kitchener stepped back aboard his little boat and left, having satisfied himself the campaign was lost, and recommended that Gallipoli be evacuated.

A sideshow of the Great War, some would call Gallipoli. Still, a legend had been born there that would prevail, and while those young men lying dead on that ridge would be forever remembered by Australians, William Kenyon and his lost cause had already been forgotten.

Afterword

In 2015, the 150th anniversary of the end of the American Civil War, and of the visit of the CSS *Shenandoah* to Australia, historians and Civil War researchers in Victoria marked the occasion with events intended to raise awareness of this little-known link between the two countries.

No-one in Australia knows the *Shenandoah* story better than Civil War researcher and event organiser Barry Crompton. As secretary of the Melbourne branch of the Civil War Round Table – a movement formed in Chicago in the 1940s to study and debate the American war – he has dedicated some 30 years of his life to sifting fact from fiction, and putting flesh on bare bones of history.

Asked why he studies the American Civil War, he'll tell you it was, at the same time, the last classical war and the first modern war – fought with old-fashioned musket and newfangled rifle, with frontal charges and in trenches. It brought the world the telegraph; rail networks; ironclads; submarines; the Gatling gun;

advances in medicine, manufacturing and photography; prisoner-of-war camps; and the International Red Cross. It was also the first war in which, courtesy of an improved and cheaper postal system, letters sent home to loved ones left us a unique and valuable archive of the thoughts and feelings of the common soldier and sailor.

In 2015, Barry Crompton travelled to the United States to visit Captain Waddell's grave in Annapolis, Maryland, and to view the *Shenandoah* collection at the Museum of the Confederacy, in Richmond, Virginia. The collection includes the *Shenandoah*'s flag. Originally taken for safekeeping by Lieutenant Dabney Scales after the surrender, the Stainless Banner is the only Confederate flag to have circumnavigated the Earth, and was the last rebel flag hauled down.

Returning to Australia, Crompton, who guides walking tours of 1860s Melbourne, located the site in Port Melbourne that had once been the home of Confederate marine William Kenyon. The house was identifiable when last he visited the area, in the 1990s, but unfortunately has since been redeveloped as an apartment complex, totally altering the landscape. So there will never be a plaque on Kenyon's wall.

Crompton walked and travelled by light rail the four-kilometre route taken in 1865 by sightseers on the Sandridge Railway, from the centre of Melbourne to Williamstown pier. From there, they would take lighters (small boats) out to see the *Shenandoah*.

Anniversary events organised by the Civil War Round Table, in collaboration with other enthusiasts, maritime history groups and local historians, included a 150th anniversary dinner at the Melbourne Club, a Buccaneers' Ball at Craig's Hotel in Ballarat, exhibits of Civil War memorabilia, including photographs of the

Shenandoah's officers, taken in Melbourne, lectures by historians, and daily parades and drills by the *Shenandoah* Crew, a group of re-enactors who raised the Stainless Banner and fired a replica cannon.

Williamstown local historian Leigh Goodall told the author, 'Even here in Williamstown, where it all happened, very few people know the story.'

Goodall was actively involved in moves to conserve the historic Williamstown docks, where the raider was repaired, where thousands of Victorians flocked to swarm over her decks, and from where the 42 Australian Confederates rowed out to secretly join the rebel cause. His home, the former Telegraph Hotel, a short distance from the docks, was a favourite haunt of the Southerners during their time in Williamstown, and he has decorated its outside walls with giant murals of the *Shenandoah*.

Goodall has done this for a singular purpose – to keep history alive. 'People see the murals and ask what it's all about,' he says. 'When I tell them the story of the *Shenandoah*, the usual reaction is "That really happened here? How come I've never heard about it?".'

It's often the case that untold or little-known stories remain so because they have been dismissed as merely 'local history'. The presumption is that the record of past events in a particular geographical area is somehow unconcerned with and unrelated to the big picture, and is the province not of 'serious' historians but of amateurs, archivists and dabblers in family lore and parochial trivia.

Much interest and scholarship is focused on the timeline of events that have 'altered the course of history' – the making and unmaking of kings and countries; deeds of the high and mighty – and rightly so.

However, the way Leigh Goodall sees it, all history is local – and he's absolutely right.

The big picture, after all, is a tapestry made of countless smaller threads. The local affects the national and thence the international. And, as we have seen, there can be few better examples than the story of the *Shenandoah*.

Notes

Introduction

1 Debate with Stephen A. Douglas, 15 October 1858, quoted in Davis, *At the Precipice: America North and South during the Secession Crisis*, University of North Carolina Press, 2010, p217

2 Robert E. Lee, Letter to Mary Custis Lee, 27 December 1856

Chapter 1: Lands of cotton

1 Fitzpatrick, *The Diaries of George Washington*, 1748–1799, vol 4, p176

2 Speech in the House of Commons, 12 May 1789

3 Ephesians, 6:5, *New International Version*

4 Wesley, J., *Thoughts Upon Slavery*, Joseph Cruikshank, Philadelphia, 1774

5 Whitfield, *Works*, vol 2, letter to Mr B., 22 March 1751

6 Ibid.

7 US Census, 1860

8 *The Gettysburg Compiler*, 27 April 1918, p2

9 Hammond, *Plantation Manual, 1857–58*, University of South Carolina, Columbia, 1985

10 Hammond, *Selections from the Letter and Speeches of the Hon. James H. Hammond*, J.F. Trow&Co., New York, 1866, p124

11 *The Rockhampton Bulletin*, 23 January 1868

12 *Australian Town and Country* (Sydney), 8 March 1873, p21

Chapter 2: Daughter of the stars

1 McNulty, F., 'The True Story of the *Shenandoah*, Told by an Officer of the Last Confederate Privateer', *Southern Historical Society Papers*, vol 21, 1893, reprinted in the *Launceston Examiner*, 24 March 1894, p10

2 Hunt, C., *The* Shenandoah; *or the Last Confederate Cruiser*, Carlton, New York, 1866, p95

3 Chew, F., Papers, Southern Historical Collection, University of North Carolina, quoted in Crompton, *The Visit of the CSS* Shenandoah *to Australia*, Archer Memorial Civil War Diary, Melbourne, 2010, p5

4 *Creswick & Clunes Advertiser*, 30 January 1865, p3

5 Horan (ed.), *CSS* Shenandoah: *The Memoirs of Lieutenant Commanding James I. Waddell*, Naval Institute Press, Annapolis, 1996, p124

6 Ibid., p123

7 Lepa, *The Shenandoah Valley Campaign of 1864*, McFarland & Co, Jefferson, 2003, p17

8 Whittle, W., 'The Cruise of the *Shenandoah*', *Southern Historical Society Papers*, vol XXXV, December 1907, p231

9 *Cincinnati Daily Gazette*, 28 February 1865, Vol 76, No 183

10 Moore, *Women of the War: Their heroism and self-sacrifice*, Scranton & Co, Hartford, 1866

Chapter 3: Welcome strangers

1 *The Sydney Morning Herald*, 26 January 1865, p4
2 *The Argus*, 26 January 1865
3 Frost, *A Face in the Glass: The journal and life of Annie Baxter Dawbin*, Heinemann, Melbourne, 1992, p289
4 Grey Papers, 1863, quoted in Hibbert, C., *Queen Victoria: A Personal History*, HarperCollins, London, 2000, p307
5 Ibid., pp68–69
6 Hilton, *A Mad, Bad and Dangerous People? England 1783–1846*, Clarendon Press, Oxford, 2000, p500
7 *The Argus*, 3 January 1865
8 *Creswick & Clunes Advertiser*, 1 February 1865, p3

Chapter 4: Other men's battles

1 *The Argus*, 17 February 1865, p1
2 Crompton, *Civil War Participants Born in Australia and New Zealand*, Archer Memorial Civil War Library, Melbourne, 2010
3 Oath taken by miners on the Eureka goldfield, 30 November 1854
4 Twain, *Following the Equator*, American Publications, Hartford, 1897
5 *The Argus*, 8 September 1854, p5
6 Marshall, *The Journey of Crazy Horse: A Lakota History*, Penguin, New York, 2004, xiv
7 Panzeri, *Little Big Horn 1876*, Osprey, Botley, 1995, p57
8 *New York Herald Tribune*, July 1876

Chapter 5: The very model of a Southern gentleman

1 Horan (ed.), *CSS Shenandoah: The Memoirs of Lieutenant Commanding James I. Waddell*, Naval Institute Press, Annapolis, 1996, p53
2 Ibid., p54

3 Ibid., p63
4 Ibid., p65
5 Freeman, *Lee's Lieutenants: A Study in Command*, Scribner, New York, 1946, vol 1, p82
6 Horan, p66
7 Ibid.
8 Ibid., p67
9 Ibid., p68
10 Ibid., p69
11 Ibid., p70
12 Ibid., p73

Chapter 6: Into the breach

1 Thomas Dartmouth, 'Jump Jim Crow', circa 1830
2 *The Sydney Morning Herald*, 17 February 1863, p4
3 *The Argus*, 16 February 1863, p4
4 *The South Australian Advertiser* (Adelaide), 16 February 1863, p2
5 Horan (ed), *CSS* Shenandoah: *The Memoirs of Lieutenant Commanding James I. Waddell*, Naval Institute Press, Annapolis, 1996, p76
6 Philip John Pinel, Journal, 1855–1867, part 1
7 Confederate States of America, Proclamation, 17 April 1861
8 Official Records of the Union and Confederate Navies in the War of Rebellion, series 2, p64
9 Dowdy, C., *Robert E. Lee: A Biography*, Victor Gollancz Ltd, London, 1970, p394
10 *The Argus*, 16 February 1863, p4
11 *The Patriot & Union* (Harrisburg, Pennsylvania), 16 February 1863
12 *The Index*, 4 February 1864, p1
13 Ibid.

14 Hunt, *The* Shenandoah; *or the Last Confederate Cruiser*, Carlton, New York, 1866, p14
15 Whittle, 'The Cruise of the *Shenandoah*', *Southern Historical Society Papers*, vol XXXV, December 1907, p237
16 Bulloch, J.D., *The Secret Service of the Confederate States in Europe*, vol 2, G.P. Putnam's Sons, New York, 1884, pp133–134
17 Ibid., p137
18 Whittle, p238
19 Hunt, p13

Chapter 7: First prize
1 Whittle, 'The Cruise of the *Shenandoah*', *Southern Historical Society Papers*, vol XXXV, December 1907, p238
2 Horan (ed.), CSS Shenandoah: *The Memoirs of Lieutenant Commanding James I. Waddell*, Naval Institute Press, Annapolis, 1996, p94
3 Whittle, p238
4 Bulloch, J.D., *The Secret Service of the Confederate States in Europe*, vol 2, G.P. Putnam's Sons, New York, 1884, p146
5 McNulty, F., 'The True Story of the *Shenandoah*, Told by an Officer of the Last Confederate Privateer, St Louis Republic', relayed by *Launceston Examiner*, 24 March 1894, p10
6 Whittle, Journal, Museum of the Confederacy, Richmond, Virginia
7 Ibid., pp94–95
8 *The Index*, 19 October 1864
9 Riley, Interview with Fred McNulty, *The Atlanta Constitution*, November 1893, reprinted in *Southern Historical Papers*, Vol 21, p165
10 Whittle, Papers, 1855–1910, edited as *The Voyage of the CSS Shenandoah: A Memorable Cruise*, University of Alabama Press, 2005, p56

11 Hunt, C., *The* Shenandoah; *or the Last Confederate Cruiser*, Carlton, New York, 1866, pp30–31

12 Hunt, pp31–32

13 Whittle, Papers, pp56–57

14 Hunt, p32

15 Riley, p165

16 Horan, p107

17 Riley, p166

18 Horan, p117

19 Mason, Journal, Museum of the Confederacy, Richmond, Virginia, December 1864

20 Whittle, Papers, p96

21 Horan, p118

22 Ibid.

23 Hunt, p72

24 Ibid., p118

25 McNulty, p10

26 Ibid.

27 Ibid., p119

28 Hunt, p74

29 McNulty, p10

30 Ibid., pp119–120

31 Glenn, J., *The Washingtons: A Family History*, vol 2, Savas Publishing, El Dorado Hills, 2014, no pagination

32 Hunt, p75

33 Hunt, pp79–81

Chapter 8: The grey and the good

1 Hunt, C., *The* Shenandoah; *or the Last Confederate Cruiser*, Carlton, New York, 1866, pp76–77

2 Horan (ed), CSS Shenandoah: *The Memoirs of Lieutenant Commanding James I. Waddell*, Naval Institute Press, Annapolis, 1996, p125

3 McNulty, F., 'The True Story of the *Shenandoah*, Told by an Officer of the Last Confederate Privateer, St Louis Republic', relayed by *Launceston Examiner*, 24 March 1894, p10

4 Mill, *Considerations on Representative Government*, Parker, Son & Bourn, London, 1861, chapter 16

5 Hunt, p97

6 Ibid., p98

7 Ibid., p97

8 Ibid., pp100–101

9 *The Age*, 27 January 1865, p3

10 *The Bendigo Advertiser*, 31 January 1865, p2

11 Horan, pp129–130

12 Frost, *A Face in the Glass: The journal and life of Annie Baxter Dawbin*, Heinemann, Melbourne, 1992, p290

13 Hunt, p111

14 Ibid.

15 Riley, interview with Fred McNulty, 'The CSS *Shenandoah* Cruise by one of its officers, Dr McNulty', *The Atlanta Constitution*, November 1893, reprinted in *Southern Historical Papers*, vol 21, p171

16 *The National Intelligencer*, January 1865, quoted in Kimmel, *The Mad Booths of Maryland*, Dover, 1969, p177

17 Ibid., p126

18 Ibid., p104

19 Horan, p127

Chapter 9: Buttons and beaux

1 Mason, Journal, quoted in Crompton, B., *Civil War Participants Born in Australia and New Zealand*, Archer Memorial Civil War Library, Melbourne, 2010, p20

2 *The Ballarat Star*, 1 February 1865, p2

3 *The Sydney Morning Herald*, 7 May 1855

4 *The Argus*, 11 April 1855
5 Victorian Parliamentary Papers, Commission of Inquiry into Conditions on the Gold Fields, A 76/1854–55, Vol II
6 *The Sydney Morning Herald*, 3 July 1861
7 Lining, Journal, quoted in Crompton, *The Visit of the CSS Shenandoah to Australia*, Archer Memorial Civil War Diary, Melbourne, 2010, p15
8 Hillgrove, T., *Hillgrove's Ballroom Guide*, New York, 1868
9 Hunt, C., *The* Shenandoah; *or the Last Confederate Cruiser*, Carlton, New York, 1866, pp107–109
10 *The Ballarat Star*, 11 February 1865, p2

Chapter 10: The trouble with Charley

1 Whittle, W., 'The Cruise of the *Shenandoah*', *Southern Historical Society Papers*, vol XXXV, December 1907, p250
2 Whittle, Journal, Museum of the Confederacy, Richmond, Virginia, 8 December 1864
3 Williams, Affidavit, 16 February 1865
4 Horan (ed.), *CSS* Shenandoah: *The Memoirs of Lieutenant Commanding James I. Waddell*, Naval Institute Press, Annapolis, 1996, p131
5 Whittle, December 1907, p251
6 Ibid., p132
7 *The Age*, 16 February 1865, p5
8 *The Argus*, 15 February 1865, p5
9 Ibid., p133
10 *The Age*, 17 February 1865, p2
11 *Punch*, quoted in Pearl, C., *Rebel Down Under*, Heinemann, Melbourne, 1970, p135
12 Ibid., p136
13 Horan, pp 133–134
14 Ibid., p135

15 Ibid.
16 Gurner, J., *Life's Panorama: Being Recollections and Reminiscences*, Lothian, Melbourne, 1930, p65

Chapter 11: A sailor's farewell

1 Horan (ed), CSS Shenandoah: *The Memoirs of Lieutenant Commanding James I. Waddell*, Naval Institute Press, Annapolis, 1996, p139
2 Hunt, C., *The* Shenandoah; *or the Last Confederate Cruiser*, Carlton, New York, 1866, pp109–110
3 Edgar Allan Poe, 'The Bells', 1848
4 William Blanchard to William Seward, Roll 3, Despatches from United States Consul in Melbourne, National Archives and Records, Maryland, 23 February 1865
5 *The Mercury*, 2 March 1865, p2
6 *The Australasian*, 25 February 1865, p11
7 *The Argus*, 27 February 1865, p4

Chapter 12: All Confederates now

1 *Shenandoah* log, 18 February, quoted in Crompton, *The Visit of the CSS* Shenandoah *to Australia*, Archer Memorial Civil War Library, Melbourne, 2010, p23
2 Lee, R.E., Letter to General P. Beauregard, 3 October 1865
3 Hunt, C., *The* Shenandoah; *or the Last Confederate Cruiser*, Carlton, New York, 1866, pp102–103
4 Ibid., pp114–115
5 Ibid.
6 Lining, C., Journal, quoted in Crompton, *The Visit of the CSS* Shenandoah *to Australia*, Archer Memorial Civil War Diary, Melbourne, 2010, p28
7 Whittle, 'The Cruise of the *Shenandoah*', *Southern Historical Society Papers*, vol XXXV, December 1907, p251

8 Horan (ed), *CSS Shenandoah: The Memoirs of Lieutenant Commanding James I. Waddell*, Naval Institute Press, Annapolis, 1996, p140

9 Seddon, *Regulations for the Army of the Confederate States*, Confederate States of America War Department, 1863, p412

10 Hunt, p116

11 Horan, pp141–142

12 Ibid., p143

13 Mahin, *One War at a Time: The International Dimensions of the Civil War*, Brassey's, Washington DC, 1999, pp68–69

14 Hibbert, C., *Queen Victoria: A Personal History*, HarperCollins, London, 2000, pp 276–277

Chapter 13: The last of Charley

1 *The Argus*, 18 March 1865, p5

2 Ibid.

3 *Creswick & Clunes Advertiser*, 22 March 1865, p2

Chapter 14: The captain and the king

1 *The Alta California*, 30 March 1865, p2

2 Horan (ed), *CSS Shenandoah: The Memoirs of Lieutenant Commanding James I. Waddell*, Naval Institute Press, Annapolis, 1996, pp143–144

3 Ibid., pp145–146

4 Ibid., p146

5 Ibid., pp146–147

6 Ibid., p150

7 Dowdy, C., *Robert E. Lee: A Biography*, Victor Gollancz Ltd, London, 1970, p578

8 Ibid.

9 Ibid.

10 Montague, A., Letter to undisclosed recipient, 30 April 1865, montaguemillennium.com

11 *The Sydney Morning Herald*, 10 April 1865, p8

12 Horan, p145

13 Ibid., p153

14 Ibid., p154

15 Riley, interview with Fred McNulty, *The Atlanta Constitution*, November, 1893, reprinted in *Southern Historical Papers*, Vol 21, p168

16 Dowdy, p585

17 Ibid., p590

Chapter 15: The curious case of Eugenio Gonzales

1 *The Argus*, 7 February 1865, p5

2 *The Argus*, 21 April 1865, p5

3 Neild, J., 'On a Case of Feigned Haemoptysis and Collapse', *Australian Medical Journal*, August 1865, pp258–266

Chapter 16: The way north

1 Earl Russell, Despatch to Governor Sir C.H. Darling, 26 April 1865

2 Tucker and Cooper, 'Jeff in Petticoats', 1865

3 *Southern Historical Society Papers*, August 1877

4 Horan (ed), CSS Shenandoah: *The Memoirs of Lieutenant Commanding James I. Waddell*, Naval Institute Press, Annapolis, 1996, p157

5 Riley, interview with Fred McNulty, *The Atlanta Constitution*, November, 1893, reprinted in *Southern Historical Papers*, Vol 21, p168

6 Ibid., p158

7 Chew, Journal, 28 May 1865, p27

8 Whittle, *The Voyage of the CSS* Shenandoah: *A Memorable Cruise*, University of Alabama Press, 2005, p154

Chapter 17: The last shot

1 Horan (ed), *CSS* Shenandoah: *The Memoirs of Lieutenant Commanding James I. Waddell*, Naval Institute Press, Annapolis, 1996, pp160–161
2 *The Argus*, 1 June 1865, p4
3 Davidson, H., Letter to J.A. McNeil Whistler, University of Glasgow Library, 7 February 1868
4 Granger, General Orders No. 3, Headquarters, District of Texas, 19 June 1865
5 Proclamation 134 – Granting Amnesty to Participants in the Rebellion, with Certain Exceptions, 29 May 1865
6 *The Geelong Advertiser*, 26 June 1865, p2
7 *The Argus* (Melbourne), 20 June 1865
8 Ibid.
9 Horan, p167
10 Riley, interview with Fred McNulty, *The Atlanta Constitution*, November 1893, reprinted in *Southern Historical Papers*, Vol 21, p168
11 Whittle, W., Journal, Museum of the Confederacy, Richmond, Virginia, p166
12 Ibid.
13 Horan, p165

Chapter 18: 'An old grey-headed devil'

1 Horan (ed), *CSS* Shenandoah: *The Memoirs of Lieutenant Commanding James I. Waddell*, Naval Institute Press, Annapolis, 1996, p166
2 Ibid.
3 Ibid., p167
4 Ibid.
5 Whittle, W., Journal, Museum of the Confederacy, Richmond, Virginia
6 Horan, p168

7 McNulty, F., 'The True Story of the *Shenandoah*, Told by an Officer of the Last Confederate Privateer', *Southern Historical Society Papers*, vol 21, 1893, reprinted in *The Launceston Examiner*, 24 March 1894, p10

8 Ibid.

9 Horan, p169

10 Ibid.

11 *San Francisco Evening Bulletin*, 19 August 1865, published in Federal Writers Project, Fairhaven, Massachusetts, American Guide Series, 1939, pp12–13

12 *San Francisco Evening Bulletin*, 19 August 1865

13 Horan, p169

14 Ibid., p170

15 Ibid., p171

16 Mulderink, E., *New Bedford's Civil War*, Fordham University Press, 2002, p142

17 Horan, p169

18 *Shenandoah* log book, 1 July 1865, quoted in Pearl, C., *Rebel Down Under*, Heinemann, Melbourne, 1970, p151

19 Horan, p173

Chapter 19: All pirates now

1 *The San Francisco Bulletin*, 6 January 1872

2 Gapps, S., 'Australian Piratical Tales', Australian National Maritime Museum, *Signals* 97, December 2011–February 2012

3 Horan (ed), CSS Shenandoah: *The Memoirs of Lieutenant Commanding James I. Waddell*, Naval Institute Press, Annapolis, 1996, p175

Chapter 20: The darkest day

1 *Shenandoah* Log Book, 2 August 1865, quoted in Horan (ed), CSS Shenandoah: *The Memoirs of Lieutenant Commanding James I. Waddell*, Naval Institute Press, Annapolis, 1996, p176

2   Whittle, 'The Cruise of the *Shenandoah*', *Southern Historical Society Papers*', vol XXXV, December 1907, p257

3   Ibid.

4   Horan (ed), *CSS* Shenandoah: *The Memoirs of Lieutenant Commanding James I. Waddell*, Naval Institute Press, Annapolis, 1996, p176

5   Whittle, W., Journal, Museum of the Confederacy, Richmond, Virginia, pp182–183

6   Horan, p176

7   Ibid., p177

8   Anderson, Letter to P.H. Anderson, *The Cincinnati Commercial*, reprinted in *The New York Tribune*, 22 August 1865

9   *The Argus*, 12 August 1865, p4

Chapter 21: Oh, Pattie!

1   Whittle, W., Journal, Museum of the Confederacy, Richmond, Virginia, p183

2   Ibid., p185

3   Riley, interview with Fred McNulty, *The Atlanta Constitution*, November 1893, reprinted in *Southern Historical Papers*, Vol 21, p169

4   Horan (ed), *CSS* Shenandoah: *The Memoirs of Lieutenant Commanding James I. Waddell*, Naval Institute Press, Annapolis, 1996, pp178–179

5   Geiger, M., *Financial Fraud and Guerrilla Violence in Missouri's Civil War*, 1861–1865, Yale University Press, 2010, p104

6   *The New York Times*, 22 September 1863, p4

7   Whittle, p199

8   Ibid., p199

9   Ibid.

10 Ibid., p201

11 Ibid.

12 Ibid., p202

13 Ibid., p203

14 Ibid.

15 Dowdy, C., *Robert E. Lee: A Biography*, Victor Gollancz Ltd, London, 1970, p734

16 *The Empire*, 13 October 1870, p3

17 Whittle, p204

18 Lebo, J., 'Man Before Marconi', *QST Magazine*, August 1948, pp42–44

Chapter 22: 'All hands to bury the dead'

1 Whittle, W., Journal, Museum of the Confederacy, Richmond, Virginia, p206

2 Lord Byron, 'The Corsair', Canto III, 1814

3 John, 11:25, *New International Version*

4 Whittle, p209

Chapter 23: Liverpool and Limbo

1 Horan (ed), *CSS* Shenandoah: *The Memoirs of Lieutenant Commanding James I. Waddell*, Naval Institute Press, Annapolis, 1996, p181

2 Whittle, W., Journal, Museum of the Confederacy, Richmond, Virginia, p209

3 McNulty, F., 'The True Story of the *Shenandoah*, Told by an Officer of the Last Confederate Privateer', *Southern Historical Society Papers*, vol 21, 1893, reprinted in *The Launceston Examiner*, 24 March 1894, p10

4 Horan, p182

5 Ibid.

6 War of the Rebellion, Official Records of the Union and Confederate Navies, series 1.3: pp749–838

7 *The Empire*, 7 November 1865, p4
8 *The San Francisco Evening Bulletin*, 16 November 1865, p3
9 *The Illustrated London News*, 18 November 1865, vol 47, no 1343, p494
10 Whittle, p213
11 Horan, p183
12 *The Liverpool Mercury*, 9 November 1865
13 Horan, p178

Chapter 24: Bad blood

1 Clark, K., *Defining Moments: African-American Commemoration and Political Culture in the South 1863–1913*, University of North Carolina Press, 2005, p210
2 Forrest, N., Report to Polk, 15 April 1864, quoted in Grant, U.S., *Personal Memoirs*, Charles L. Webster & Company, New York, 1885–86, p391
3 Eicher, D., *The Longest Night: A Military History of the Civil War*, Simon & Schuster, New York, 2001, p657
4 Horan (ed), CSS Shenandoah: *The Memoirs of Lieutenant Commanding James I. Waddell*, Naval Institute Press, Annapolis, 1996, p183
5 Hunt, C., *The Shenandoah; or the Last Confederate Cruiser*, Carlton, New York, 1866, pp261–62
6 Ibid., p262
7 Ibid., p263
8 Ibid., p263–264
9 Waddell, Letter, 27 December 1865, quoted in Hunt, p183
10 Hunt, pp224–226
11 Waddell, Letter, 27 December 1865, quoted in Hunt, pp268–271
12 Ibid.

Chapter 25: The long way home
1 *Confederate Veteran Magazine*, November 1920
2 Whittle, W., Journal, Museum of the Confederacy, Richmond, Virginia, p44
3 Report of the State Board of Lunacy and Charity of Massachusetts, 1889, p43
4 Roosevelt, T., Address in Roswell, Georgia, *Almanac of Theodore Roosevelt*, 20 October 1905, theodore-roosevelt.com
5 *The Williamstown Chronicle*, 1 July 1876, p3
6 Adamson, Letter to J. Bancroft Davis, 2 March 1872
7 Correspondence Concerning Claims Against Great Britain Transmitted to the Senate of the United States, 1872, vol 3, p426
8 Ibid.
9 National Archives, Washington DC, Despatches of US Consuls in Australia, quoted in Crompton, B., *Civil War Participants Born in Australia and New Zealand*, Archer Memorial Civil War Library, Melbourne, 2010, p36
10 Nast, T., 'The apple of discord at the Geneva Tribunal', *Harper's Weekly*, 5 October 1872
11 Lounsbury, T., "'To' and the infinitive", *Harper's* Magazine, April 1904

Chapter 26: The horse has bolted
1 *The Nashville Times* (Queensland), 28 March 1868, p3
2 *The Queenslander*, 18 April 1868, p8
3 Proclamation 179 – Granting Full Pardon and Amnesty for the Offence of Treason Against the United States During the Late Civil War, 25 December 1868
4 Foreign Enlistment Act 1870 (33 & 34, Vict. C90)
5 *The Spectator*, 6 August 1870, p3

Chapter 27: The blame game

1 *The New York Times*, 2 December 1875
2 *The Queenslander*, 15 January 1876, p19
3 *South Australian Chronicle and Weekly Mail*, 22 January 1876, p11
4 *The Sydney Morning Herald*, 5 May 1876
5 *The Vernon Pioneer*, 28 April 1878
6 *The Vernon Pioneer*, 3 May 1878
7 Fawcett, B., *100 Mistakes that Changed History*, Berkley Books, New York, 2010, p42

Chapter 28: Requiem for a lost cause

1 Fewster, K., *Frontline Gallipoli – C.E.W. Bean's diary from the trenches*, Allen & Unwin, Sydney, 1983, p176

References

Adamson, Letter to J. Bancroft Davis, 2 March 1872

Anderson, Letter to P.H. Anderson, *The Cincinnati Commercial*, reprinted in *The New York Tribune*, 22 August 1865

Australian Town and Country (Sydney)

Bulloch, J.D., *The Secret Service of the Confederate States in Europe*, vol 2, G.P. Putnam's Sons, New York, 1884

Chew, F., Papers, Southern Historical Collection, University of North Carolina, quoted in Crompton, *The Visit of the CSS Shenandoah to Australia*, Archer Memorial Civil War Diary, 2010

Clark, K., *Defining Moments: African-American Commemoration and Political Culture in the South 1863–1913*, University of North Carolina Press, 2005

Confederate States of America, Proclamation, 17 April 1861

Confederate Veteran Magazine, November 1920

Correspondence Concerning Claims Against Great Britain transmitted to the Senate of the United States, 1872, vol 3

Creswick & Clunes Advertiser

Crompton, B., *Civil War Participants Born in Australia and New Zealand*, Archer Memorial Civil War Library, Melbourne, 2010

Crompton, B., *The Visit of the CSS* Shenandoah *to Australia*, Archer Memorial Civil War Library, Melbourne, 2010

Dartmouth, Thomas, 'Jump Jim Crow', circa 1830

Davidson, H., Letter to J.A. McNeil Whistler, University of Glasgow Library, 7 February 1868

Debate with Stephen A. Douglas, 15 October 1858, quoted in Davis, *At the Precipice: America North and South during the Secession Crisis*, University of North Carolina Press, 2010

Dowdy, C., *Robert E. Lee: A Biography*, Victor Gollancz Ltd, London, 1970

Earl Russell, *Despatch to Governor Sir C.H. Darling*, 26 April 1865

Eicher, D., *The Longest Night: A Military History of the Civil War*, Simon & Schuster, New York, 2001

Fawcett, B., *100 Mistakes that Changed History*, Berkley Books, New York, 2010

Fewster, K., *Frontline Gallipoli – C.E.W. Bean's diary from the trenches*, Allen & Unwin, Sydney, 1983

Fitzpatrick, *The Diaries of George Washington*, 1748–1799, vol 4

Foreign Enlistment Act 1870 (33 & 34, Vict. C90)

Forrest, N., Report to Polk, 15 April 1864, quoted in Grant, U.S., *Personal Memoirs*, Charles L. Webster & Company, New York, 1885–86

Freeman, *Lee's Lieutenants: A Study in Command*, Scribner, New York, 1946

Frost, *A Face in the Glass: The journal and life of Annie Baxter Dawbin*, Heinemann, Melbourne, 1992

Gapps, S., 'Australian Piratical Tales', Australian National Maritime Museum, *Signals* 97, December 2011–February 2012

Geiger, M., *Financial Fraud and Guerrilla Violence in Missouri's Civil War, 1861–1865*, Yale University Press, 2010

Glenn, J, *The Washingtons: A Family History*, vol 2, Savas Publishing, El Dorado Hills, 2014

Granger, General Orders No 3, Headquarters, District of Texas, 19 June 1865

Gurner, J., *Life's Panorama: Being Recollections and Reminiscences*, Lothian, Melbourne, 1930

Hammond, G., *Plantation Manual 1857–58*, University of South Carolina, Columbia, 1985

Hammond, G., *Selections from the Letter and Speeches of the Hon. James H. Hammond*, J.F. Trow & Co., New York, 1866

Hibbert, C., *Queen Victoria: A Personal History*, HarperCollins, London, 2000

Hilton, B., *A Mad, Bad and Dangerous People? England 1783–1846*, Clarendon Press, Oxford, 2000

Horan (ed.), *CSS Shenandoah: The Memoirs of Lieutenant Commanding James I. Waddell*, Naval Institute Press, Annapolis, 1996

Hunt, *The Shenandoah; or the Last Confederate Cruiser*, Carlton, New York, 1866

Lebo, J., 'Man before Marconi', *QST Magazine*, August 1948

Lee, R.E., Letter to General P. Beauregard, 3 October 1865

Lepa, *The Shenandoah Valley Campaign of 1864*, McFarland & Co, Jefferson, 2003

Lining, C., Journal, quoted in Crompton, *The Visit of the CSS Shenandoah to Australia*, Archer Memorial Civil War Library, Melbourne, 2010

Lord Byron, 'The Corsair', 1814

Lounsbury, T., '"To" and the infinitive', *Harper's Magazine*, April 1904

Mahin, *One War at A Time: The International Dimensions of the Civil War*, Brassey's, Washington DC, 1999

Marshall, *The Journey of Crazy Horse: A Lakota History*, Penguin, New York, 2004

McNulty, F., 'The True Story of the *Shenandoah*, Told by an Officer of the Last Confederate Privateer', *Southern Historical Society Papers*, vol 21, 1893, reprinted in *The Launceston Examiner*, 24 March 1894

Mill, *Considerations on Representative Government*, Parker, Son & Bourn, London, 1861

Montague, A., Letter to undisclosed recipient, 30 April 1865

Moore, *Women of the War: Their heroism and self-sacrifice*, Scranton & Co, Hartford, 1866

Mulderink, E., *New Bedford's Civil War*, Fordham University Press, New York, 2002

Nast, T., 'The apple of discord at the Geneva Tribunal', *Harper's Weekly*, 5 October 1872

National Archives, Washington DC, Despatches of US Consuls in Australia, quoted in Crompton, B., *Civil War Participants Born in Australia and New Zealand*, Archer Memorial Civil War Library, 2010

Neild, J., 'On a Case of Feigned Haemoptysis and Collapse', *Australian Medical Journal*, August 1865

New York Herald Tribune

Official Records of the Union and Confederate Navies in the War of Rebellion, series 2

Panzeri, *Little Big Horn*, Osprey, Botley, 1995

Pinel, Philip John, Journal, 1855–1867, part 1

Proclamation 134 – Granting Amnesty to Participants in the Rebellion, with Certain Exceptions, 29 May, 1865

Proclamation 179 – Granting Full Pardon and Amnesty for the Offence of Treason Against the United States During the Late Civil War, 25 December, 1868

Punch, quoted in Pearl, C., *Rebel Down Under*, Heinemann, Melbourne, 1970

Report of the State Board of Lunacy and Charity of Massachusetts, 1889

Riley, interview with Fred McNulty, *The Atlanta Constitution*, November 1893, reprinted in *Southern Historical Papers*, Vol 21

Robert E. Lee, Letter to Mary Custis Lee, 27 December 1856

Roosevelt, T., Address in Roswell, Georgia, *Almanac of Theodore Roosevelt*, 20 October 1905, theodore-roosevelt.com

Ruffin, E., Diary, 17 June 1865

San Francisco Evening Bulletin

Seddon, Regulations for the Army of the Confederate States, Confederate States of America War Department, 1863

Shenandoah log book, 18 February 1865, quoted in Crompton, *The Visit of the CSS* Shenandoah *to Australia*, Archer Memorial Civil War Library, Melbourne, 2010

Shenandoah log book, 1 July 1865, quoted in Pearl, C., *Rebel Down Under*, Heinemann, Melbourne, 1970

Shenandoah log book, 2 August 1865, quoted in Horan (ed), *CSS* Shenandoah: *The Memoirs of Lieutenant Commanding James I. Waddell*, Naval Institute Press, Annapolis, 1996

South Australian Chronicle and Weekly Mail (Adelaide)

Southern Historical Society Papers, August 1877

The Age (Melbourne)

The Alta California

The Argus (Melbourne)

The Australasian (Melbourne)

The Ballarat Star

The Bendigo Advertiser

The New International Version Bible

The Cincinnati Daily Gazette

The Empire (Sydney)

The Geelong Advertiser (Victoria)

The Gettysburg Compiler

The Illustrated London News

The Index

The Liverpool Mercury

The Mercury (Hobart)

The Nashville Times (Queensland)

The National Intelligencer, January 1865, quoted in Kimmel,
    The Mad Booths of Maryland, Dover, 1969

The New York Times

The Patriot & Union (Harrisburg, Pennsylvania)

The Queenslander (Brisbane)

The Republican Standard (Bridgeport)

The San Francisco Evening Bulletin

The South Australian Advertiser (Adelaide)

The Spectator (London)

The Standard (New Bedford)

The Sydney Morning Herald

The Times (London)

The Vernon Pioneer (Alabama)

The Williamstown Chronicle

Twain, M., *Following the Equator*, American Publications,
    Hartford, 1897

US Census, 1860

Victorian Parliamentary Papers, Commission of Inquiry into
    Conditions on the Gold Fields, A 76/1854–55, Vol II

Waddell, Letter, 27 December 1865, quoted in Hunt, C., *The
    Cruise of the* Shenandoah, G.W. Carlton, New York, 1867

'War of the Rebellion', *Official Records of the Union and
    Confederate Navies*, series 1.3

Wesley, J., *Thoughts Upon Slavery*, Joseph Cruikshank,
    Philadelphia, 1774

Whalemen's Shipping List and Merchants' Transcript (New Bedford)

Whitfield, G., Works, vol 2, Letter to Mr B., 22 March 1751

Whittle, W., Journal, Museum of the Confederacy, Richmond, Virginia

Whittle, W., Papers, 1855–1910, edited as *The Voyage of the CSS Shenandoah: A Memorable Cruise*, University of Alabama Press, 2005

Whittle, W., 'The Cruise of the *Shenandoah*', *Southern Historical Society Papers*, vol XXXV, December 1907

Wilberforce, W., Speech in the House of Commons, 12 May 1789

William Blanchard to William Seward, Roll 3, Despatches from United States Consul in Melbourne, National Archives and Records, Maryland, 23 February 1865

Appendix I

Shenandoah *complement at Madeira (partial)*

Captain James Iredell Waddell
Lieutenant William Conway
   Whittle
Lieutenant Sidney Smith Lee
Lieutenant Dabney Minor
   Scales
Acting Sailing Master Irvine S.
   Bulloch
Engineer Matthew O'Brien
Engineer W.H. Codd
Engineer John Hutchinson
Engineer Ernest Mugguffeney
Surgeon Charles E. Lining

Paymaster Breedlove Smith
Midshipman O.A. Brown
Midshipman John T. Mason
Assistant Surgeon Fred J.
   McNulty
Master's Mate Cornelius E.
   Hunt
Master's Mate John T. Minor
Master's Mate Lodge Colton
Boatswain George Harwood
Carpenter J. O'Shea
Gunner J.L. Guy
Sailmaker Henry Alcott

Appendix II

The 42 Melbourne recruits

Amended from the list according to William Temple, whose evidence for the *Alabama* Claims was of doubtful accuracy.

Petty officers
Robert Dunning, captain of
    the foretop
Thomas Strong, captain of the
    mizzen-mast
Charles Cobbey, gunner's mate
John James, carpenter's mate
John Spring, captain of the hold
Ernest W. Burt, doctor's steward
James McLaren, master-at-arms
William Smith, ship's cook
David Alexander, corporal of
    marines
George P. Canning, sergeant of
    marines

Marines
William Kenyon
Henry Reily
Robert Brown

Sailors
John Blacker, captain's clerk
John Collins
Thomas Foran
Lawrence Kerney
John McDonal
John Ramsdale
Franklin Gower
John Kilgower
Thomas Swanton

John Moss

James Fegan

Samuel Crooks

John Simmes

John Hill

William Hutchinson

Thomas Evans

Charles H. Morton

George H. Gifford

Henry Canning

James Ross

John Williams

Duke Simmons

Firemen

Thomas McLean

William Brice

William Green

William Burgess

Joseph Mullineux

Henry Sutherland

James Stranth

Appendix III

Ships captured by the Shenandoah

There are discrepancies among lists by Captain Waddell, various ship's officers and other sources. The list below is based on that of Master's Mate Cornelius Hunt.

Abigail, New Bedford, captured 27 May 1865, $16,705

Adelaide, Baltimore, captured December 1864 (exact date not listed), $24,000

Alina, Searsport, captured 30 October 1864, value $95,000

Brunswick, New Bedford, captured 28 June 1865, $16,272

Catherine, New Bedford, captured 25 June 1865, $26,174

Charter Oak, San Francisco, captured 5 November, $15,000

Congress, New Bedford, captured 28 June 1865, $55,300

Covington, New Bedford, captured 28 June 1865, $30,000

D. Godfrey, Boston, captured 8 November 1864, $36,000

Delphine, Bangor, captured 29 December 1864, $25,000

Edward, New Bedford, captured 4 December 1864, $20,000

Edward Carey, San Francisco, captured 1 April 1865, $15,000

Euphrates, New Bedford, 22 June 1865, $42,320

Favorite, Fairhaven, captured 28 June 1865, $57,896

General Pike, New Bedford, captured 25 June 1865, $30,000

General Williams, New Bedford, captured 28 June 1865, $44,750

Gypsey, New Bedford, captured 25 June 1865, $34,369

Harvest, Honolulu, captured 1 April 1865, $34,759

Hector, New Bedford, captured 1 April 1865, $58,000

Hillman, New Bedford, captured 28 June 1865, $33,000

Isaac Howland, New Bedford, captured 28 June 1865, $75,112

Isabella, New Bedford, captured 25 June 1865, $38,000

James Murray, New Bedford, captured 28 June 1865, $40,550

Jireh Swift, New Bedford, captured 22 June 1865, $61,960

Kate Prince, Portsmouth, New Jersey, captured 12 November
    1864, $40,000

Lizzie M. Stacey, Boston, captured 13 November 1864, $15,000

Martha, New Bedford, captured 28 June 1865, $30,307

Milo, New Bedford, captured 28 June 1865, $30,000

Nassau, New Bedford, captured 28 June 1865, $40,000

Nile, New London, captured 28 June 1865, $25,550

Nimrod, New Bedford, captured 25 June 1865, $29,260

Pearl, New London, captured 1 April 1865, $10,000

Sophia Thornton, New Bedford, captured 22 June 1865, $70,000

Susan, New York, captured 10 November 1864, $5,436

Susan Abigail, New Bedford, captured 25 June 1865, $6,500

Waverly, New Bedford, captured 28 June 1865, $62,376

William C. Nye, New Bedford, captured 25 June 1865, $31,512

William Thomson, New Bedford, captured 22 June 1865, $40,925

Acknowledgements

I am indebted to my old friend Paul O'Brien – not only a great artist but the possessor of a keen eye for the arcane – who set me on the trail of Australians who fought in the American Civil War.

That trail would have been all but impossible to follow had it not been for the invaluable resources of the Museum of the Confederacy, the State Library of New South Wales, the State Library of Victoria, the Trove collection of the National Library of Australia, the US National Archives, Official Records of the Union and Confederate Navies, the Australian National Maritime Museum, and the Civil War Round Table.

My thanks to Steve Ramsey for his expert advice on all things nautical; to Carol Felone, for granting me permission to quote from a letter by her great-grandfather Almer Montague, a Union soldier who witnessed the surrender of Lee at Appomattox; to my publisher Alison Urquhart for her vision and support; to my excellent editor Anne Reilly, a writer's dream; to Leigh Goodall for his dedication to keeping history alive; and with particular gratitude to Barry Crompton, the very model of an historical researcher.

Index

Loved the book?

Join thousands of other readers online at